ALSO BY HERBERT MITGANG

BIOGRAPHY
Abraham Lincoln: A Press Portrait
The Fiery Trial: A Life of Lincoln
The Man Who Rode the Tiger: The Life and Times of
    Judge Samuel Seabury

REPORTAGE
Dangerous Dossiers: Exposing the Secret War
Against America's Greatest Authors
Freedom to See: Television and the First Amendment

HISTORY
The Letters of Carl Sandburg
Washington, D. C. in Lincoln's Time
Spectator of America
America at Random: Topics of The Times
Civilians Under Arms: Stars and Stripes, Civil War to Korea

LITERATURE
Words Still Count with Me: A Chronicle of Literary Conversations
Working for the Reader: A Chronicle of Culture,
Literature, War and Politics in Books

NOVELS
The Return
Get These Men Out of the Hot Sun
The Montauk Fault
Kings in the Counting House

PLAYS
Mister Lincoln

ONCE UPON A TIME IN

New York

Jimmy Walker,
Franklin Roosevelt,
and the Last Great Battle
of the Jazz Age

Herbert Mitgang

THE FREE PRESS

THE FREE PRESS
A Division of Simon & Schuster Inc.
1230 Avenue of the Americas
New York, NY 10020

The Free Press and colophon are trademarks of
Simon & Schuster Inc.

Designed by Kim Llewellyn

Manufactured in the United States of America

10 9 8 7 6 5 4 3 2 1

Library of Congress Cataloging-in-Publication Data

Mitgang, Herbert.
    Once upon a time in New York : Jimmy Walker, Franklin Roosevelt,
  and the last great battle of the Jazz Age / Herbert Mitgang.
      p. cm.
    Includes bibliographical references and index.
    1. Walker, James John, 1881–1946. 2. New York (N.Y.)—Politics
  and government—1898–1951. 3. Roosevelt, Franklin D. (Franklin
  Delano), 1882–1945. 4. Political corruption—New York (State)—New
  York—History—20th century. 5. Corruption investigation—New York
  (State)—New York—History—20th century. 6. Tammany Hall.
  7. Walker, James John, 1881–1946—Friends and associates.
  8. Mayors—New York (State)—New York Biography. 9. Governors—New
  York (State) Biography. I. Title.
F128.5.M73   2000   99-16631   CIP
974.7'104'0922—dc21
[B]

ISBN 0-684-85579-8 (alk. paper)

For my parents,
Benjamin and Florence Mitgang

*I'd rather be a lamppost in New York City
than Mayor of Chicago.*

—JAMES J. WALKER

The old gay Mayor, he ain't what he used to be.

—FRANKLIN P. ADAMS

I'm a Democrat still. Very still.

—ALFRED E. SMITH

If you were any dumber, I'd make you a commissioner.

—FIORELLO H. LA GUARDIA

All life is nine to five against.

—DAMON RUNYON

There is nothing I love so much as a good fight.

—FRANKLIN D. ROOSEVELT

Contents

Cast of Characters   xi

Prologue: That Was a Time....   1

1 A Bullet for Big Arnie   5

2 The Boozy Era   23

3 The Gang's All Here   37

4 Night Mayor of New York   59

5 Lullaby of Broadway   79

6 Hares and Hounds   97

7 The Tin Box Brigade   107

8 Ring Around the Rackets   125

9 Little Boy Blue Blows His Horn   143

10 F.D.R. vs. the Boy Friend   167

11 F.D.R., Esq.—Judge and Jury   183

12 The Knave of Hearts   205

13 "Jimmy, You Brightened Up the Joint!"   217

Epilogue: A New Political Era   231

A Note on Sources   237

Acknowledgments   243

Index   245

Cast of Characters

JAMES J. WALKER
Mayor of the City of New York.

FRANKLIN DELANO ROOSEVELT
Governor of New York State during Walker hearings, Democratic presidential candidate.

FIORELLO "LITTLE FLOWER" H. LA GUARDIA
Ex-congressman, the New York mayor who defeated Tammany Hall's hacks.

ALFRED E. SMITH
Ex-governor of New York, defeated presidential candidate, Tammany elder statesman.

SAMUEL SEABURY
Former State Supreme Court judge, chief counsel investigating Mayor Walker and citywide corruption.

BETTY "MONK" COMPTON
Jimmy Walker's mistress, Broadway musical comedy actress.

HON. THOMAS "TIN BOX" FARLEY
Sheriff of New York County, Tammany Hall Sachem.

HON. JAMES "JESSE JAMES" MCQUADE
Sheriff of Kings County, Tammany Hall Sachem.

JOHN F. CURRY
Former sewer inspector, Chief Sachem of Tammany Hall.

ARNOLD ROTHSTEIN
New York City's gambling czar, murdered.

JOSEPH F. CRATER
State Supreme Court Justice, disappeared, whereabouts unknown.

MISS POLLY ADLER
New York City's foremost vice "entrepreneuse."

THOMAS C. T. CRAIN
District attorney of New York County, under investigation for
incompetence.

JANET ALLEN "ALLIE" WALKER
Jimmy Walker's loyal wife.

JOHN "RED MIKE" HYLAN
Ex-mayor, Tammany loyalist, judge of the Children's Court of Queens
County.

PAUL BLOCK
Wealthy owner of the *Brooklyn Standard-Union*, source of a secret
brokerage account shared with Mayor Walker.

GROVER A. WHALEN
Official greeter, police commissioner.

Prologue

That Was a Time. . . .

After a late dinner in their Manhattan hideaway on a star-kissed night in the autumn of 1928, Mayor James J. Walker and his showgirl mistress, Betty Compton, motored to Westchester in his chauffeured, silver-trimmed Duesenberg to hear Vincent Lopez's orchestra play dance tunes at Joe Pani's Woodmansten Inn. The nightclub was a favorite hangout for respectable suburbanites, revelers from New York City carrying their own silver flasks of Prohibition whisky, and members of the underworld and their women, some of whom were rumored to be their wives.

That evening Betty was in high spirits. She turned to Lopez and said, "I feel like Cinderella." Betty insisted on dancing and coaxed Walker out on the floor. He reluctantly agreed to take a few turns before going back to their table. She kicked off her satin slippers and asked Lopez to autograph them as a souvenir. The bandleader borrowed a fountain pen and did so to please Betty and his pal Jimmy, who asked her to restrain herself. He had only been drinking ginger ale at the club.

Suddenly, there was a stirring at one of the important tables nearby. A well-dressed man who seemed to know the mayor strolled over and whispered something in his ear.

Walker looked startled. He and Betty quickly rose from their ring-side table and hurried to the cloakroom. Lopez left the bandstand and followed them as the mayor's car pulled up to the entrance. It was a little past midnight. Walker apologized for having to leave so early; after all, he was not called the Night Mayor of New York for nothing. He told the bandleader that they had to return to Manhattan immediately.

"Arnold Rothstein has just been shot, Vincent," the mayor said. "That means trouble from here on."

His instinct was on target; there would be even more trouble than he could possibly have imagined. Jimmy Walker's own conduct in and out of office was about to become the centerpiece of the greatest investigation of municipal corruption in American history.

All across the United States, journalists and other wiseacres would soon have a field day with the popular mayor's personal problems and public trials. Not since the notorious Tweed Ring was exposed in the nineteenth century would New Yorkers become so aroused and, strangely, amused. The indignant "Goo-Goos"—the Good Government advocates—smelled blood in the corridors of City Hall. Even so, it was hard to be considered an idealist at a time when idealism in government seemed old-fashioned. If you were an outspoken reformer in the freebooting 1920s, you were just not with it. A benevolent form of blinkered corruption bestrode the city.

Ben Hecht, the Chicago reporter who become a playwright (*The Front Page*) and screenwriter, observed: "Walker is a troubadour headed for Wagnerian dramas. No man could hold life so carelessly without falling down a manhole before he is done."

Before mounting the witness stand, Walker cheerfully said: "There are three things a man must do alone. Be born, die, and testify." Sharply dressed for his show-and-tell trial, wearing a blue double-breasted suit with a matching blue shirt, blue tie, and blue handkerchief, the mayor commented: "Little Boy Blue is about to blow his horn—or his top."

While being cross-examined in the county courthouse in Manhattan by the intrepid Samuel Seabury, the anti-Tammany patrician who was the proud namesake of the first Episcopal bishop in the United

States, Walker told reporters: "This fellow Seabury would convict the Twelve Apostles if he could." The mayor kept his cool—and gained the applause of his cheering admirers with a wisecrack: "Life is just a bowl of Seaburys."

But the mayor's nightclubbing lifestyle was overshadowed as other major personalities were coming forward on the American political stage. In 1928 Al Smith was running for president and Franklin Roosevelt for governor; the following year, Mayor Jimmy Walker would run for reelection against Congressman Fiorello La Guardia. In these contests, the murder of politically connected Arnold Rothstein affected the power of Tammany Hall's Sachems, whose tentacles reached into every corner of the city—and into every voting booth.

In the balance stood the man Roosevelt called the Happy Warrior—Alfred E. Smith, the first Catholic to be nominated for president. Would a regionally divided nation be ready to put aside its religious and racial differences and vote for him? Would Al Smith be able to distance himself from his image as a social reformer who grew up on the rough-and-tumble sidewalks of New York and be accepted as a leader of national stature? He had called for repeal of Prohibition, a central issue around the country. But as H. L. Mencken astutely wrote: "Those who fear the Pope outnumber those who are tired of the Anti-Saloon League."

In the wings hovered one of the boldest personalities in the electoral history of the Empire City—Fiorello La Guardia, a Republican Congressman in a Democratic town. He was of half-Italian, half-Jewish origin, a street fighter who reflected the hopes of the ethnic neighborhoods more than any other politician. The Little Flower, a former president of the city's Board of Aldermen, aspired to be the next mayor of New York—if Jimmy Walker and the Tammany operatives stumbled.

Franklin D. Roosevelt observed the repercussions of the Rothstein assassination and the burgeoning investigations in New York City with the greatest personal interest. If the Tammany leaders did not erect any last-minute roadblocks, his dream of being nominated and elected as the thirty-second president of the United States when his turn came might become a reality.

Roosevelt was known for his eloquence, good looks, and recognizable name. No one who knew him could deny his personal bravery in making a comeback after polio had destroyed his ability to walk alone; in four determined years he had graduated from crutches to canes on Democratic political platforms. "If he burned down the Capitol," said the humorist Will Rogers, "we would cheer and say, 'Well, we at least got a fire started anyhow.'"

But some political analysts considered him a lightweight. In words that he would later have to swallow, Walter Lippmann, the influential columnist, declared: "Franklin D. Roosevelt is no crusader. He is no tribune of the people. He is no enemy of entrenched privilege. He is a pleasant man who, without any important qualifications for the office, would very much like to be President."

In a bizarre way, the notorious gangland murder of Rothstein called attention to the weakness of the district attorney and the police department and touched off the trials of Jimmy Walker and Tammany Hall. Suddenly, Governor Roosevelt found himself facing down the kingmakers and corrupters within his own party in the City of New York. Would Roosevelt show that he was capable of independent behavior—or would he cave in for political expediency? As a presidential contender, Roosevelt was about to have his mettle tested.

ONE

A Bullet for Big Arnie

Arnold Rothstein sat at his corner table in Leo Lindy's shrine to brisket, boiled chicken, and belly lox at 1626 Broadway, his back to the wall, picking with a gold toothpick at the cherry-cheesecake crumbs lodged between his teeth and gums. With a flick of his manicured thumbnail, he relit his batonlike Havana with a match that instantly flared up and flamed out.

In the powerful precincts of Tammany Hall, whose district leaders provided protection for a price, as well as in the better circles of the underworld, Big Arnie was greatly respected as a shrewd over-achiever in a dangerous line of work.

One after another, the runners handling racetrack bets and a piece of the action from floating craps and card games approached his private table with the day's receipts. They bowed their heads like courtiers before a monarch who holds a royal flush. Rothstein's nimble mind computed the numbers and the vigorish from clients foolish enough to fall behind in their debts. Collections for the bootlegging and narcotics businesses he bankrolled were handled elsewhere by "the boys"—silent enforcers in gray fedoras, with bulges beneath their coat jackets, men whose names usually ended in vowels.

Rothstein lived quietly in the Fairfield Hotel at 20 West Seventy-second Street, one of several buildings he owned, but he made Lindy's his informal headquarters. It was an easy run in his Rolls-Royce to the restaurant between Forty-ninth and Fiftieth on Broadway. Leo "Lindy" Lindemann sat at the cash register, greeting the regulars and encouraging them to try the flanken with white horseradish today; unsuccessfully, Mrs. Lindemann discouraged the patronage of the gamblers and mobsters. She preferred the gossip columnists, actors, and second bananas who dropped in for a bite to eat after the theater and the last show at the Gaiety on Forty-sixth Street and the other burlesque houses off the Main Stem.

Not far away, at *his* special table, Damon Runyon, the Hearst newspaper columnist—who came from Manhattan, Kansas, but much preferred this Manhattan—was making mental notes for the prototypes of Harry the Horse, Milk Ear Willie, Big Nig, and Sorrowful Jones. They were fairly closely based on the con artists and sporting ladies who surrounded him at the fictional restaurant he called Mindy's. These characters in his first book, *Guys and Dolls,* would later become the basis for the classic Broadway musical.

The time was the 1920s, and Tammany's James John Walker, the elegant Beau James, was serving as the popular mayor of New York City. In a lawless era, when almost anything went, the lives and fortunes of the mayor and the gambler were destined to intersect in sinister ways.

Big Arnie was New York's gambling czar. He was a fence and a smuggler, a fixer of horse races and baseball scores. Students of American fiction know Arnold Rothstein under a different moniker: Meyer Wolfshiem. (That was the name F. Scott Fitzgerald originally gave him in *The Great Gatsby.* In later editions of the novel, the name is spelled "Wolfsheim.") Fitzgerald wrote that Wolfshiem was the gambler who fixed the 1919 World Series; it helped to define Wolfshiem's character.

That year, the Chicago White Sox were favored to beat the Cincinnati Reds. Gamblers bribed a group of White Sox players to throw the games. It was surmised that Rothstein arranged the fix. Underworld snitches informed Rothstein in plenty of time for him to place his own bets. He had been approached at Jamaica Racetrack in Queens by a go-between and told that the Series could be fixed for $100,000—a bribe of $20,000 each to five Sox players. With that advance knowledge, but without himself investing, Rothstein made a bundle betting against the Black Sox, as they came to be called.

Fitzgerald altered the facts, but captured the truth about Rothstein during a conversation between Nick Carraway, the narrator, and Gatsby:

> "He becomes very sentimental sometimes," explained Gatsby. "This is one of his sentimental days. He's quite a character around New York— a denizen of Broadway."
>
> "Who is he anyhow—an actor?"
>
> "No."
>
> "A dentist?"
>
> "Meyer Wolfshiem? No, he's a gambler." Gatsby hesitated, then added coolly: "He's the man who fixed the World Series back in 1919."
>
> "Fixed the World Series?" I repeated.
>
> The idea staggered me. I remembered of course that the World Series had been fixed in 1919 but if I had thought of it at all I would have thought of it as a thing that merely happened, the end of some inevitable chain. It never occurred to me that one man could start to play with the faith of fifty million people—with the single-mindedness of a burglar blowing a safe.
>
> "How did he happen to do that?" I asked after a minute.
>
> "He just saw the opportunity."
>
> "Why isn't he in jail?"
>
> "They can't get him, old sport. He's a smart man."

Fitzgerald liked to tell friends that he had actually met Rothstein. When he and Ring Lardner, the short-story writer, were Long Island neighbors in Great Neck (West Egg in the novel), Lardner once introduced Fitzgerald to the gambler. It could have been at the home of Herbert Bayard Swope, the fabled reporter and editor of the *New York World* ("the OLD *World*," to newspaper lovers), who gave weekend parties for the swells and the molls at his estate that overlooked the fictional "courtesy bay" (actually, Manhasset Bay) and Daisy Buchanan's green light. Lardner's modest house was within shouting distance of the Swope estate.

Although Rothstein was never known to have bequeathed his winnings from a fixed daily double to a nonprofit foundation for the improvement of the breed, animal or human, he did contribute to American literature by unwittingly lending his reputation, if not his name, to Fitzgerald's story of unrequited dreams in the "fresh, green breast of the New World" that the novelist envisioned on "two eggs" of land protruding into Long Island Sound.

Big Arnie could hardly be called one of Gotham's beloved citizens, although he claimed that his personal philosophy was summed up in one word: "friendship." One of his own lawyers, William J. Fallon, described Rothstein as "a man who dwells in doorways. A gray rat, waiting for his cheese." Sometimes friendships failed, and rats squabbled.

Rothstein, well-mannered and soft of speech, did not fit the popular stereotype of the professional gambler. But his associates were chary of trifling with him. He had an overweening confidence in his own brain. At one time August Belmont ruled Rothstein off Belmont Park. Later he was reinstated. Rothstein said that he had simply gone to Belmont and convinced him that his enormous winnings were the product of superior intelligence. The banker was said to admit that Rothstein's moral code was better than those of many of his business associates.

On November 4, 1928, after visiting some of his cronies in a floating card game in the Park Central Hotel, Rothstein was shot in the groin by what police said was an unknown assailant. Broadway intelligence said Rothstein had welshed on one of his big gambling debts and was being called to account.

A story got around in bookmaking circles that, had he lived, Rothstein would have collected nearly a million dollars betting that Franklin D. Roosevelt would win the race for governor of New York and that Alfred E. Smith, the former governor running for president of the United States, would lose to Herbert Hoover, two days after the shooting. It didn't matter to the gambler that one was a Democrat and the other a Republican; worshippers of the large green denominations from the U.S. Treasury didn't play politics. Rothstein was right on the money for both candidates. If he had lived that long, he could have paid his debts—but someone was impatient.

The attempted killing was page-one news even in the staid *New York Times*. The above-the-fold headline, in the broadsheet's traditional Latin Condensed type, read:

ROTHSTEIN, GAMBLER, MYSTERIOUSLY SHOT; REFUSES TO TALK

"When *The Times* prints scandalous news," explained Adolph S. Ochs, the publisher, "it's sociology."

Slowly, the facts began to emerge about the mysterious hit on Rothstein. Only weeks before, he had declared that he had given up gambling in favor of the real estate business. At one time he owned and subleased one thousand furnished apartments in the city. The regular crossover between his legal and illegal enterprises enabled him to move comfortably among the Tammany politicians who ruled the neighborhoods as independent enclaves. Rothstein often boasted that he had friends in the Social Register who frequented the finest speakeasies in Manhattan. There, behind sliding peepholes and closed doors, socialites paid well to drink his illegal Canadian whisky. What's more, the women in sexy bias-cut satin dresses thought they were privileged characters when they rubbed shoulders with glamorous gangsters.

Still alive the day after taking a bullet in his gut, Rothstein wouldn't talk about the identity of the gunman, but detectives and police reporters began to assemble the fragmentary evidence picked up from informers in the alleys and streets around Hell's Kitchen on the tough West Side.

At eleven o'clock on the night of the shooting, the police found Rothstein in a state of collapse in the Fifty-sixth Street service entrance of the Park Central Hotel on Seventh Avenue. He had asked the doorman to call a doctor and a taxicab. It was first believed that Rothstein had been shot on the east side of Seventh Avenue. Police theorized that he had plodded grimly across the avenue, pushed through the hotel's main entrance into the corridor, and made his way to the service entrance to find a taxi.

But other clues cast doubt on this theory. A taxi driver, Albert Bender, told the police that a pistol had fallen on the sidewalk, as if it had been tossed from a sedan that he had seen. Then he changed his story; it might have been hurled from an apartment facing Seventh Avenue. The .38-caliber revolver, its handle chipped as if in an effort to hide fingerprints, was found. The police picked up five unexploded shells in the gutter.

At Polyclinic Hospital, doctors discovered that the bullet had entered Rothstein's abdomen. News of the shooting quickly traveled up and down Broadway. Within an hour, dozens of his friends lined the corridors of the hospital. Among the first to get there was a gentleman who answered only to the name Butch. He was willing to offer his blood for a transfusion; the offer was accepted.

Rothstein, who often carried as much as $100,000 in thousand-dollar bills in his front and side pockets, had a mere $6,500 in his wallet. Detectives from the West Forty-seventh Street station house questioned him about the incident: Did he know the gunman, or was the assailant a stranger? Apart from giving his age and home address, Rothstein remained mute. At 2:15 in the morning of November 5, the surgeons operated. At first, they probed in vain for the bullet; a few hours later they removed a thick nickel-jacketed lead slug. It proved to be the missing bullet that had been fired from the stubby .38-caliber Colt revolver found outside the Park Central.

In the middle of the night, a new group of police officers arrived and took up positions outside Rothstein's room and at the hospital entrance. The men in blue were there because a tipster had reported that hired gunmen were assembling who planned to finish off the wounded gambler. Rothstein owed big, possibly plus vigorish.

A police captain with a touch of the philosopher told reporters that

a man with as many friends as Rothstein was bound to have a few enemies as well. He revealed that a little more than a year ago, "somebody
in the rackets tried to take him for a ride." Instead of accepting the invitation, Rothstein ducked back into his office when he saw the door of
the automobile swing open and the barrels of long guns inside.

Thereafter, Rothstein hired a bodyguard to protect him around the
clock. One of his bodyguards was Abe Attell, a canny ex–featherweight
boxing champion. It so happened, insiders winked, that Attell was in
Chicago when the Black Sox World Series was fixed. Another bodyguard was none other than Jack "Legs" Diamond, a trigger-happy
gangster, who was paid a thousand dollars a week to protect Rothstein.

As an apprentice thief with the Gopher Gang in Chelsea on Manhattan's West Side, Legs got his nickname because of the speed he
showed after stealing packages in warehouses and off trucks. A more
romantic explanation later circulated: that he was called Legs because
of his gracefulness on the dance floor. His specialties were the
Charleston and the Black Bottom.

In his dot-dot-dot gossip column, Walter Winchell branded him
"On His Last Legs" Diamond because he had been shot at so many
times by rival gangsters. Legs was a fearless gunsel and an enemy of
Dutch Schultz, the beer baron whose real name was Arthur Flegen-
heimer. Both were in the speakeasy and policy rackets games. Sometimes their territories overlapped, an unhealthy condition for anyone
who didn't know his geography. The Dutchman's protector was Jimmy
Hines, a West Side Tammany leader, who later went to jail for "licens-
ing" the racketeers in Hell's Kitchen.

Legs owned a piece of the Hotsy Totsy Club, a Prohibition joint on
Fifty-fourth Street and Broadway. There he could be seen with his
girlfriend, Kiki Roberts, a Ziegfeld Follies looker whose actual name
was Marion Strasmick. After surviving dozens of shotgun pellets that
peppered his slim body, Legs was tracked down in Albany. As he lay in
a drunken stupor, a volley of bullets fired directly into his face, his
head, and the back of his neck finally finished him off. Not long afterward, Dutch Schultz took a fatal hit himself, in Newark. The Dutchman's deathbed ravings became the stuff of wonder and legend,

including one memorable line: "Mother is the best bet, and don't let Satan draw you too fast."

On *his* deathbed after two more transfusions, Rothstein still refused to reveal the name of the gunman or the reason why he had been shot. After the effects of the anesthetic given him for the operation had passed, Rothstein fell into a deep sleep. Waiting for him to wake up were Captain Edmund Meade, two detectives, Patrick Flood and John Green, and a stenographer from police headquarters. Detective Flood had known the gambler for a long time. He moved close to the bed. A look of recognition glinted in Rothstein's brown eyes.

"Hello, Paddy," he said weakly.

"Who shot you?" asked Flood.

"Got nothing to say," said Rothstein. "Nothing, nothing. Won't talk about it."

At the insistence of the doctors the detectives abandoned their efforts and were ordered to leave the room. Rothstein's mind clouded.

His parents and estranged wife, Caroline, who lived at 912 Fifth Avenue overlooking Central Park on the Upper East Side, were in the hospital when the doctors informed them he was sinking. They immediately summoned his lawyer, Maurice F. Cantor, who rushed to his bedside.

Counselor-at-law Cantor was one of Rothstein's links to the Tammany political machine. At the same time that his prominent client lay wounded in the hospital, Cantor was campaigning for state assemblyman as the Democratic candidate in the Eleventh Assembly District in Manhattan.

Rothstein and Cantor were alone together for an hour. The gambler delivered instructions about the disposition of his fortune, supposedly including a list of persons to whom he owed money and those who owed money to him. He died on November 6, 1928, leaving an estate estimated to be worth between five and ten million dollars.

More important events than the infamous gambler's death dominated the headlines. Two days later, the returns of the presidential and gubernatorial elections were played on page one in a 48-point banner in *The New York Times* that read:

HOOVER WINS, THANKS NATION; ROOSEVELT CLAIMS HIS VICTORY

The lead article reported that Governor Smith said he would never run for public office again, but "I will never lose my interest in public affairs, that is a sure thing." Smith claimed to have no regrets about the campaign, but he looked less than his usual buoyant self on the night of the election: "The cigar, which was clamped between his teeth, never lighted until it was dropped to the floor after the radio had bluntly announced 'a Hoover landslide,' after which it was replaced by a fresh cigar that he smoked pleasantly."

Actually, Smith's desire to be President did not end with his defeat. Four years later he still hoped to capture his party's nomination. When Smith was denied the chance to run again, he turned bitter, abandoned his progressive goals for the blue-collar workers, and instead joined forces with big businessmen. He became president, at $50,000 a year, of the corporation formed to erect the Empire State Building. Although Smith received almost fifteen million votes—the largest number ever attained by a Democrat in a national race up to that time—about 21.5 million ballots were cast for Hoover. Smith was repudiated by his own party in the South and, even more humiliating, in his own state.

"Well," he acidly commented, "the time hasn't come yet when a man can say his beads in the White House."

But the Happy Warrior was pleased that Roosevelt would replace him in Albany. Smith had thought that his own chances for victory would be enhanced with Roosevelt's name on the same ticket and had pressured him to run. Although Smith and Roosevelt were not close intimates, both were loyal Democrats and allies on matters of social reform legislation for New York State.

Thinking that he had lost the race for governor, Roosevelt had gone to bed early. In the morning, he discovered that he had won by a slim margin of about 24,500 out of 4.2 million votes cast. How did Roosevelt succeed and Smith fail in New York? Smith's religion, of course, was a deciding factor in his defeat. As a national candidate, Smith spent much of his time campaigning outside New York, believing that his popularity would assure victory in his home state.

Roosevelt, by contrast, campaigned in almost every town and city, upstate and downstate—from Oswego to Elmira, Dunkirk to Batavia, Watertown to Boonville, Rome to Herkimer, Schenectady to Albany, and across the five boroughs of New York City. During his gubernatorial speeches, he invariably praised Smith's presidential candidacy. But he also hammered away at his own proposed legislation and human concerns. In a typical speech on the campaign trail, Roosevelt said:

"In social legislation, in education, in health, in better housing, in the care of the aged, we have gone far, but we must go farther." He also showed concern for the millions of New Yorkers who depended on farming: "While there have been prosperity and growth in the cities, their measure has not extended to the rural communities. This is in part a national problem, but it also calls for immediate action in our own state."

In retrospect, Roosevelt's campaign for governor was a preview of his future campaign for president.

Almost immediately, there was talk that Albany would be Roosevelt's stepping-stone to Washington. Even before he was sworn in as the new governor, *The New York Times*'s editorial page summed up his qualifications for the presidency:

"Governor-elect Roosevelt is within reach of the Democratic party's leadership. The manner in which this happened has many of the aspects of romance. Born a Roosevelt and a Democrat by preference, he first won his spurs by opposing Tammany as a State Senator in the legislature. In the Wilson regime as Assistant Secretary of the Navy, he took the path of his more famous kinsman, Theodore Roosevelt. He was nominated for Vice President in 1920 but his party was defeated. Crippling health suddenly afflicted him. But destiny was not through with Franklin D. Roosevelt. Despite his physical infirmity, he threw himself into the cause of Governor Smith's candidacy in 1924 and again in 1928. Not only is Roosevelt a victor in New York but he is warmly regarded by the Southern Democracy."

The editorial exaggerated Roosevelt's anti-Tammany position at that time. It was Charlie Murphy, the Tammany boss, who had engineered the Roosevelt nomination for vice president in 1920. A candidate tied to Al Smith and Jimmy Walker could not help being linked to Tammany Hall but, as a resident of Hyde Park in Dutchess County, F.D.R. was not under the control of the Manhattan leadership. Nevertheless, the new governor recognized Tammany's vote-counting ability in city and state affairs.

Indeed, Mayor Walker had nominated Roosevelt for governor at the party's state convention and campaigned for him. In his resplendent oratorical style, Walker called Roosevelt "a real, genuine, 100 percent American, and by that I mean a man who has studied and who knows the Declaration of Independence and refused to forget what has been written in that immortal document."

Beyond the Hudson, not everyone gave Roosevelt a similar stamp of approval. H. L. Mencken satirized him: "Roosevelt is one of the most charming of men, but like many another very charming man he leaves on the beholder the impression that he is also somewhat shallow and futile. It is hard to say precisely how that impression is produced; maybe his Christian Science smile is to blame, or the tenor overtones in his voice."

After the election, the dozen morning and evening daily newspapers in New York (this figure does not even count the foreign-language press) picked up the scent of the hunt for Rothstein's killer. Spurred by Good Government reformers, the public demanded action by the district attorney and police department. From stoolies on parole and streetwise small-timers in the underworld, detectives began to piece together a mosaic of information about the crime.

On the night of the shooting, Rothstein was sitting at his usual table at Lindy's, noshing and sipping coffee with some friends, when a call came through to him at 10:45 P.M. He spoke briefly and then picked up his hat and coat. "George McManus wants me over at the Park Central," he told his friends. Then he left alone, without a bodyguard. Rothstein himself did not carry a weapon; that was not his style or the source of his power.

McManus, a gambler, was one of the out-of-towners with bankrolls of unknown origin who enjoyed life along the Rialto. Detectives claimed that he had been among the eight players in a card game in which Rothstein had lost $303,000. Of that small fortune, Rothstein still owed $219,000. McManus himself had lost $51,000 early in the same game, before the cards began to fall his way. It was understood by the players that Rothstein had not exactly welshed on his gambling debt; he promised to pay up as soon as he could get the cash together. Even to big-time gamblers in those free-spending years before the Wall Street crash, a couple of hundred grand was serious money.

When settlement time came a few days later, Rothstein said he was short of ready cash, owing to his heavy investments in real estate. He failed to mention that, simultaneously, his secretive heroin and cocaine investments demanded large amounts of ready money because narcotics was strictly a cash-and-carry business.

The big winner in the game was believed to be one "Nigger Nate" Raymond, who had known Rothstein for at least ten years. Nathan Raymond, a California businessman with vague connections to the sports world, had a swarthy complexion; hence his nickname. Rothstein still had $60,000 in his pocket that night, but he refused to divvy it up among the winners. After all, $60,000 was little more to him than what the boys at Lindy's called walking-around money.

"I'm Rothstein," he boasted. "My name ought to be good for the money." He added that he would probably have to sell one of his apartment houses to raise the cash to pay off his losses.

Two months passed. Rothstein still had not come up with the money for Nigger Nate and the other gamblers. On the weekend of the shooting, Rothstein and Raymond ran into each other in front of

Lindy's. Rothstein reassured him, "Nate, I'll give you some of that money on Monday."

Ten minutes before he left Lindy's to go to the Park Central in response to the phone call, Rothstein emerged from his Rolls-Royce and told Eugene Reiman, his longtime chauffeur and confidant, to go either to his home or to his office, at 45 West Fifty-seventh Street, and "get some dough." Reiman departed, picked up the money, and returned to Lindy's.

There he was told that Rothstein had been "slugged" and taken to Polyclinic. The chauffeur immediately drove to the hospital and saw Rothstein in the emergency room. They were never alone together. The detectives did not say what happened to the dough Reiman was supposedly carrying to Rothstein.

A persistent report went around that a pair of gangsters had been hired by one or more of Rothstein's creditors to demonstrate that they meant business and, the weekend he was shot, said the gossips, was the last chance he was going to get to pay up. According to an unnamed pigeon questioned by the detectives, one of the gunmen lost his temper when Rothstein ridiculed him. He took out the Colt .38, angrily pointed the gun as if he were going to shoot Big Arnie in his testicles, and pulled the trigger, perhaps accidentally. The shot was a little high, but the bullet did its work even more effectively in the gambler's gut.

A Chesterfield overcoat with George McManus's name embroidered inside was found in Room 349 at the Park Central. McManus had rented the room using the name George Richards. But McManus was nowhere to be found; he had disappeared from his usual gambling haunts and speakeasies right after the shooting. Detectives had reason to believe that he was the nervous triggerman who had been insulted by Rothstein.

Three weeks after Rothstein was buried in a bronze coffin following a traditional Jewish service at Union Field Cemetery in Brooklyn, McManus turned himself in. His lawyer arranged for him to surrender to John Cordes, a detective, while getting a shave and a haircut in a barbershop on 242nd Street in upper Manhattan, far from the madding

Broadway crowd. Cordes and McManus greeted each other like old acquaintances. Reading a magazine, the detective waited patiently in a nearby chair for the suspected killer to have his shave and hot towel finished before taking him downtown.

McManus admitted that he was the one who had called Rothstein at Lindy's and summoned him to the Park Central Hotel. He revealed that on the night of the big card game a few months before, Rothstein's usual luck had run out and he ran up debts to several gamblers, including a group of California racetrack characters and someone known only as the St. Louis Kid. In the game, $500,000 in cash or IOUs was in circulation. At first, the men gambled with dice. Then straight poker was taken up, followed by stud poker.

To speed up the action, the gamblers turned to "high spade." This was played by cutting a deck, the winner being the holder of the highest spade. According to McManus, that night Rothstein dropped $340,000 at high spade.

Rothstein had the reputation of being a prompt payer of his IOUs. But this time, not only did he fail to come through, he announced his suspicion that the big game had been crooked. This accusation from a gambling veteran at first seemed like a copout along Broadway, but when he repeated the charge, it was accepted that he might well have been duped. His accusation infuriated the men who had been trying to collect. Rumors soon reached informants up and down the West Side that Rothstein was going to be killed.

When Rothstein heard that he was a marked man, he said, "I'm not going to give them a cent, and that goes for the gamblers and the gorillas. If they're looking for me, I can be found any night at Lindy's." In politics and crime, in those days, reputation was everything.

McManus, whose brother Thomas "Hump" McManus also operated floating card games, evidently was trusted by the wary Rothstein, who otherwise would not have gone alone to the hotel room. The brothers McManus were more or less respected as honest men engaged in dishonest activities. They knew how to keep the cops from making raids. Hump McManus had once been a first-grade detective assigned to police headquarters; retired, he still had connections that were useful in the gambling world.

Arnold Rothstein's murder had caused Mayor Walker and Tammany's Sachems a good deal of embarrassment. It was brazen, yet no indictment was made after McManus turned himself in. Among those criticizing City Hall for failing to solve the Rothstein case and bring his murderer to justice was Congressman Fiorello La Guardia. Jimmy Walker would not hear the last of him, then or in the years to come.

Manhattan's own "Little Flower" was a rare but popular Republican representative in a Democratic controlled city. La Guardia was a formidable campaigner and a thorn in Walker's side during every election. While he and Governor Roosevelt were on opposite sides politically, their thinking was alike on social and economic issues affecting the man in the street. La Guardia and New York's Republican leaders were determined to make capital out of the Rothstein murder.

The general public, following the newspapers, began to wonder if there was something wrong with the way the police department was being run. There were unfounded and unproven allegations of a possible cover-up in this case. Of Rothstein's drug trafficking, *The Sun,* a New York newspaper that often sounded like a house organ for the Republican party, editorialized:

"All intelligent citizens know that such a business as Rothstein's included many assets of evil and could not be conducted without the knowledge of men in authority. His operations were too large and his scope too generous to escape scrutiny—unless official eyes were intentionally deflected the other way."

The weak District Attorney's Office was unable to find eyewitnesses among the professional gamblers, who could not speak without risking their own necks or kneecaps. So far as the men in Room 349 at the Park Central were concerned, they all might have been playing a friendly game of casino for pennies.

Although the detectives produced little specific evidence, the high police command felt that an arrest had to be made to show that they were doing something. They wanted to respond to the constant calls for action made by political columnists and editorial writers. McManus was indicted for first-degree murder.

When the Rothstein case broke, Joseph A. Warren was the police commissioner. Warren was considered a man of integrity, but police knowledge was clearly not his main qualification for the post. When Jimmy Walker was serving as a state assemblyman early in his career, he had an office in Warren's law firm, and Warren often looked after Walker's clients when the assemblyman was occupied in Albany. A year before Rothstein's murder, Walker had persuaded Warren to take the commissioner's job. He considered Joe Warren a close friend, who could be trusted not to interfere with gambling in the Tammany club-houses.

Unfortunately, the job was too much for Warren. He began to suffer emotionally and was close to a nervous breakdown even before the Rothstein murder. Under pressure from his own mentors in Tammany Hall, who realized that the unsolved murder was causing them political damage, Walker issued an ultimatum to his friend Warren: Dig up more information about Rothstein's murder, or retire. Warren stepped down as police commissioner, entered a sanatorium in Connecticut and, less than a year after being forced out by his former law associate, died of a paralytic stroke.

Mayor Walker had Warren's replacement in mind even before his failing police commissioner resigned. Grover Aloysius Whalen had once served as commissioner of plant and structures, an influential Tammany job, under Mayor John "Red Mike" Hylan. The carrot-topped mayor was a former motorman on Brooklyn's elevated railway lines who had lost his job after "rounding a curb too quickly." Whalen had once served as Mayor Hylan's personal secretary, and both were close to Tammany Hall.

A glad-hander with a magnificent waxed mustache and a fine set of glistening teeth, Whalen was general manager of Wanamaker's department store in 1928. Administrative experience was his main qualification for the sensitive police department post. It did him no harm that, like Jimmy Walker, the Tammany Hall Sachems, and most of the department heads in the NYPD, he had Irish-American roots.

Mayor Walker was impressed by Whalen's wealthy connections. And Whalen's flashiness and expensive wardrobe were compatible with Walker's style.

Of Whalen's appointment, Arthur "Bugs" Baer, a popular humorist, wrote: "Grover made as handsome a figure as ever nodded from the waist. He had the perfect teeth of an aluminum comb, and a wire walker would have mistaken the part in Grover's hair for a continuation of his act."

Speaking of Whalen's personality, Gene Fowler, a Hearst newspaper stalwart, commented, "Add spats, and stir with a cane."

With his perennial homburg tilted at a rakish angle, and a gardenia in his lapel, Police Commissioner Whalen greeted dignitaries on the steps of City Hall, ordered new uniforms for the cops, and, to show his own Americanism, encouraged anticommunist demonstrations in the streets.

The case against McManus dragged on through the courts for almost a year before he was brought to trial. A noted criminal lawyer, James Murray, represented him and succeeded in having him released on bail of $50,000. The release was challenged in the Appellate Division of the State Supreme Court and all the way up to the state's highest court, the Court of Appeals, but McManus remained a free man.

Finally, the trial ended with a hung jury. The Criminal Court judge directed a verdict of not guilty.

Police Commissioner Whalen blamed others. "The failure to present incontrovertible evidence sufficient for a conviction was due entirely to the laxity of the police who had been assigned to the case originally and the commanding officers of the detective and uniformed forces at the time of the murder," he said. "The case has never been fully explained, and as the laws of our country provide, every man must be considered innocent until proven guilty."

And so, in 1930, George McManus walked.

As for Nigger Nate Raymond, detectives discovered that he was a wealthy "sportsman" from San Francisco but something less than a sterling character in the annals of sportsmanship. He had been barred from all baseball parks in the Pacific Coast League for complicity in bribery scandals. After returning to San Francisco, he rented a private plane and in it married Claire Omley, a movie actress. Among the witnesses at the wedding, which took place in the skies over northern Mexico, was Jack Dempsey, the former heavyweight champion of the world.

So far as is known, Nigger Nate never collected his big score from the deceased gambler's estate. Nobody went to jail for the murder of Arnold Rothstein.

TWO

The Boozy Era

Not long after the acquittal of the leading suspect in the murder of Arnold Rothstein, a second mystery arose to embarrass Whalen's police department and Walker's administration.

Joseph Force Crater, a state Supreme Court justice sitting in Manhattan, disappeared. He was one of Governor Roosevelt's appointments, a bow to Tammany Hall: Judge Crater was close to the Democratic machine. On the way up the political ladder, he served as president of the Nineteenth Assembly District's Cayuga Democratic Club on the Upper West Side. Crater was regarded as an upstanding man. In his choker collar, spats, and black robe, he looked every inch the dignified jurist.

On a summer's night in 1930 when he was last seen, Judge Crater had bought a single ticket to *Dancing Partners,* at the Belasco Theatre on West Forty-fourth Street. Either he had not gone to the show at all or he had walked out after the first act to keep an appointment. He went to Billy Haas's Restaurant on West Forty-fifth Street, a show business hangout, hoisted a few Prohibition drinks with his friends, waved good-bye with his Panama hat to Sally Lou Ritz, a striking Follies girl, and walked into the night and posterity. His disappearance wasn't reported to the public for a full month.

Then sordid facts about Crater's finances and private life emerged. At the same time that he lived respectably as a devoted husband on lower Fifth Avenue, he kept a divorcée in an apartment in midtown. His frequent recesses and adjournments were the subject of courtroom speculation by dirty minds about where and how he spent his afternoons—his personal matinees.

Judge Crater's reputation rested less on his abilities as a student of Sir William Blackstone's commentaries on the law than on glowing reports from producer Florenz Ziegfeld's heavenly showgirls. He was known to be a big spender and skirt chaser. City Hall scribes, a source of fun-and-games news that wasn't always printable, enjoyed spreading the rumor that Judge Crater's extraordinary sexual equipment enabled him to play the Ziegfeld chorus line with exceptional success.

One of Crater's girlfriends, Lorraine Fay, thought she was the forty-one-year-old judge's one and only and planned to file a breach-of-promise suit against him. Another girlfriend, Marie Miller, was an attractive nightclub hostess. A third, Elaine Dawn, a former Ziegfeld girl, also worked in a nightclub after her days on the kick line were over. The most vivid of the tabloids, the suitably named *Evening Graphic,* known for its fake photo montages that featured intimate bedroom escapades, offered a simple explanation for Crater's vanishing:

"Sex is the direct reason for nine-tenths of missing persons."

Looking into Crater's financial records for clues to his disappearance, investigators found that shortly after becoming a judge he took $22,500 out of his bank account—the exact amount of a year's salary on the Supreme Court. The inference was drawn that he had paid his Tammany masters for the privilege of dispensing justice. The investigators also found that he participated in shady real estate deals.

Around the police shacks in the boroughs and in Room 9 at City Hall, where the gentlemen of the press hung their upbrimmed fedoras, some reporters guessed that Judge Crater had accumulated bribes while on the bench, and then fled with one of his floozies. Eventually, he became Case No. 13595 in the records of the Bureau of Missing Persons. The city government expended an estimated quarter of a million dollars to track him down.

For years afterward, sightings of Judge Crater were reported in good-time resorts all over the world. But Case No. 13595 was never solved. To this day, it's still on the books.

The murder of Arnold Rothstein and the mystery surrounding Justice Crater's disappearance stuck in the public's mind. The reputations of important personalities in city and state politics—including the mayor and the governor—came into question. Rexford G. Tugwell, one of Roosevelt's closest advisers and a member of his original "Brain Trust" in Albany, said that New York liberals saw "weakness instead of shrewdness" in the governor's reluctance to discipline Tammany and blow the whistle on Jimmy Walker and his ineffectual commissioners.

W. Kingsland Macy, the powerful Republican boss in the polo-playing precincts of Suffolk County in Long Island's horse country, attempted to gain political capital by the scandals. He called for the state legislature to investigate the governance of New York City, long a Democratic stronghold. Broadway, the GOP leader said, is "the most densely populated and most effectively police-patrolled area in the city or in the United States." How, Macy wondered, could the Rothstein murder have taken place without the police identifying and tracking down the perp or perps?

Pursuing his own ambitions, the U.S. attorney for the Southern District of New York, Charles H. Tuttle, got into the act because he hoped to run on the Republican ticket against Governor Roosevelt. What helped Tuttle to gain the nomination was his revelation that Rothstein wasn't just a big-time betting man but also "the prime factor in a colossal and criminal combination operating in narcotics here and abroad."

Spurred by Kingsland Macy, Republicans put heat on Governor Roosevelt. They introduced a bill to start an investigation of New York City's affairs. But the Tammany leaders—most of whom held well-paid no-show jobs as county clerks and keepers of various seals and records—were not anxious to have the state look too closely at the inside workings of the Walker administration.

Retaliating, the Democrats offered a resolution in the state legislature calling for an investigation of all the towns and villages in Macy's home territory. One of Tammany's elder statesmen maintained that "a little light should be shed on Suffolk County, too." Indeed, the wealthy county was known as a hotbed of cronyism in awarding contracts for repaving its endless roads and in cutting real estate deals with local Republican officials. The Democratic resolution failed, but the Republican bill made it through the Republican-ruled legislature.

Governor Roosevelt vetoed the state legislature's first attempt to examine the Walker administration. In rejecting the Republican effort, which was clearly designed to embarrass him in 1930, Roosevelt declared:

"I do not base my official disapproval on the obvious political aims, as shown by the announcement of its purpose in the press before it was introduced. Such an inquiry defies precedents and adds unheard-of duties to the Governor to meddle in the affairs of every city and county."

But a few years later—as more evidence of malfeasance, misfeasance, and nonfeasance came to the surface about Jimmy Walker and the departments of the City of New York—F.D.R. was forced to authorize a state investigation at the very moment that he began to make plans to pursue the presidency.

The ground had begun to shift under Walker and Tammany's leaders. Reform groups and the press demanded action; at the same time, Roosevelt did not want to succumb to obvious Republican political pressure in Albany. It was a delicate balancing act: the governor still needed Tammany's support in New York City. But by 1932—a presidential election year—Roosevelt had to show the national Democratic leadership that he could be independent and stand up against corruption and criminality in his own state.

Police Commissioner Whalen needed to do something to appear active and divert attention from the Rothstein fiasco. With Mayor Walker's approval, he decided to cleanse the city of New York—not of its organized criminals and gangsters but of its "Reds."

As for Walker, a notorious nonreader, his knowledge of Marxism would barely have filled a thimble. His interest in foreign affairs was limited to what gossip he had traded at expensive watering holes and Michelin-starred restaurants during his frequent junkets to Europe.

"It seemed evident that New York was becoming a hotbed of communism," Whalen said. "There may not have been many in the Party then, but they were all real Tartars, making up for any lack of numbers by their energy and ability to outshout others. It was here in New York that their far-reaching program for the future of the Party in America was being prepared."

Nowadays we tend to think of anticommunist witch-hunts as a product of the wild McCarthyite accusations of the early 1950s. In fact, relatively few people were prosecuted or deported during that time, although reputations were destroyed and individuals lost jobs, particularly in the entertainment field. The 1920s, by contrast, were rife with police actions against thousands of people and with abrogations of the First Amendment in the name of anticommunism.

To compare militant trade union members, and the student radicals arguing about socialism and fascism on the campuses of Brooklyn College and City College, with the hordes of Genghis Khan, as Commissioner Whalen did, sounded far-fetched to New York's civil libertarians. But no one stopped him.

Whalen's operation would, in fact, resemble that of A. Mitchell Palmer, the attorney general of the United States from 1919 to 1921, whose infamous raids against Reds lumped together college-cafeteria radicals, Socialists, anarchists, members of the International Workers of the World, and activists on union picket lines. Palmer's right-hand man in the pursuit of those branded alien radicals was J. Edgar Hoover, head of the Department of Justice's General Intelligence Division, who was rewarded for his Red-hunting activities by being named director of the FBI.

Jimmy Walker's favorite commissioner—at least, his favorite for the moment—said that one of the toughest problems he faced as the city's top cop was how to break up Communist demonstrations held in public squares. To do so, Whalen decided to infiltrate the Communist

Party with fifty young probationary officers. They actually joined the Party, paid their dues, and participated in the endless lectures and debates on the glories of Marxism and dialectical materialism.

Under the command of the Bronx chief of detectives, Henry Bruckner, these special cops were formed into an anti-communist "Intelligence Squad." From a secret headquarters, the police spies sent daily reports through their own switchboard directly to the police commissioner, who then shared the information with Mayor Walker.

"Red infiltration was the greatest enemy of this country and our city," Whalen claimed. In his opinion, New York's other problems—the schools, subways, housing, welfare, crime in the streets, bribery and corruption—were less important than chasing homegrown Reds who carried not weapons but banners.

The police commissioner, a good family man, particularly disliked women radicals:

"The girls in these Communist groups were urged to wear long hatpins in their berets so that at a moment's notice they could pull them out and use them effectively against horses, policemen and detectives as they surged back and forth in the crowds. These women Communists were taught to yell hysterically in rasping, fiendish voices in order to create panic and give the impression that a massacre was taking place. Some women would fall in assumed unconsciousness before the oncoming police and horses, and others were directed to jump at the police and tear at their faces with fingernails."

When a crowd of 100,000 demonstrators gathered in and around Union Square for a march on City Hall to air their grievances about police harassment directly to Mayor Walker, Commissioner Whalen assembled an army of cops to thwart them. The force included a thousand police reserves, three hundred mounted police, and a hundred motorcycle cops. Whalen enlisted the fire department to help his armed forces. Firemen with wrenches stood by at all the hydrants in and around Union Square, prepared to turn them into water cannons against the people. Blocked by the police and firemen, the demonstrators were unable to march below Fourteenth Street.

Thereafter, Whalen's men in blue—otherwise known as New York's Finest—were nicknamed Whalen's Cossacks.

Unlike Walker, Whalen was not beholden to Tammany Hall, because he had a job waiting for him at Wanamaker's whenever he decided to quit. He was sworn in as police commissioner on December 18, 1928, but after a year and a half he resigned and returned to his more lucrative job running the department store. Though there was no open break with the mayor, Whalen felt that Walker had ceased to approve of some of his policies. He was informed by someone on the inside at City Hall that the mayor had said, "Well, we won the election. Now Grover can go." Even if the remark was only a wisecrack, such talk did not endear the mayor to the police commissioner.

The true reason for the break in their friendship was never disclosed by either public official. But some of Whalen's associates believed that it had to do with the conditions he imposed upon Walker before agreeing to take office. In his 1955 autobiography—Whalen, who thought rather well of himself, unabashedly titled it *Mr. New York*—he revealed these terms:

1. That the Mayor would not make any requests of the Police Commissioner for appointments, transfers or promotions during my tenure of office.

2. That I would reduce any police officer whose advancement in the Department had been due to political "pull."

3. That I would immediately retire the Chief Inspector and the Commanding Officer of Detectives regardless of their friendship with the Mayor and replace them with men of my choice without consulting the Mayor.

4. That my term as Police Commissioner would be for one year only.

5. That I would tolerate no interference in cracking down on professional gambling, including any that might be going on in Tammany clubhouses.

6. That I would reorganize the Police Department on a sound basis.

These terms were tough; almost insulting. To Whalen's surprise at the time, Mayor Walker replied that he would accept all of them. But the conditions cut too close to the bone of political appointments.

Some years later, Whalen said, "During my tenure as Police Commissioner, Jimmy Walker never violated any of the terms of the agreement but, as I had predicted, I lost his friendship."

Speaking of Jimmy Walker's choice of Whalen in the first place, Congressman Fiorello La Guardia said: "It takes more than a silk hat and a pair of spats to make an efficient Police Commissioner in the City of New York."

Despite his Red-bashing, Whalen did not change the lax conditions in the force during his brief tenure. Had he been allowed to stay on longer, there might well have been some improvements in the management of the police department.

Actually, in the era of Prohibition, the job of police commissioner was a nearly impossible assignment.

"The twin symbols of the 18th Amendment were the Tommy gun and the poisoned cup," observed Herbert Asbury, a social historian. The Eighteenth Amendment to the U.S. Constitution, which went into effect in 1920, banned the "manufacture, sale, or transportation of intoxicating liquors." From then until its repeal by the Twenty-first Amendment in 1933, the country was divided between "wets" and "drys"—those who wanted to repeal the Amendment, as a well-intentioned failure to regulate people's lives, and those who believed that booze was the root of all evil.

It was a debate that had been going on almost from the beginning of the Republic. Thomas Jefferson encouraged the development of viniculture as an alternative to the production of hard liquor, while James Madison believed that "for the good of the country" young men should abstain altogether. Abraham Lincoln, who did not drink, recalled that during his youth in Indiana and Illinois, intoxicating liquors came forth "like the Egyptian angel of death, commissioned to slay, if not the first, the fairest born in every family."

Yet for all its good intentions, Prohibition chiefly succeeded in turning ordinary citizens into lawbreakers. As Mark Twain said of earlier efforts to regulate the sale of liquor, "Prohibition only drives drunkenness behind doors and into dark places, and does not cure or even diminish it."

New York was already considered sin city by bluenoses when Jimmy Walker became mayor in 1926. The Methodist Board of Temperance, Prohibition and Public Morals called New York "a foreign city run by foreigners for foreigners and according to foreign ideas." The Episcopalians said, "We regard voluntary total abstinence from all intoxicants as the obligation of the city."

The Prohibition laws resulted in bootlegging and the making of bathtub gin and other home brews that could kill as well as intoxicate. It also caused hijacking—truckloads and boatloads of whisky were stolen from rival gangs, often at the point of a sawed-off shotgun. A subculture of lawbreaking developed to circumvent the Federals and the local gendarmerie. Beer and liquor flowed into New York, Chicago, New Orleans, and San Francisco. Canada and Mexico were the major sources of rum-running. Liquor flowed across some four thousand border crossings between the United States and Canada alone. Boats carrying whisky landed at all the Great Lakes ports. When the waterways were frozen, sleds were used to transport whisky over Lake Erie. There were fifteen hundred Prohibition agents, but they were greatly outnumbered by the bootleggers.

The Federals wanted New York's police to do more about finding and shutting down stills and speakeasies. There was a feeling in Washington and Albany that Mayor Walker winked at the lawbreakers. Upright officials in both political parties felt that His Honor set a poor example by dropping in at nightclubs during his nocturnal rounds. The uptown "speaks" favored by Walker were patronized by playboys and ladies of the night; more than Scotch was for sale there. And everyone knew that some of the tonier nightclubs were controlled by gangsters.

In the Southern District of New York, Mabel W. Willebrandt, an assistant U.S. attorney who supervised the Prohibition agents, feuded with Mayor Walker about his failure to enforce Prohibition. With a touch of sarcasm, she said that the mayor himself would make a first-class inspector of nightclubs.

Walker was ready with a wisecrack: "If I were to qualify as an inspector I don't think I should need to become a reckless purchaser of orchids or of Staten Island Champagne to learn facts that are known to virtually everyone."

His retort was directed against Mrs. Willebrandt and her federal agents: she had encouraged them to buy orchids and champagne for their wives and girlfriends while on the job. By playing the role of big spenders, the agents were able to stay undercover—until they flashed their badges at the end of a boozy evening.

Prohibition brought its share of laughs but also its share of hardships to the many people who did not patronize the fancy speakeasies. There were illegal corner and basement saloons where workingmen gambled their wages for the hard stuff, where prostitutes plied their trade, where drunks were rolled, and where ward bosses bought votes for a bottle of hooch.

Two publicity-minded federal agents, Moe W. Smith and Isadore (Izzy) Einstein, kept the tabloids busy describing their exploits busting the owners of stills and speakeasies. They didn't mind if the boys with clunky Speed Graphics accompanied them on their appointed rounds, as long as their pictures later turned up in the newspaper rotogravure sections.

The euphonious team of Izzy and Moe tickled the local burghers with their antics. Even if their disguises didn't fool anyone, their clownlike rubber noses and false whiskers became the team's hallmarks. In Harlem they wore blackface—fooling only themselves; in the classier nightclubs, tuxedos; in country clubs, knickers. What they could not hide was their girth. Izzy was five feet tall and tipped the scales at 225 pounds. Moe outweighed him.

Once, Izzy Einstein met Albert Einstein and asked him about his line of work. "I discover stars in the sky," said the famous scientist. Izzy replied, "I'm a discoverer, too, only I make my discoveries in the basements."

In five years, Izzy and Moe arrested more than four thousand violators of the law and smashed five million bottles of bootleg beer and whisky. Instead of winning medals and promotions, however, the two agents were invited to retire "for the good of the service," probably because they had drawn too much attention to themselves.

Izzy and Moe ended their careers as life insurance salesmen and respected members of the Grand Street Boys Association, a social club that encouraged good deeds on the Lower East Side and raised money for charities. The club was one of Jimmy Walker's favorite hangouts.

During his brief tenure in office, Commissioner Whalen claimed that there were 32,000 speakeasies in New York City. They were discovered in the most unlikely places: tearooms, restaurants, cellars, the penthouses of apartment buildings on both sides of Central Park. One speakeasy was fronted by a synagogue.

The inlets of Long Island served as ports of call for small boats unloading hard liquor. Once in a while, bathers at Coney Island, New York's playground for the poor and middle classes at the ocean end of Brooklyn, heard the boom of small cannon as the Coast Guard fired warning shots across the bows of unregistered speedboats suspected of carrying contraband whisky. Sometimes the whisky was dumped to lighten an unregistered vessel so it could make a fast getaway. To the delight of beachcombers from Coney Island to Montauk Point, 120 miles away at the eastern tip of Long Island, cases of whisky sometimes washed up on the sands.

Garages in the two-family houses of Brooklyn were often rented as hiding places for the small trucks that transported liquor from ships to landfalls after dark. In the neighborhoods of Bensonhurst and Bay Ridge, bottles of booze could be heard rattling in and out of the garages in the middle of the night. It was the better part of wisdom for homeowners picking up a few extra dollars not to ask what the unmarked trucks carried.

Fortunes were made by gangsters as well as by otherwise legitimate businessmen engaged in importing and selling liquor to a thirsty nation. The price of illicit whisky rose by an average of 520 percent during the thirteen years of Prohibition. Raids on speakeasies and gambling dens—and payoffs to the police—were so common that they were hardly worth reporting unless celebrities were caught.

Once caught in farcical style were James J. Walker and Betty Compton, according to the *The East Hampton Star,* Long Island's trusted local newspaper, which normally devoted itself to gardening advice from the Ladies Village Improvement Society, the fortunes of the high school football team, and high-tide news for the commercial fishermen operating beyond the Montauk Point lighthouse. In 1929, a headline in the paper read:

WALKER'S TOUCH OF COMEDY ENDS MONTAUK RAID TALK

The article went on to say that Mayor Walker had been cornered in a gambling raid at the Montauk Island Club but had claimed he was only having dinner in the club's restaurant. The Suffolk Country district attorney—a gentleman with the unlikely name of Wednesday Blue—declined to press charges against the mayor of New York City.

"As long as the Mayor admits he was around when the raid occurred," said Mr. Blue, "that satisfies me. I'm willing to let it go at that."

What *The Star* failed to mention was that Betty Compton had been playing hazard for high stakes in the club's casino—with Jimmy Walker standing at her elbow—when the sheriff's deputies arrived. Walker deserted his ladylove and, borrowing a waiter's apron, tried to disguise himself as a member of the dining room staff. Nobody believed him, of course, yet everybody concerned winked as Jimmy and Betty sailed into the sunset on a yacht that belonged to one of his rich pals and was anchored in Montauk Harbor.

An Association Against the Prohibition Amendment was formed by wealthy industrialists a few years after the law went into effect. They believed that the Eighteenth Amendment increased their taxes and gave too much power to the federal government. A majority of sympathetic Congressmen challenged the Eighteenth Amendment in the early 1930s; it was repealed soon after President Roosevelt took office.

For repeal, the traditional long-term process of ratification by the state legislatures was avoided by an extraordinary method. For the first time since the Constitution itself had been ratified, Congress called for separate ratifying conventions in each state, whose delegates would be elected for the specific purpose of saying yes or no to the Twenty-first Amendment. The nationwide total was almost 73 percent. After this vote, the states were again in control of liquor laws. Several states held steadfast to Prohibition even after federal repeal, but New York became a wet state.

Prohibition played a role in the 1928 presidential election between Alfred E. Smith and Herbert Hoover. In the compaign, Hoover called the federal law "a great social and economic experiment, noble in motive and far-reaching in purpose." Smith, following the Democratic party line, wanted regulation left to the states. Hoover's defense of the Eighteenth Amendment did not help him when he ran against Governor Roosevelt in 1932.

Perhaps Jimmy Walker's greatest moment of glory would come on a fine spring day in 1932 when, dressed in striped trousers, with a flower in his lapel, he led a demonstration up Fifth Avenue during the "beer parade" that marked the end of Prohibition. It was his last hurrah; the worst was yet to come.

The boozy years were drawing to a close.

By now, one-third of the nation was (in F.D.R.'s phrase) "ill-housed, ill-clad and ill-fed." During his first presidential campaign, in words that ignited the dreams of the public—as no other president has in the twentieth century—Roosevelt declared:

"Throughout the Nation, men and women, forgotten in the political philosophy of the Government of the last years, look to us here for guidance and for more equitable opportunity to share in the distribution of national wealth. On the farms, in the large metropolitan areas, in the smaller cities and in the villages, millions of our citizens cherish the hope that their old standards of living and of thought have not gone forever. Those millions cannot and shall not hope in vain. I pledge you, I pledge myself, to a New Deal for the American people."

Even as major felonies occurred in the streets, and corruption was rampant in the business of the city, people recognized the need for a National Recovery Act to revive their personal lives by creating jobs. "N.R.A.—We Do Our Part" became a New Deal slogan that appeared on billboards and in the windows of nearly every home and business. The end of Prohibition meshed with the beginning of the New Deal. By breaking the bonds of criminality that accompanied Prohibition, legitimate businessmen, engaged in the manufacture and transportation of wines, beer, and liquor, could flourish openly without payoffs to gangster elements.

It was not simply Jimmy Walker's open flouting of the liquor laws during his nighttime peregrinations that would bring him down. Governor Roosevelt, in fact, was also a voice against Prohibition: "The methods adopted since the World War with the purpose of achieving a greater temperance by the forcing of Prohibition have been accompanied by complete and tragic failure," Roosevelt said. "It has led to the general encouragement of lawlessness, corruption, hypocrisy, crime and disorder."

A more devastating factor than booze was at work in the Empire City. It was the inability of Walker's district attorneys and police officials to crack other kinds of cases—political ones involving the Tammany hacks and felons in his City for Sale—that fundamentally divided Walker and Roosevelt. Simultaneously, citizen reformers and newspaper editorials clamored for action against the bigtime gangsters and well-known corrupters.

THREE

The Gang's All Here

During Franklin Roosevelt's and Jimmy Walker's early careers in the Democratic party, before World War I, it was recognized that Tammany Hall stood at the center of political power in New York City and sometimes could influence legislation in Albany. Almost every well-paid position in a city department was cleared through the borough leaders—and many jobs could be bought. Doing business with the municipal government also carried a price tag. The corrupted were in cahoots with the corrupters. A quick license, a fake billing, a rakeoff, a moneyed handshake, a wink . . . and the fix would be in.

The big town's agencies and services were for sale. So were the civil and criminal courts. Nominees for the bench were selected by the Tammany chieftains, not by the bar associations or judicial reform groups. Payoffs flowed upward to the Hall from the clubhouses. Everybody understood that this was the way the system worked, the way to get things done.

A permit to make a cut in the sidewalk for a gas station? $50. A variance to add another floor to a skyscraper without a legal setback to let a little sunshine in? That'll be $3,000 for the building inspector, plus another $5,000 lagniappe for "the organization" at Tammany's impressive new headquarters, built on Seventeenth Street and Union

Square in 1929. What's the under-the-table payment for a pier on the Hudson River to dock your transatlantic liner? Well, how does $50,000 in unmarked, untaxed bills sound?

Even if you got a $5 traffic ticket for speeding in your Packard (or Studebaker or Nash or Jordan, any of those elegant, romantic roadsters with rumble seats and running boards), you took it around to your local Democratic clubhouse. There young lawyers on the make volunteered their time and fixed your ticket. Favors brought obligations, greasing the way for ambitious loyalists who hoped to earn a place on the ballot themselves someday.

In gratitude to the district leader, your whole family voted the straight Democratic line in the next election. It didn't matter that some of the old folks couldn't pronounce the names of the candidates or scrawl much more than their signatures; all they had to know was that you marked an "X" next to every five-pointed Democratic star on the ballot.

The Republicans? Tammany's leaders liked to say that the Grand Old Party represented the wealthy and those who pretended to be—the uptown swells who lived on the right side of the New York Central tracks, the straw bosses in starched Arrow Collars whose forebears had arrived long before the turn of the century—not the people in the neighborhoods where most of the working families lived; not "our kind."

After all, the Democrats sneered, look at the Republican presidents running the country in the 1920s: Harding, Coolidge, Hoover. The very mention of their names caused disdain among the Democratic faithful in New York State.

Then, of course, there were progressive-minded politicians like the Roosevelts.

To be sure, there were Roosevelts and Roosevelts—Republican Theodore from Oyster Bay, on the north shore of Long Island, and Democratic Franklin from Hyde Park, on the Hudson Highlands. The two men were distant kinsmen. Franklin's bride, Eleanor Roosevelt, was his cousin as well as Theodore Roosevelt's niece. At Franklin and Eleanor's wedding in 1905, Theodore Roosevelt gave the bride away.

Teddy Roosevelt had emerged as the leader of reform Republicans in the New York State Assembly in the early 1880s. Then he mounted his steed as colonel of a volunteer cavalry unit, the "Rough Riders," in Cuba during the Spanish-American War, and heroically rode off to the governorship in 1899. Elected vice president in 1900, he succeeded the assassinated William McKinley in September 1901.

Franklin Roosevelt turned to the Democratic party from another direction, as part of the reform movement of the Progressive Era. F.D.R.'s father, James, was a registered Democrat and had been a life-long supporter of New York governor, and then president, Grover Cleveland in the 1880s and 1890s. As governor, Cleveland had distanced himself from Tammany Hall. The Cleveland Democrats still carried weight in New York State politics. Personally and politically, it was only natural that Franklin Roosevelt be nominated by Dutchess County's Democrats for state senator in 1910.

F.D.R. was not Tammany's man, then or later, but in Albany he saw the need to get along with all factions of the Democratic party. The Tammany Democracy in Albany included Alfred E. Smith, a future governor, and Robert F. Wagner, a future U.S. senator. Early on, Smith dismissed the new senator from Dutchess County as a brash young man, more interested in civil service reform than social legislation. But Roosevelt was a quick study and soon found himself in agreement with Smith and Wagner, the cities' leading spokesmen in Albany. Indeed, it can be said that Roosevelt first learned about political compromise and the need for social reform from both of them.

From the beginning of his political journey, Roosevelt knew something that Tammany and some of the newspaper columnists who considered him only a dilettante didn't know: Almost from the time he was elected president of the Harvard *Crimson* in 1903 and entered Columbia University's law school the following year, F.D.R. had envisioned himself as a future president of the United States. With or without Tammany's support, he would work relentlessly to achieve that dream.

"Politics is business; that's what's the matter with it. The corruption that shocks us in public affairs we practice ourselves in our private concerns."

So wrote Lincoln Steffens, one of the pioneering muckrakers against municipal corruption, in *The Shame of the Cities*. But Steffens was only a journalist, a member of a lowly profession that perforce stands on the outside looking in. To know Tammany from the inside demanded a "philosopher" in the tradition of the legendary George Washington Plunkitt, a Democratic ward boss on the Lower East Side of Manhattan in the 1880s. The gregarious and loquacious Plunkitt transacted all his business from what he called his office: the bootblack stand in front of the New York County Courthouse.

Plunkitt lives in history for coining the phrase "honest graft." He received four salaries—simultaneously—for serving as a magistrate, alderman, county supervisor and state senator. With a straight face, he defined the difference between business and larceny:

"The politician who steals is worse than a thief. He is a fool. With the grand opportunities all around for the man with a political pull there's no excuse for stealing a cent. It makes me tired to hear old codgers boasting that they retired from politics without a dollar except what they earned in their profession or private business. If they lived today they would be just the same as the rest of us. There ain't any more honest people in the world just now than the convicts in Sing Sing. Not one of them steals anything. Because they can't, my boy, because they can't.

"As for me, I see my opportunities and I take them. Honest graft."

Jimmy Walker came out of a long tradition of acceptable bribery and official looting—and, somewhat surprisingly, patriotism. As a proper Tammany man by inheritance and preference, Walker sometimes wrapped himself in the flag during his speeches. New Yorkers lapped up his patriotic platitudes in behalf of God, country, and the greatest city in the world.

In Walker's time, Tammany was still considered a benevolent political organization. The sachems served as the motor running the Democratic party in New York City, and party traditions mattered. The organization was established more than two centuries ago as the Society of St. Tammany, or Columbian Order, by William Mooney, a Continental Army veteran. The name derived from Tamanend, a legendary

Indian chief who had a reputation for wisdom and love of liberty. The society's original purpose was pure: to help the cause of American independence.

In the post–Revolutionary War period, Tammany men affected Indian names and titles. Originally, there were thirteen trustees, after the original thirteen states. The president, or leader, was the Grand Sachem. The title of Great Grand Sachem was conferred upon the president of the United States; Andrew Jackson was the last president so honored. Unlike the politicos who influenced elections in other states by the force of local personalities, Tammany was a long-lived New York institution.

Below the Sachems came the Sagamore (master of ceremonies), the Scribe (secretary), and the Wiskinskie (doorkeeper). The Indian dress gradually became purely ceremonial, but the titles of Grand Sachem, Sachem, and Wiskinskie continued. Eventually, top hats replaced feathered headgear, but they served the same purpose: to signify beribboned Authority. Another carryover from the founding days was the use of the term "Wigwam" for the organization's meeting hall.

The democratization of the ballot box was one of Tammany's original goals; the society helped to bring about the removal of the property qualification for voting. The broadened franchise brought Tammany a greater following in New York City. Almost at the same time, Tammany members in the city government began to use their powers in corrupt ways. One of the first Grand Sachems to be convicted was Matthew L. Davis, who defrauded banks and insurance companies of several million dollars in the 1820s. When some of the Sachems were caught in swindles, the society learned how to use its influence to bring about light prison terms.

The pattern of election, dictation, and corruption in Tammany Hall began to flourish in the middle of the nineteenth century. One of Tammany's most notorious leaders was Fernando Wood, who had served in Congress and been involved in commercial and political fraud—perfect training for accumulating Tammany boodle. As the Democratic mayor of New York, Wood ruled in an era of gangs that performed as bullyboys for the machine during elections.

When he was denied renomination—not for wrongdoing but because of his eccentric, obsessive behavior—Wood organized a faction of Tammany named Mozart Hall, after its meeting place. Though they professed loyalty to the Union cause, elements in both Tammany and Mozart Hall were Southern sympathizers. During the Civil War, the Lincoln administration considered Fernando Wood and his "Peace Democrats" troublemakers if not actually treasonous.

The post–Civil War era introduced Tammany's most inventive scoundrel, William Marcy Tweed. He was perhaps the greatest spoilsman in American municipal history as well as a master of subterranean politics. Tweed was the first to have bestowed on him the title "Boss" that preceded the names of future leaders.

After being elected to the Board of Supervisors in New York, he formed what became known as the Tweed Ring. Its purpose was to lobby in support of bills for unnecessary supplies—again and again and again. As soon as he became head of Tammany Hall, Tweed increased the "tax" on contractors supplying materials to the city from a "normal" 10 percent to 35 percent. He created fictitious public institutions, put in his friends as officers, then billed the city for millions of dollars to run the nonexistent agencies.

Nearly every city job from janitor to judge could be bought. The Tweed Ring nomination to such a lucrative office as county clerk, for example, cost $40,000. It was well worth the bribe to the lucky incumbent.

In its proudest hour, *The New York Times* published evidence that blew the Tweed Ring wide open in 1871 and thereafter. It fired off a long editorial salvo, "The Democratic Millennium," which began: "We should like to have a treatise from Mr. Tweed on the art of growing rich in as many years as can be counted on the fingers of one hand. You might begin with nothing and in five or six years you can boast of your ten millions. How was it done? We wish Mr. Tweed to tell us."

The independent newspaper kept up the drumbeat while other papers, generally partisan in those days, including *The World* and *The Sun,* scolded *The Times*'s crusade, saying its anti-Tweed editorials harmed New York City's credit in Wall Street and the banking and business community. The only help *The Times* received came from

Thomas Nast, the editorial cartoonist for *Harper's Weekly,* the political and literary journal; Nast's biting pen etched memorable images of the Ring of corruption. Nast created the Tammany tiger (the idea stemmed from the tiger's head that decorated Tweed's volunteer fire engine company), the Republican elephant, and the Democratic donkey—symbols employed by cartoonists to this day.

The main cover for Tammany's phony appropriations at the time was a new county courthouse, built near the then new City Hall. A half-dozen courthouses could have been built for the money spent on its faked costs. One phantom firm alone received $6 million in two years "for supplying furniture and carpets." (The infamous building remains in City Hall Park today. Justice is no longer meted out there, but passersby with a sense of history still refer to it as the Tweed Courthouse.) *The Times* attacked the building costs vociferously.

Retaliating, Boss Tweed and his lieutenants devised a scheme to buy *The Times* for $5 million and thus silence it. In response, the newspaper printed an editorial that said "no money" could induce the hard-pressed owners to sell a single share of stock to Tammany "or to anyone associated with it or indeed to any person or party whatever until the struggle is fought out."

Historians have calculated that, at a minimum, Boss Tweed and his cronies stole $75 million from the city. After being indicted and convicted, Tweed uttered an unforgettable line as he entered prison. When the warden of the Blackwell's Island penitentiary asked his occupation, Tweed drew himself up and said: "Statesman!"

After Boss Tweed's reign, Tammany leaders attempted to reform their old practices. Instead of "Boss" before the names of the Grand Sachems, the word "Honest" appeared—thus such leaders as "Honest John" O'Neill and "Honest John" Kelly. These sobriquets, however, did not save some of the leaders from spending time behind bars.

The most powerful Tammany Sachem in the twentieth century was Charles Francis Murphy, who ruled the Hall from 1902 to 1924, a time when Jimmy Walker was making a name for himself as a party loyalist while representing New York City in the State Assembly and Senate in Albany. In the same years, F.D.R. served as a state senator and assistant secretary of the Navy; he was the vice presidential nominee in 1920, and made the "Happy Warrior" speech nominating Al Smith for president at the Democratic convention in 1924.

Murphy, a respected saloonkeeper, got himself appointed to the lucrative post of docks commissioner of the busy Port of New York. In the four saloons he owned, decorum was the rule and no women were allowed. Personally, he was considered a good family man who could never be accused of such everyday vices as smoking or drinking.

Al Smith and Jimmy Walker both admired Murphy's democratic touch. Rather than appearing at the hall itself in the evening, "Silent Charlie" often kept office hours under a street lamp on Second Avenue and Twentieth Street, in the Gashouse District where he grew up. There the people could pay him their respects and request a boon. He had three short answers: "Yes," "No," and "I'll look into it." Murphy once explained why he measured out his words so carefully: "Most of the troubles of the world could be avoided if men opened their minds instead of their mouths."

Financially, Boss Murphy was in fine shape. In the course of his tenure as docks commissioner, he banked a million dollars. New York, after all, was a busy and lucrative port—especially for the commissioner. After dining at Delmonico's Restaurant in midtown with his acolytes and the city's rich and powerful, the "Commissioner"—a title he cherished long after he was out of office—often relaxed on his large estate in Hampton Bays, where he built his own private nine-hole golf course.

Nine holes, not eighteen. Obviously, Murphy was a frugal man; after his magnificent funeral at St. Patrick's Cathedral, it was discovered that he left an estate amounting to $2, 170, 761.

Big Tim Sullivan, an ally of Silent Charlie Murphy, controlled his own fiefdom on the East Side of Manhattan below Union Square. Sullivan was also known by his original nickname, Dry Dollar (from his habit, in the days when he too was a saloonkeeper, of carefully wiping the bar before anyone placed money on it). He was a leader who took care of his constituents, including judges he had put on the bench. In turn, they took care of him when his friends were involved in bankruptcy and other litigation.

Big Tim also looked out for Arnold Rothstein. Sullivan "licensed" Rothstein's gambling establishments. In return for immunity from police raids, a percentage of Rothstein's income from his clubs went to the Tammany leader.

What Big Tim Sullivan could do best was win elections. He once admitted to a crony that the best "repeaters" at the polls were men who wore whiskers:

"When you've voted 'em with their whiskers on, you take 'em to a barber and scrape off the chin fringe. Then you vote 'em again with side lilacs and a mustache. Then to a barber again, off comes the sides and you vote 'em a third time with the mustache. If that ain't enough and the box can stand a few more ballots, clean off the mustache and vote 'em plain face. That makes every one of 'em good for four votes."

It's easy to think of the era of Tammany dominance as an unbroken chain of corrupt, money-driven, antidemocratic governance. And it is true that certain temptations persist whenever one party controls local nominations and elections. After all, even in the 1990s, New York politics had to concern itself with ferreting out organized crime in local, monopolistic industries. Actually, Tammany changed with the times. In later years, it even had its own reformers. Boss Murphy's successor, between 1924 and 1929, was George W. Olvany, who had a comparatively clean reputation and came in at the strong suggestion of Al Smith.

It was said that Olvany was the only member of the Board of Aldermen who had remained seated when a youngster poked his head into a meeting and shouted, "Alderman, your saloon is on fire!"

Olvany was a Greenwich Village boy who somehow avoided membership in the Hudson Dusters, the local barefisted gang, and instead played with Jimmy Walker and went to church with Al Smith. He progressed through the clubs to become deputy fire commissioner, sheriff's counsel, and (for six months) a criminal court judge. No sooner did he step into the leadership of the Hall, however, than he began to make party professionals long for Silent Charlie Murphy.

Olvany's trouble was that he had a big mouth, into which he often put both feet. For instance, in the apostolic publication *World's Work,* he wrote with Celtic pride: "The Irish are natural leaders. The strain of Limerick keeps them at the top. They have the ability to handle men. Even the Jewish districts have Irish leaders. The Jews want to be ruled by them."

Nor did Tammany veterans appreciate Olvany's righteousness and bragging about Jimmy Walker's clean government: "If there is the slightest suspicion of grafting fastened upon anyone in our organization, his resignation is demanded at once. We will not tolerate it for a moment. I state with positive conviction that New York is the best-governed city in the world. There is less corruption in New York than in some cities one-tenth its size."

Whether this was wishful thinking or foolish political boasting, most of Olvany's colleagues in the organization undoubtedly would have disagreed. For the most important "clean" Tammany man at the time, Al Smith, was too smart and too honest to boast. As governor and as a Democratic standard-bearer for president, Smith had attained national stature.

In many ways, Smith was a fighting governor, who blazed the trail of social legislation that Franklin D. Roosevelt would follow when he became governor. Smith took special pride in the state's Labor Department, which set higher safety standards in factories and encouraged compensation claims by the 400,000 workers in the state who were injured in industrial injuries every year. That same attitude was evinced in the stronger labor laws that Governor Roosevelt carried from Albany to Washington.

At the height of his power in the 1920s, Smith was also admired beyond the borders of his own country. One of the keenest assessments of him was made by André Siegfried, a French political scientist, in his 1927 book, *America Comes of Age*. Siegfried wrote:

"Al Smith has attained national prestige, partly by his honesty and his ability, but mainly owing to his origins in the slum quarters of New York. The enormous mass of immigrants rightly look upon him as their mouthpiece, for he is Catholic, though not the tool of the Church; a man of the people in every fibre and yet not an extremist; and above all he proclaims a new Americanism in which the Nordic

Protestant tradition counts for nothing. In spite of his crudeness, this Irish-American stands for the best in the non-Anglo-Saxon community, and the foreign population feels for the first time that he gives them access to power and honors."

When Walker pledged to be "a Tammany Hall Mayor" who would always follow the Hall's "leadership and advice," Smith, who particularly disliked Walker's philandering because it harmed the Democratic party's image—and his own presidential aspirations—warned him to change his ways, or else. As a longtime friend who grew up in the same culture, Smith told him bluntly:

"Jimmy, the wind is getting stronger and you're going to be blown sky-high."

In the past, reformers had usually challenged Tammany's chokehold on the city from outside the confines of the Hall. Edwin L. Godkin, the founding editor of *The Nation,* wrote: "The three things a Tammany leader most dread are, in the ascending order of repulsiveness, the penitentiary, honest industry and biography."

One such quixotic "biographer"—the Reverend Charles H. Parkhurst of the Madison Square Presbyterian Church, who was also a busy member of the Society for the Prevention of Crime—blamed Tammany for the city's rampant vice in the gay 1890s. He correctly surmised that payoffs to the police and public officials were necessary for the brothels and gambling dens to be tolerated.

Delivering a sermon on St. Valentine's Day—a time normally associated with thoughts of love rather than kinky sex—Dr. Parkhurst aroused his parishioners as he addressed them in fire-and-brimstone language:

"There is not a form under which the Devil disguises himself, that so perplexes us in our efforts, or so bewilders us in the devising of our schemes, as the polluted harpies that, under the pretense of governing this city, are feeding day and night on its quivering vitals. While we fight iniquity, Tammany shields and patronizes it; while we try to convert criminals they manufacture them; and they have a hundred dollars invested in manufacturing machinery to our one invested in converting machinery."

Dr. Parkhurst's own adventures while searching for evidence in the nether regions of organized sin helped lighten the mood of his parishioners and all New Yorkers who enjoyed reading about his peregrinations. Parkhurst insisted on witnessing New York's vice up close and in person.

What Dr. Parkhurst saw while touring the dens of wickedness for weeks shocked him out of his wits. To look like a patron, he disguised himself by wearing checked black-and-white trousers, a red flannel scarf, and a slouch hat. He did not have to add false whiskers; he wore his own real ones. Dr. Parkhurst discovered ten-cent whisky saloons frequented by children; opium dens; "tight houses" (so called because the ladies there cavorted in skimpy skivvies); and five-cent lodging houses frequented by derelicts who emerged only at election time as Democratic voters for a bottle of booze.

Dr. Parkhurst visited Hattie Adams's famous brothel, where a "dance of nature" was performed by five young ladies, each dressed in a demure Mother Hubbard gown. The ladies then doffed all their garments and frolicked around the room bare-assed, playing leapfrog. In the spirit of fun, they jumped over Dr. Parkhurst's accomplice, Charles W. Gardner, a detective hired for $6 a night to show him the town.

The good Reverend watched the naked women without flinching, slowly sipped his beer, and took notes. When Hattie herself pulled on Dr. Parkhurst's whiskers, he bristled and warned her not to attempt any further familiarities.

The crusading Dr. Parkhurst demanded of Gardner, "Show me something worse!"

After downing a fortifying drink of Cherry Hill whisky in a saloon on Cherry Street, "he acted as if he had swallowed a whole political parade, torchlights and all," the detective said. They moved on to the Golden Rule Pleasure Club on West Third Street, where Dr. Parkhurst was greeted by Scotch Ann, an imaginative madam who escorted him to a row of cubicles, offering him a variety of sexual games that were forbidden in the Good Book, sometimes leading to death by stoning.

"In each room sat a youth whose face was painted, eyebrows blackened, and who spoke in the high falsetto voice of a young girl," Parkhurst discovered. When Scotch Ann explained what unusual pleasures awaited him in the cubicles, the clergyman decided that he had seen enough.

"Why, I wouldn't stay in that house for all the money in the world!" Dr. Parkhurst declared, and fled past Scotch Ann into the clean night air.

Speaking out against the vice purveyors, Dr. Parkhurst described them and their Tammany protectors as "a lying, perjured, rum-soaked and libidinous lot. Anyone who, with all the easily ascertainable facts in view, denies that drunkenness, gambling and licentiousness in this town are municipally protected, is either a knave or a fool."

Despite Parkhurst's brave undercover work, no significant changes were made in the vice-ridden Tenderloin, the sporting-house area in the West Twenties and Thirties between Sixth and Eighth Avenues. It was called the Tenderloin by an otherwise honest police captain, Alexander S. Williams, who decided to pick up a little graft by leaving a quiet residential neighborhood and transferring to the district. "I've had nothin' but chuck steak for a long time," he said, "and now I'm goin' to get a little of the tenderloin." Because of his liberal use of the nightstick, Captain Williams was nicknamed Clubber. The reformers found that the cops increased arrests of street prostitutes and saloon girls because they could not be shaken down as easily as brothelkeepers. But the police made sure that the houses of ill-repute on their beat were not raided. The brothels run by Hattie Adams, Scotch Ann, and scores of other enterprising madams all over town were accepted by the city fathers as a "legitimate" part of the underground economy.

As for Dr. Parkhurst, he kept hammering away in his sermons at the seamy side of life in New York. In 1918, he retired as pastor of Madison Square Presbyterian Church and began writing a newspaper column for one of his old enemies, William Randolph Hearst. In 1927, at the age of eighty-five, he married his longtime secretary (his first wife had died six years before). Dr. Parkhurst lived to see a reform administration take over City Hall in 1933. That year, at the age of ninety-two, he expired.

Another fierce Tammany "biographer," overlapping with Jimmy Walker in Manhattan politics, was Fiorello H. La Guardia, affectionately known in the tabloids as the Little Flower. As much as Walker, ethnic New York flowed in his veins. Fiorello was born at 177 Sullivan Street on the Lower East Side of Manhattan, the son of Italian immigrants—a Jewish mother, Irene Luzzatto Coen, from Trieste, and an Italian agnostic father, Achille La Guardia, from Foggia. He was raised on military posts in the West, where his father was an Army bandmaster. At the age of nineteen, Fiorello joined the U.S. Consular Service and was stationed in Trieste and Budapest, where he acquired a knowledge of French, German, Italian and Croatian. La Guardia could campaign and curse in a half-dozen languages, and he was able to do both in the linguistic mosaic of Manhattan.

After becoming a lawyer, he ran for Congress as both a Progressive and Republican in the Tammany-controlled Twentieth Assembly District, which lay mostly on the East Side of Manhattan, and also included East Harlem. He scored an astonishing victory and was elected in 1916. When the United States entered World War I, he learned to fly and enlisted in the Army's fledgling Aero Service, rising to the rank of major overseas. All his life, he was proud to be called Major.

After the war, he accepted an offer to run for president of the New York City Board of Aldermen, and won again—the first Republican to do so. In Boss Tweed's day, the aldermen were referred to, with some justification, as the Forty Thieves. Things hadn't changed too much in the city's legislative body in the 1920s; it was among the aldermen that La Guardia observed the excesses of the Tammany machine close up. He exposed the fact that a Tammany leader's son obtained for $7,500—and without bidding—a city pier contract worth hundreds of thousands of dollars. After a brief stint as president of the board, La Guardia was reelected to Congress in 1922, becoming the leading

House liberal in fighting against Prohibition, racism, and the prevailing doctrine of laissez-faire for big business.

As a Republican in both New York and Washington, La Guardia was the odd man *in*. "I stand for the Republicanism of Abraham Lincoln," he explained, "and let me tell you that the average Republican leader east of the Mississippi doesn't know any more about Abraham Lincoln than Henry Ford knows about the Talmud." The crack against Ford referred to his anti-Semitism.

La Guardia's short temper and voluble style sometimes troubled even his admirers. His close friend Adolf A. Berle, Jr., a Columbia law professor who was a Roosevelt Brain Truster, once said of him, "If Fiorello was a demagogue, he was a demagogue in the right direction."

When Mayor Walker ran for a second term in 1929, his opponent was Congressman La Guardia. Could Fiorello stand a chance against the Tammany machine and the popular mayor? La Guardia thought so. "There's a long shot winning in Saratoga every day," he said. "There is one thing I know how to do and that is to beat Tammany Hall."

Citing his record as a vote-getter, La Guardia's loyal Italian followers recited:

> Seven times he's won elections,
> Seven times he's reached the top.
> He is proud he's an American,
> And he's proud he is a Wop!

The Hearst newspapers supported Mayor Walker. While most of the other New York dailies leaned toward the Republicans during elections, *The New York Times* offered its readers an independent balance sheet of Jimmy Walker's assets and liabilities in its inimitable, objective style:

THE MAYOR HE MIGHT BE

If the people of this city were asked to sum up the official character of Mayor Walker nine out of ten of them would dwell upon his great personal charm, his talent for friendship, his broad sympathies embracing all sorts and conditions of men, his ready wit, his brilliance as a speaker at every kind of gathering or function, his skill as a politician, his gift for winning support from the most unlikely quarters. These estimates of the Mayor are true enough, but they ignore certain things in him which he usually keeps in the background, but which mark him out as a man naturally fitted for a great executive position.

Mr. Walker has a singularly alert intelligence. He is quick not only in epigram and repartee, but in grasp of the essentials of a governmental problem laid before him. Probably no man in New York better understands its public business. What has been done, Mr. Walker has at the end of his fingers; what should be done at the end of his tongue. His versatility, his ingenuity in finding ways out of difficulties, his swift dispatch of affairs demanding his attention, his adroitness in dealing with opposition and in composing controversies—all these are high qualities in a public servant and should equip him for a most useful career.

After this extravagant introduction to Walker's instincts and talents, the anonymous *Times* editorial writer let the other shoe drop and said what he (there were no women on the editorial board then) really meant to say:

What has been lacking has been the steady application of uncommon abilities to the uncommonly complicated and arduous work of the office. The city has stood by and seen, as it were, great powers going to waste. Citizens have not so much minded Mr. Walker's frequent absences, or his obvious delight in the social side of life, but they have regretted that he has not devoted himself more exclusively and sternly to the big job placed in his hands. Everybody who knows Mr. Walker well is confident that he has in him the makings of a remarkable chief magistrate of this city. The Mayor that he has been gives only a hint of the Mayor that he might be.

As for La Guardia, *The Times* noted that he was a worthwhile legislator with a strong record in Congress, a New Yorker who was close to his constituents, and a onetime president of the Board of Aldermen with a knowledge of city affairs. But as usual he was running as a Republican, and the newspaper, which normally leaned toward incumbent Democrats, did not break ranks with its independent electoral history and endorse him.

Republican party enrollment citywide was less than half that of the Democrats. Running against the odds, La Guardia accused Walker of playing by the Tammany rules. He even claimed that the mayor and the police department knew who had killed Arnold Rothstein but did nothing to bring the murderer before the bar of justice. Despite La Guardia's strong campaign—he spoke Yiddish in Brooklyn's Jewish neighborhoods and Italian in Manhattan's Little Italy—Mayor Walker won by better than a two-to-one margin, 865,000 to 368,000, with Norman Thomas, the Socialist candidate, receiving 175,000 votes.

Walker's humor had often saved the day (and night) during the campaign. When La Guardia attacked him for getting his salary raised from $25,000 to $40,000 a year, he responded: "Why, that's cheap! Think what it would cost if I worked full time!"

Tammany leaders celebrated his victory with block parties and Walker visited the clubhouses to thank his supporters. On the quiet, he lifted a glass with old friends. His favorite drink was champagne or a Black Velvet, a mixture of champagne and Guinness stout.

For La Guardia, the defeat was only temporary; his career was destined to blossom again. "To the victor belongs the responsibility for good government," the Little Flower said. Although badly defeated, he had helped to open a window on corruption and Tammany's role in city affairs.

Walker said, "I hope this will be the last of the time-worn, moth-eaten imaginary slogan, 'anti-Tammany.'" But it would be his last run for public office before human termites were discovered undermining the foundations of City Hall.

Even some Democratic politicians worried about Jimmy Walker as mayor, not so much because of his lifestyle, though it demanded greater financial resources than he earned legitimately, but because of his inability to guard against the greed of others. They recognized

Walker as an attractive vote-getter who was exalted by the electorate, yet harbored friendly doubts about him.

One of the most powerful doubters was Edward J. Flynn, the man to see in the Bronx, whose background was similar to Walker's: he was a son of Irish immigrants, a graduate of Fordham Law School, an attorney, and a state assemblyman. After a move to make him president of the Board of Aldermen collapsed, he became sheriff of Bronx County, a sinecure that operated under a fee system: the sheriff and his underlings collected fees for serving numerous writs and other court papers.

The sheriff's office was ideal training for the spoils system and advancement to county leader. In effect, Flynn became political boss of the Bronx, with the advice and consent of Tammany Hall in Manhattan. Unlike some of his confreres in the Wigwam on Union Square, he was generally respected by his constituents.

Boss Flynn observed Jimmy Walker at close range for many years. His assessment of the mayor's character was as perceptive as Governor Al Smith's. Flynn regarded Walker with a mixture of warmth and despair:

"No one in New York politics was more personable or more generally liked than Jimmy Walker. No one could become really angry with him. When, as frequently happened in my relations with him, he would do something that annoyed me, I found that his manner was so boyishly disarming that my resentment usually evaporated. This was a beguiling characteristic, but one which was destined ultimately to give him much trouble. Many of the people who surrounded him were superficial and rapacious. He found it hard to believe that any of his friends were bad—or even wrong. In the end, Jimmy became the victim of some of these so–called 'friends.'"

In retrospect, Flynn had to admit that during the Walker administration New York had "the worst example of the 'spoils system' that could be imagined."

As a Democratic leader, Flynn was of a higher caliber than the political bosses who ruled the boodle departments in Brooklyn and Manhattan. Governor Roosevelt appointed Flynn his secretary of state in Albany, and he remained a close political ally of the future president.

To be sure, there were early indications that Jimmy Walker was on the take to support his expensive habits, which included making improvements on his home. One of his favorite millionaires, Jules Mastbaum, quietly paid for the repairs on his house on St. Luke's Place. "Go ahead and fix up the place and send me the bill," Walker's generous friend offered. The cost was $25,000. It was later discovered that Mastbaum had also been an intermediary in a deal that got the Mayor $26,500 in bonds and involved a payoff for a public transportation franchise.

Another one of Walker's fawning millionaires, A. C. Blumenthal, a man-about-town and theatrical producer, put his private railway car at the mayor's disposal when Walker was invited to make a speech at a dedication of a Confederate army monument in Georgia. It was never made clear why Walker was chosen, unless it was for his oratorical skills and ability to please any audience—even if doing so meant playing to their prejudices and rewriting the past.

Speaking of the Civil War at the ceremony, Mayor Walker cast the bloody conflict in terms the audience wanted to hear:

"It was a real he-war, and it was predicated largely upon the theory that some men held in respect to the sovereign rights of the individual states. The South of the sixties of the last century fought for states' rights, and today, in the twentieth century, I believe you gave up the fight too soon."

The audience cheered his remarks. At a banquet afterward, Mayor Walker spoke of his affection for his beloved father and for General Robert E. Lee, somehow linking them in his pantheon of heroes.

The New York *Herald Tribune* was unimpressed by Walker's junkets or by his ready excuse that he was "working" as a "goodwill ambassador" for the city. In an editorial comment, the newspaper noted that, during his first two years in office, the mayor had spent 143 days out of New York, visiting Hollywood, Houston, San Francisco, Atlanta, Florida, Louisville (for the Kentucky Derby), Paris, London, Berlin, Rome, and Dublin, with a few side trips to Bermuda and Havana.

Nearly one year later, Walker's total days spent away from his office would be higher, and he still seemed very secure. When he appeared in a self-aggrandizing film, *The New York Times* reported: "The Mayor, with grace and ease many a movie star might envy, played the principal role in a Movietone production of 'Building with Walker,' produced in the open air at Broadway and 47th Street. The Mayor's monologue, which might have been entitled 'My City,' was followed by scenes of subway construction, with steam-shovel accompaniment, interspersed with musical interludes by a band."

In November 1928, just after Arnold Rothstein lost his life, Alfred E. Smith was defeated in his campaign for president by Herbert Hoover. And though Franklin D. Roosevelt won the governership by a narrow plurality of 29,000 votes against Albert Ottinger, his Republican opponent, what counted to Tammany Hall was that the legislature in Albany was now Republican in both houses.

With Roosevelt in the governor's chair, the reformers were on the march. In his first inaugural address, on January 1, 1929, Roosevelt graciously praised his predecessor, Alfred E. Smith, as a "public servant of true greatness" and then pledged that the state would not become involved in "partisan politics" during his administration. The next day, in his first annual message to the legislature, Roosevelt began to outline his programs.

His words foretold the vastly larger-scaled National Recovery Act, which he would establish during his first term in the White House.

Roosevelt expressed concern for the alarming number of farms abandoned because of the agricultural depression that had existed since 1920. He proposed a fairer adjustment of assessments and taxes to help family-owned farms exist. Both the farmer and the consumer would gain, he said, if "the problem of distribution" could be solved.

Then Roosevelt addressed the needs of working men and women in the cities and towns. "When I consider the extraordinary progress which has been made in labor and social legislation," he said, "I am reminded of the fact that eighteen years ago, when I was a member of the legislature, any person advocating a large part of the laws which have been enacted would have been called a dangerous radical." (That—and worse—is exactly what he was branded in Albany and Washington.) But, Roosevelt added, criticism was the price that had to be paid for social progress throughout history.

"While much has been accomplished so far, we cannot stand still, and I recommend to you the following program which I believe to be the needs of the day:

"A real eight-hour day and forty-eight-hour week for women and children in industry.

"The establishment for them of an advisory minimum or fair wage board.

"The extension of workmen's compensation to give its benefits to all occupational diseases.

"The continuation of such provisions of the emergency rent laws as are necessary.

"Declaration by law that the labor of a human being is not a commodity or an article of commerce."

This last recommendation was not so much a legal remedy as a philosophical expression of sympathy for people who worked with their hands—a Rooseveltian Emancipation Proclamation for labor in the twentieth century.

As the Depression struck the nation in October 1929, Governor Roosevelt's programs to improve working conditions and aid the unemployed were enacted. In his last annual message to the legislature before he moved on to Washington, Governor Roosevelt expressed for the state a commitment that would later resound for the country:

"The actual present conditions of life which face at least two millions of the citizens of our State compel a reiteration of the principle to which we are committed—that the people of the State of New York cannot allow any individuals within her borders to go unfed, unclothed, or unsheltered. From that fundamental springs all the work of relief now in progress."

In Manhattan, another story was slowly beginning to surface that threatened the stability of government and the public's belief in the integrity of some of their officials.

Yet even while rumbles of discontent with City Hall were heard in the broadsheet newspapers, Jimmy Walker himself still remained the prodigal son of Tammany's Sachems. Occasional questions were raised about his personal and ceremonial activities, but he remained popular with the tabloids and the electorate. Few citizens—or journalists—were aware of the degree of corruption that existed inside the municipal government.

Scandal was in the air, but the majority of the people believed it had nothing to do with their own Jimsie. Only half in jest, an unnamed crony of the mayor was quoted as saying, sotto voce, "One thing about Jimmy, he may steal a dime, but he'll always let you take a penny."

The Tammany Sachems and their loyalists still gathered in their new Wigwam on Union Square, confident that nothing would change in the Democratic-controlled precincts of the city. So, raising mugs of bootleg beer, the party faithful sang their ancient theme song:

> *Tammany, Tammany,*
> *Swamp 'em, swamp 'em*
> *Get the wampum,*
> *Taammanee!*

But Jimmy Walker's rhinestone world was about to be exposed to daylight by the Goo-Goos, by the Seabury investigation, and, to Tammany's surprise, by Governor Roosevelt himself.

FOUR

Night Mayor of New York

New Yorkers adored Mayor James J. Walker. He was one of them: a hometown boy, part Kilkenny sentimentalist, part Greenwich Village boulevardier, an Irish charmer with the gift of gab who was good for a laugh at his own expense—and theirs. Among his many contributions to political and human discourse were some memorable one-liners:

"I'm trying to find out if Diogenes was on the level."

"No girl was ever ruined by a book."

"There are two places where politicians end up, the farm or the breadline. I am a farmer—at the moment."

"A reformer is a guy who rides through a sewer in a glass-bottomed boat."

Tammany Hall, too, admired Jimmy Walker. He was electable, he didn't rock the boat, and he played by their rules.

True, he spent his nighttime hours with the bobbed-hair beauties in the Ziegfeld Follies and his daytime hours greeting celebrities on the steps of City Hall—or on longer and longer vacations away from his clean desk.

At least, he believed in live-and-let-live for the city's working stiffs, all those noble straphangers clinging for dear life on the BMT and IRT lines. He was aware that the United States was a nation of immigrants, that New York was the cultural capital of the country, and that Broadway and Forty-second Street was the crossroads of the world.

No one could accuse him of intolerance toward the electorate. He respected the rainbow of colors and mosaic of religions living in the balkanized enclaves of Manhattan, Brooklyn, the Bronx, Queens, and Staten Island. After an average forty-eight-hour workweek, it was still only a Buffalo-nickel ride for people on the subway, the elevated, the trolley, or the ferry all the way to the end of the line and home again, and he was mayor for all of them.

When speaking of his youth growing up in Greenwich Village, on a square between Seventh Avenue and Hudson Street called St. Luke's Place, he waxed sentimental:

"I saw the skyline grow, and I saw the city grow, and sometimes I wonder if it was worth the price we paid. In those days we did not need interracial movements or goodwill groups. Then a neighborhood group meant so much.

"Here in the most cosmopolitan community since the beginning of time, a city composed of sons and daughters of every one of the forty-eight states, and with men and women from every country in the civilized world, we worked together. Here where there were and are more Irishmen than in Dublin, more Germans than in any city other than Berlin, and more Jews than in Palestine—here we lived together in peace, like one great family, and should so live today and tomorrow.

"We all went to school together, went to work together, and to the theater and to the fields of sport—with little rancor, no real hatred. We lived like human beings, who asked only the opportunity to work out our earthly existence and worship our God according to the dictates of our conscience."

Elected mayor at the age of forty-five in 1925, Walker wore the big town's heart on his hand-tailored sleeve. He was a dude for all seasons who always dressed to kill. The sidewalks of New York resounded beneath his pointy-toed black shoes, which were carefully cradled in four-button gray spats. He loved to lead a parade up Fifth Avenue—or any other street where the crowds could cheer him as he smiled and waved his shiny silk topper.

Jimmy Walker's wardrobe was very much a part of his personality and theatricality in office. He changed his outfit three times a day—twice during office hours and once again for his nighttime peregrinations. Various matching outfits were parked in different places for quick changeovers: his tailor's shop at the Ritz-Carlton, at City Hall, and wherever he slept that evening.

Ever since he entered public life, before the Great War, Jimmy Walker had employed a private tailor who cut his suits to order. Jeann Friedman, who had emigrated to the United States from Hungary, designed two basic ensembles for him. The first was called the Hyde Park. It featured a plain jacket with prominent lapels and a pinched waist, a waistcoat, and matching striped trousers. The second, the Biarritz, was deliberately informal but, if anything, even more studied, according to George Walsh, an editor and biographer. It combined a flannel jacket with tweed knickers. In both ensembles, the trousers, which measured exactly ten inches wide at the knees and nine and a quarter inches at the bottom, buttoned directly on his waistcoat so they could hang in a straight line, with no break at the instep.

"He designed all his clothes and he was a tailor's dream," Mr. Friedman said. "Whenever he needed a dressing gown or pajamas, I would accompany him to Sulka's and help him supervise his own design for these garments."

Undoubtedly, the cost of Walker's wardobe alone exceeded his yearly salary as a state senator or as mayor of New York.

"There is no law to define the kind of clothes a Mayor must wear," Jimmy Walker said, criticizing his critics. "If I thought that I might serve the taxpayers better by appearing at City Hall clad in overalls, or even a snood, I should do so. But until we have an ordinance to the contrary, I shall bathe frequently, as is my custom, and change my linen often, as is my perhaps eccentric desire, and patronize the tailor of my own choice."

He also loved to give speeches before political and charitable organizations. Here he was at his best, in the opinion of his close friend and fellow skirt-chaser George Jessel, a stand-up monologist and showbiz impresario:

"Jimmy Walker and I have been a team as after-dinner speakers at a thousand different affairs, including churches, synagogues, and every conceivable charity, regardless of race, creed or color," Jessel said. "Jimmy is the greatest impromptu speaker of his or anybody else's time. The greatest example of his presence of mind happened during his last campaign for the mayoralty, with Dudley Field Malone, Collector of the Port of New York, and myself."

The three friends were making a series of political speeches in the Bronx, from early in the morning until midnight. Tired as they were after returning downtown, Walker suddenly remembered that there was one more affair they had neglected to attend, a dinner at the Biltmore Hotel in Manhattan. Although he was hoarse, the mayor insisted on doing his duty for the electorate one more time.

"We hurried up to the Cascade Room, where a group of men were seated, and somebody was making a speech," Jessel said. "What and who these men were, neither Jim nor I knew. We were rushed to the dais and the speaker stopped immediately at our entrance. There was applause and Jim whispered to me, 'Start talking, George, stall for a few minutes till I find out what this is all about."

The boastful Jessel—he called himself the Toastmaster General of the United States—warmed up the audience with a speech replete with platitudes masquerading as wisdom. Jessel began: "Gentlemen, this is an evening to be remembered, a memory to conjure with." Then he delivered a series of set gags, most of which began, "A funny thing happened on the way down here tonight . . ." Nobody laughed; he had no idea what nationality these people were. All he knew was that they were sitting on their hands.

In an aside to Walker, Jessel muttered, "They're all yours, Jim." Facing the audience, Jessel wound up, "Now, gentlemen, I bring you the Magistrate of this, our great city, Father Knickerbocker's truly begotten son, James J. Walker."

Taking his time, Mayor Walker stood up, cocked his head, and began with his own all-purpose routine: "Gentlemen, in this kaleidoscopic era that we live in, this great melting pot, where from all walks of life men come closer together, it is needless for me to tell you what the

people of Polish birth have meant to the progress of the City of New
York. I can take you back to the great General Thaddeus Kosciuszko in
1776..."

There was no reaction from the audience; they were definitely not
Polish. Undaunted, Walker continued:

"And the simple Italian ditchdigger, imbued with the spirit of the
great Giuseppe Garibaldi, has been more helpful to Greater New York
than anyone I can think of."

Again, no sign of recognition; they were definitely not Italians.
Walker continued with his praise of ethnic New Yorkers, until he finally ran out of countries, except for Denmark and a few South American nations. At last, he had a memory flash and remembered the
name of the organization. Brightening, Walker began:

"If only the streets of New York were as clean as those of Copen-
hagen, the great capital of Denmark..."

The Danish-American New Yorkers cheered Walker for the first
time. With a faint smile, he continued to describe the virtues of their
country. "From then on," Jessel claimed, "Jimmy had their votes in his
pocket."

So boasted the Toastmaster General, who would give anything for
a punchline.

Robert Moses, the nonpareil parks and highway administrator of
New York City and State, also admired Mayor Walker's ability to think
on his feet. Moses, who prided himself on his own eloquence, remembered when Walker was one of the scheduled speakers at the hun-
dredth anniversary of the Erie Canal, which links New York City with
the Great Lakes. The long-winded speakers included the grandson of
DeWitt Clinton, builder of the big ditch, who droned on for forty-five
minutes, and the lawyer for the Port Authority, who spoke for nearly
an hour. The bored crowd began to leave just as Jimmy Walker got up
to speak.

Rising lightly to his feet, the mayor pointed to the clock and said:

"I see before me the busiest and most powerful leaders of the
world of industry. They must get back to their desks. Neither wind,
nor snow, nor rain, nor gloom of night, nor Jimmy Walker shall keep

them from their appointed rounds. Gentlemen, this meeting is adjourned for one hundred years."

But most of Mayor Walker's outings were for amusement, not speeches. In the evening, a beautiful companion sitting next to him on the buttery leather backseat of his limousine, he took off in his official town car, with his liveried chauffeur at the wheel, for a night on the town.

James J. Walker had traveled a twisting road from Greenwich Village to City Hall, with interludes along the way among Tin Pan Alley's balladeers and political pit stops in Albany's legislative halls.

He was born on June 19, 1881, at 110 Leroy Street on the Lower West Side of Manhattan. His father, William Walker, originally from a small town outside Dublin, married a Greenwich Village girl, also of Irish background, soon after he arrived in New York. It didn't take long for Tammany Hall to flow in the family's blood. Jimmy's father, a carpenter, was a friend of John R. Voorhis, a stair builder who became a police commissioner. In New York City, the police department and Tammany Hall were often Celtic kith and kin.

With the backing of the police commissioner, Tammany supported William Walker for membership on the Board of Aldermen. After serving four terms as an alderman, Mr. Walker became a member of the State Assembly in Albany and then went on to a more lucrative post: superintendent of public buildings in Manhattan.

As the family's fortunes improved, the Walkers moved to a house on St. Luke's Place. In those growing years, Jimmy Walker behaved like a good choirboy.

Young James attended St. Francis Xavier School and LaSalle School, where he developed an interest in sports. He was too small to box, but he loved to play and watch baseball. No mayor was better equipped to throw out the first ball on opening day during the era when there were still three major league teams in New York—the Yankees, the Giants, and the Dodgers. One of his friends from the old neighborhood claimed that Jimmy had once put in a season on a semi-pro baseball team in Hoboken.

Walker was a little too impatient for straight classroom work. After a year at St. Francis Xavier, he dropped out and, at the urging of his father, enrolled in New York Law School. Once again he left after a year, working as a bank messenger, then returned to law school while living under the family roof. During this time, he frequently took part in amateur theatricals and tried his hand at writing one-act plays, none of which went anywhere.

He became an aspiring songwriter in Tin Pan Alley—his main interest rather than the law books. Early in his musical career, he had two songs published—"Good-by Eyes of Blue" and "I Like Your Way." Neither ballad was successful. Then, in 1908, came his one memorable song, "Will You Love Me in December as You Do in May," with music by Ernest R. Ball. It remained a hit longer than most popular ballads before World War I and later would be played during his entrances and exits at nightclubs and whenever he mounted a public platform.

Jimmy Walker's lyrics were surprisingly romantic. His sentimental language appeared in marked contrast to the uncharitable comments that he made in the heat of political campaigns and that would haunt him later. The plain, rather unsophisticated words to his one big hit went:

> Now in the summer of life, sweetheart,
> You say you love but me,
> Gladly I'll give my heart to you,
> Throbbing with ecstasy.
> But last night I saw, while a-dreaming,
> The future, old and gray,
> And I wondered if you'll love me then, dear,
> Just as you do today.
>
> Will you love me in December as you do in May?
> Will you love me in the same old-fashioned way?
> When my hair has turned to gray?
> Will you kiss me then and say,
> That you love me in December as you did in May?

The words were apparently directed at Janet Allen, a pretty young singer he had met while playing piano in amateur theatricals. The diminutive Miss Allen—Walker called her Allie—was a little more experienced in show business than the aspiring law student. She had once played a chorus girl and understudied the leading lady in *The Duke of Duluth,* a Broadway production. During their courtship in Greenwich Village, what especially pleased Jimmy Walker was that while he played the piano Janet sang all his songs.

Jimmy earned $10,000 in royalties from the sale of sheet music, and spent much of it on his wardrobe. Already he was wearing custom-made suits, shirts, and shoes and sporting a walking stick. At the same time, he could now afford to take Allie to Rector's for an expensive dinner between her jobs in vaudeville. He also took Allie home to his mother and father and the rest of his family on St. Luke's Place.

After a few years, they became engaged, but Walker was in no hurry to get married. He was at the start of his sixteen-year career as a legislator—a job handed to him by virtue of his father's Tammany connections—traveling to Albany and enjoying its bachelor opportunities. According to his fellow legislators, he was effective as a speaker and learned how to compromise with both the upstate Republicans and the downstate Democrats. Allie waited patiently until 1912, the year Walker was finally admitted to practice law. She abandoned her Christian Science religion when they were married.

The wedding took place at St. Joseph's Church in New York; Jimmy arrived two hours late. He blamed a mishap involving the best man, who was carrying the wedding ring, and horse-drawn fire engines that delayed both of them. The best man was a fire buff, the story went, and was sidetracked by a fire on the way to the ceremony.

Later Jimmy would be famous for his lateness. He was credited with having kept President Calvin Coolidge waiting for forty minutes while on a visit to Washington. A wisecracking columnist wondered if Coolidge knew the difference. After his meeting at the White House, Walker had an appointment with Andrew Mellon, the secretary of the Treasury. He showed up an hour late. Disdainfully, Walker said, "I refuse to live by the clock."

Not long after his wedding, Jimmy returned to his old ways. He took up with a French-Canadian dancer and singer, Yvonne Shelton. His relationship with the mercurial showgirl continued for several tumultuous years. He called her Little Fellow because she was five feet tall and weighed only eighty-five pounds. She called him J.J. Yvonne liked to cook for the senator from Greenwich Village; he enjoyed her meals and whatever other pleasures she offered.

Eventually, Senator Walker and the Little Fellow drifted apart. When they broke up, in a hotel room overlooking Central Park, she reportedly told him: "This is good-bye. You're in love with a town. It's the first time I ever had to compete with that. And I'm overmatched."

Other performers in the musical comedy world were attracted to the dashing legislator with theatrical connections who worked the night beat like a newspaper reporter. The faithful Allie Walker was aware of her husband's infidelities; so were his Tammany mentors and colleagues in the state senate. But most of Jimmy Walker's liaisons at the time were passing affairs.

"Mr. Walker took naturally to the game of politics as it is played by Tammany," commented *The New York Times* of the beginning of his public career. "His first experience in the game was as a worker for the election of Seth Low, a Fusion candidate for Mayor. Under the tutelage of his father, the former Alderman and Assemblyman, Jimmy Walker was nominated and elected to the New York State Assembly in 1909. While in the Assembly, he came under the guidance of Alfred E. Smith, who had become an important figure in Albany. The Assemblyman could not have had a greater sponsor."

Al Smith served as a bridge between Walker and Roosevelt. Smith remembered with pride and humor that he and Jimmy began as Tammany flag bearers on the East Side and West Side of Manhattan during local elections. Walker would prove an apt student of party politics during his service in the legislature. "This boy is a greater strategist than General Sheridan and he rides twice as fast," Smith said. Assemblyman

Walker learned the ropes of parliamentary procedure—stalling, lobbying, and eventually achieving cross-party unity.

Occasionally, the raucous goings-on between the upstate Republican majority and downstate Democrats made the Assembly resemble the agora of ancient Athens more than an austere legislative body. They also revealed party differences that were rooted in class differences—the old-time prosperous legislators from upstate New York versus the striving sons of immigrants from New York City.

"The New York State Assembly session of 1911 had a moment when partisanship on both sides of the house was running high," Al Smith recalled. "Ed Merritt, Fred Hammond and Jesse Phillips, representing the Republican side, and I, representing the Democratic side, were engaged in a crossfire of debate on a bill that had to do with the removal of the Commission of Jurors in Nassau County. There were considerable hard feelings on both sides of the chamber when Assemblyman Wende from Buffalo rose in his place and asked for the privilege of interrupting. It was readily granted.

"Mr. Wende said, 'Mr. Speaker, I have just heard that Cornell won the boat race.'"

"Merritt said, 'That doesn't mean anything to me. I'm a Yale man.'"

"Hammond said, 'It doesn't mean anything to me. I'm a Harvard man.'"

"Phillips said, 'It doesn't mean anything to me. I am a U. of M. man.'"

Assemblyman Al Smith found himself the only one of the quartet standing—and the only one without college credentials. Nevertheless, he confidently addressed his colleagues:

"It doesn't mean anything to me because I am an F.F.M. man."

The Republicans looked puzzled. "What is that, Al?"

Smith replied, "F.F.M.—Fulton Fish Market. Let's proceed with the debate."

This was not the first time Al Smith had referred to his blue-collar upbringing. He often used homespun similes about the Fulton Fish Market. Once, describing someone he didn't like, Smith referred to him as having "an eye as glassy as a dead cod." Of another he said, "He shakes hands like a frozen mackerel."

In the Smith and Walker years in Albany, the state legislature was a training camp for wisecracks. Once Al Smith was making a speech and a heckler yelled, "Tell me all you know, Al, it won't take long." Smith replied, "I'll tell them all we *both* know and it won't take any longer."

In 1912, at the age of thirty-one, Walker passed the bar examination in Albany and was admitted to practice law. At that time, a college degree was not needed and the requirements for admission to the bar were not stringent for newly minted attorneys.

In the Assembly, Walker attracted the favorable attention of Tammany's Silent Charlie Murphy. After Walker had served a few years, Murphy tapped him to run for the state Senate. Walker had proved that he could work effectively with his fellow Democrats. In Manhattan's Assembly and senatorial districts, the Democratic nomination was tantamount to election.

Senator Walker and Assemblyman Smith became close allies. Together, over the opposition of corporation lawyers and lobbyists, they helped obtain the enactment of the state's first Workmen's Compensation Act, which placed responsibility for occupational accidents largely on employers. After six years in the upper house, Walker was advanced to Democratic minority leader with, of course, Boss Murphy's approval. Tammany and his colleagues in the legislature agreed that Walker acquitted himself creditably. Smith moved up to the governor's chair in 1919, where he advocated liberal social welfare laws.

Senator Walker was best remembered by his colleagues and the public for a wisecrack that effectively killed the so-called Clean Books Bill. This had been introduced by John S. Sumner and was supported by upstate Republicans as well as by a handful of New York City Democrats. Passages from the novels of D. H. Lawrence and other authors were read in the chamber as examples of "dirty books." (Lawrence's *Women in Love* had been written in 1916 but the British author was unable to find a publisher until 1920 in New York, where an action against its publication failed.)

Supporters of the censorial Clean Books Bill said that if such smut-filled works were permitted in the schools and on public library bookshelves, the lives of women would be placed in danger and the sanctity of marriage and the home would break down.

Turning toward Senator Sumner and his allies, Walker said, "I have heard with great interest the addresses of the gentlemen on the other side, and I have the utmost respect for what they have said. But I submit, gentlemen, that they are either naive or confused. Why all this talk about womanhood?" And then he delivered what became a clinching argument in future censorship cases: "I have never yet heard of a girl being ruined by a book." His familiar crack is usually shortened to "No girl was ever ruined by a book."

Walker's designation to run for mayor—arguably the most important job in city politics aside from whichever title was held by the leader of Tammany Hall—resulted from a split in the Democratic party. Prompted by Governor Smith, in 1925 the Tammany organization decided to deny Mayor John F. Hylan renomination. George W. Olvany, then leader of Tammany Hall, and Edward J. Flynn, the Bronx Democratic leader, stood by Governor Smith; John H. McCooey of Brooklyn and Maurice E. Connolly of Queens, the Democratic leaders in their boroughs, supported Hylan. On the sober editorial page of *The New York Times,* Hylan was called "an imperfect demagogue."

With the Sachems divided, other forces in state politics decided to offer Surrogate James A. Foley the nomination. (It was no coincidence that Surrogate Foley was the influential Charlie Murphy's son-in-law.) However, Foley declined on the grounds of ill health, preferring to remain in judicial robes. More than any other court, the Office of the Surrogate, which handled wills, estates, and guardianships, was a rich source of patronage for clubhouse lawyers and their relatives and friends.

Governor Smith believed he had exerted himself sufficiently in leading the fight to shelve Red Mike Hylan; he did not openly push for Walker as the next possible replacement. The selection of Jimmy Walker to run for the nomination against Mayor Hylan was made by George Olvany, Tammany's new chieftain. Olvany had come to power with a comparatively clean reputation. He was an Al Smith man, and nobody had ever found the governor guilty of financial shenanigans.

Walker won the nomination by a substantial majority. His Republican-Fusion opponent in the 1925 election was Frank D. Waterman, the fountain-pen manufacturer, who conducted a "Say It with Shovels" campaign to remind voters that he had forced the Hylan administration to begin subway construction. His supporters wore little brass shovels in their lapels. Although an unexciting candidate, Waterman did argue that the subway system would become politicized if Walker became mayor.

"Municipal operation would mean that every subway employee from general manager to watchman would be selected on grounds of political pull," Waterman predicted, not without reason. "Tammany control of our subways would mean Tammany free to give, without competition, contracts for cars, contracts for steel rails, contracts for equipment, contracts for all kinds of favored Tammany contractors."

Waterman's prediction came true. In the field of public transportation, Walker's business friends received contracts without bidding.

Speaking in the Great Hall of the Wigwam, Walker—without blushing—praised Tammany as "the home of an organization which has done more to fight the fight of the City of New York than any political organization that you or I have ever heard of. Nearly all the humane measures that have been written in the statute books of the State in recent years emanated from this building."

At the same time that Walker boasted of his achievements as a state legislator, he felt the need to explain his way of life:

"I am ready to admit that I would rather laugh than cry. I like the company of my fellow human beings. I like the theatre and am devoted to healthy outdoor sports. Because I like these things, I have reflected my attitude in some of the legislation I have sponsored—2.75 percent beer, Sunday baseball, Sunday movies, and legalized boxing. [Beer sales and sports and entertainment had been banned under Sunday blue laws.] But let me allay any fear there may be that, because I believe in personal liberty, wholesome amusement and healthy professional sport, I will countenance for a moment any indecency or vice in New York."

Although Walker had abandoned his songwriting dreams, Tin Pan

Alley continued to cherish him as one of its own. Irving Berlin, a close friend, took time out from his highly successful career as a businessman with his own sheet-music and recording company to write a campaign song:

> *It's a "walk-in" with Walker*
> *It's a "walk-in" with Jim*
> *He's a corker—and one of the mob*
> *A real New Yorker—who's fit for the job.*

Norman Thomas, the Socialist party stalwart, who was a candidate himself, raised the most courageous voice against Jimmy Walker. Thomas was in the tradition of such third-party and populist candidates in American history as Theodore Roosevelt (Progressive), Robert La Follette (Progressive) and Eugene V. Debs (Socialist). Beginning with his opposition to Alfred E. Smith and Herbert Hoover in 1928, Thomas would run for president on the Socialist ticket in the next five elections. He was the man to vote for if you didn't like either the Democratic or the Republican candidate.

With remarkable prescience, Thomas declared, "It is quite true that we have not shared any great enthusiasm for Mayor Hylan. We have felt that his devotion to the people, while honest enough, has been lacking in reason and understanding. But never for one instant have we shared the delusion that the people will be better off under Jimmy Walker than Mayor Hylan. The man whom Broadway calls 'our Jimmy' may be too clever to let the city slide back to the naked, roaring vice of the days of Boss [Richard] Croker, but there isn't anyone who does not know that under Walker the underworld of New York will flourish as it never flourished under Hylan. There isn't anyone who does not know that the transit interests and a lot of others will rejoice in Walker's victory."

But *The New York Times,* which simultaneously called itself both Independent and Democratic, regarded State Senator James J. Walker as a progressive:

"Among the legislation he has sponsored was a bill to unmask the

Ku Klux Klan by compelling publication of its membership roll. He has also been the sponsor of legislation providing for a liberalization of the Prohibition Law. During the administrations of Governor Smith subsequent to 1922, he made a brilliant fight for the Governor's legislative program, succeeding in 100 percent performance while the Senate remained Democratic."

On election day, Walker defeated Waterman by a plurality of 400,000 votes. All the warring elements of the Democratic party had rallied behind him. He was indeed the people's choice.

No mayor of New York took office under more favorable auspices. The primary election had shown that the public was weary of Mayor Hylan and the quarreling that had marked the meetings of the Board of Estimate.

One of Mayor Walker's first acts was to adopt a comprehensive system of subway routes. The Board of Transportation began to let contracts for one of the largest engineering undertakings in municipal history—the construction of $700 million worth of underground transportation.

Mayor Walker announced that he favored a citywide system of bus operation, and he induced the Board of Estimate to award a monopolistic franchise to the Equitable Coach Company. Subsequently, Walker's dealings with his friends at Equitable became the basis of one of the most damaging charges against him during the citywide investigations.

Two major administrative accomplishments took place during Mayor Walker's initial term in office. The first was the consolidation of all the city's public hospitals. Dr. William Schroeder Jr., the new commissioner of hospitals, was the mayor's close friend and personal physician. The second was the creation of a department of sanitation. Dr. Schroeder also headed the sanitation commission. In both jobs, his deputies were Tammany appointments. This arrangement came under sharp criticism from professionals in both departments.

The Walker administration made large appropriations for parks and playgrounds and materially improved the park system. Here was a side of Walker that belied his reputation for inactivity and showed that he could reach out to people living in the far corners of all five boroughs.

"I can never forget that Jimmy Walker gave us the city water-supply easements in Nassau County which became the backbone of the Long Island State Park system and the means of access to Jones Beach and the finest oceanfront park in the world," Robert Moses later declared. Then, in one of his flights of fancy that said as much about his own amour-propre as about Walker's, Moses added, "Jimmy was the extrovert, the spontaneous eccentric, the sidewalk favorite, the beloved clown, the idol of those who seek companionship and mercy above and beyond justice."

Actually, more credit for the establishment of Jones Beach could be given to Governor Smith, who promoted the idea of an oceanfront park area for city dwellers who wanted to avoid the Coney Island crowds and tinsel. The wealthy residents of Long Island opposed the acquisition of the land. A member of the Old Guard with a large estate complained, "Where are we going to find a place to live, with all this rabble coming in?"

"What *rabble?*" Smith riposted. "*I'm* the rabble."

Mayor Walker's accomplishments were achieved at a price. During his first term, Tammany Hall kept its hammerlock on certain administrative and appointive positions in the city government. The boroughs were divided into lucrative enclaves, each ruled by local club leaders who were allowed to get a piece of the action as long as they shared the wealth with the higher-ups in the Hall.

He had his basic salary increased by subservient city legislators from $25,000 to $40,000 a year (plus such perks as his chauffeured limousine). Eighty-five district leaders received salaries of more than $7,000 a year for no-show sinecures with fancy titles—county clerk, register, sheriff and deputy sheriff, city marshal—that often included under-the-table payments from businessmen.

Those below the leadership ranks had to content themselves with what they could get by extortion, from fixing traffic tickets to arranging for judicial "contracts" and departmental licenses. If there was an indictment to be quashed—whether it was a simple charge of breaking and entering by a neighborhood youth, or a storekeeper's violation of fire and safety laws—the normal place to appeal was the local Democratic clubhouse. There ambitious young lawyers loyally gave free legal aid, under the watchful eye of the district leader, in the hope of gaining a place of their own at the public teat.

In the spoils system that Jimmy Walker inherited but could hardly be blamed for initiating, political advancement worked like a farm team in big-league baseball. An adept lawyer (in those days law clerks earned between $5 and $25 a week) might go from the bush leagues as an assistant district attorney or law secretary to a seat in the legislature as a city councilman, state assemblyman, or state senator. From there the next step was the bench, as a magistrate, municipal court judge, criminal court judge, or state Supreme Court judge. Like Surrogate Foley's job, judgeships were often the best sinecures in the system. A surrogate had the power to name law guardians and referees to administer estates. These estates often paid large fees.

To achieve such an appointment or a place on the ballot, one gave a sizable contribution to the "club." Sometimes it was legitimate—a payment to help defray the cost of a political campaign; sometimes it was not—a contribution for which there was no accounting. Some officials and appointees paid outright bribes, and Republicans as well as Democrats were involved. Payments were made in crisp, undeclared currency, in amounts roughly equal to the first year's salary on the bench. The usual cost of a magistrate's job was $10,000; for a criminal court or Supreme Court judge, $25,000.

"The political history of our organization," Walker said glibly, "shows that the successful leaders of Tammany Hall, such as Charles Murphy, John Kelly and Richard Croker, were district leaders. There is nothing too big for a Tammany leader that democracy can give. They are the outstanding benefactors of this town."

Hypocritical as it sounded, Walker, a Tammany beneficiary like his father before him, may well have believed what he was saying. To be sure, he omitted the name of Boss Tweed from his list of so-called Tammany benefactors.

At the beginning of Walker's tenure in office, Tammany's Sachems temporarily loosened their reins. Boss Murphy had a certain dignity; his leaders always addressed him as "Mr. Murphy." He also had a businesslike reticence; it was said of Murphy that even on the Fourth of July he refused to open his mouth to sing "The Star-Spangled Banner" for fear of committing himself.

Jimmy Walker admired Charlie Murphy because he had a certain way of operating behind the scenes that gained him the respect of his Democratic party associates. They cited the fact that when Red Mike Hylan, then a Brooklyn county judge, was being considered as a candidate for mayor, Murphy asked John McCooey, Tammany's Brooklyn chieftain, "Is Hylan a man we can trust and do business with?" McCooey replied, "He certainly is—do you want to meet him?" Murphy said, "No, but I want you to ram him down my throat." Thereafter, Democratic clubs in Brooklyn attested to Judge Hylan's independence, resolutions were passed, and Boss Murphy bowed to the public clamor and accepted him as candidate for the good of the party.

Eventually, when Governor Al Smith persuaded the bosses that Hylan did not have the mental equipment for the mayor's job, a deal was struck to prevent him from running as an independent candidate. Hylan announced his retirement and promised to support Tammany's choice. A few years later, the payoff came when Mayor Walker appointed Hylan a judge of the Children's Court in Queens. Walker did get the last word, however. When Alva Johnston, one of New York's astute reporters, asked the mayor why he had appointed a man who had impugned his character, Walker replied: "The appointment of Judge Hylan means that the children can now be judged by one of their peers."

With a mixture of affection and sarcasm, Jimmy Walker's newspaper drinking pals called him the Night Mayor of New York. He wasn't offended by the title, laughing it off in the presence of his friends and accusers. Only half in jest, he frequently referred to his assistant, Charles F. Kerrigan, as the Day Mayor.

During the daylight hours, Mayor Walker did manage to keep busy as a toastmaster and off-the-cuff speaker, especially on the steps of City Hall and in ticker-tape parades. He was at his best greeting dignitaries, foreign and domestic. The public festivities gave him an excuse to get all dressed up in his cutaway, striped trousers, and four-button spats. The task of striking up the ceremonial municipal bands helped get Walker out of the office, into the streets, and onto the front pages of the tabloids.

"What a wonderful sight it was, when the weather was right and the happy, cheering crowds turned out to see great statesmen and returning heroes," recalled Grover Whalen, praising the mayor as a host for the high and mighty. "After meeting a ship from Europe after it docked on the Hudson River, we rode our royalties through the canyons of downtown Manhattan to City Hall, that graceful gem of a building, contrasting so happily with the surrounding skyscrapers, to be greeted by the smiling, personable Jimmy Walker."

Among those who received the full Walker treatment (at considerable expense to the city, especially for police and sanitation department overtime) were Queen Marie of Rumania, Crown Prince Gustavus Adolphus and Princess Louise of Sweden, Prime Minister Ramsay MacDonald of England, Charles A. Lindbergh for flying the Atlantic solo, and Gertrude Ederle for swimming the English Channel.

In honor of the visit Queen Marie paid before she went on a national tour with her children, Mayor Walker decided to present her with a hand-illuminated scroll and a special medal from the City of New York. Standing on the steps of City Hall, he was about to pin the medal on her coat, somewhere in the vicinity of her ample bosom, when he hesitated for a moment.

"Your Majesty, I've never stuck a Queen, and I hesitate to do so now."

"Proceed, Your Honor," she replied graciously. "The risk is mine."

"And such a beautiful risk it is, Your Majesty," said Jimmy Walker gallantly.

Even though Jimmy Walker's own crown was lopsided, City Hall offered him a throne room and palace. He could be depended upon to put on a royal performance for his constituents. With his quick-witted comebacks and nocturnal wanderings, there was little question that Jimmy Walker cherished the life that only New York offered.

The same could not be said for the average citizen. Cronyism, pay-offs, and corruption were costly to any man or woman—whether a shopkeeper or a home builder—doing business with the city. The financial fun and games enriched Tammany's minions and the Hall, at the expense of the public.

Certainly the Empire City had its bright side—an endless carnival of attractions and kaleidoscope of opportunities in almost every field. In later years, the essayist E. B. White expressed those feelings about the city's meaning with unmatched eloquence: "New York is to the nation what the white church spire is to the village—the visible symbol of aspiration and faith, the white plume saying the way is up."

But Jimmy Walker's way was destined to take a different, crooked turn.

FIVE

Lullaby of Broadway

Mayor James J. Walker attained the height of his fame, if not his power, during the giddy Jazz Age of the 1920s. For a while it appeared that squabbles between the Goo-Goos and Tammany, between Democrats and Republicans, would fade under the bright lights of the pre-Depression years. It was a time that Westbrook Pegler, a misanthropic Hearst columnist who constantly ranted against Franklin and Eleanor Roosevelt, called the Era of Wonderful Nonsense. So it was, for the fortunate ones.

The mayor was idolized; even his critics considered him merely a charming rogue. People enjoyed watching him dip into the Fountain of Youth fully clothed, like the reckless Scott Fitzgeralds cavorting in front of the Plaza Hotel. The under-the-table money that Walker obtained from the corporate corrupters was not really aimed at building up his personal bank account but, rather, at helping him travel through life in first class. He literally did so during his frequent crossings to Europe on bubbly transatlantic liners while singing the glories of the city of New York—"the renowned and ancient city of Gotham," in Washington Irving's romantic vision, which Walker seemed to follow.

The times were celebrated in a song written by Jack Yellen, with music by Milton Ager, that went:

Happy days are here again,
The skies above are clear again,
Let us sing a song of cheer again,
Happy days are here again!

The tune enlivened national conventions and would become the campaign song of Governor Roosevelt and future Democratic presidents.

Eventually, the economic boom that began after the First World War began to run out of steam. Yet even when prosperity failed to appear just around the corner, Mayor Walker continued to trip the light fantastic. "He wore New York in his lapel like a boutonniere," wrote one of his newspaper friends. By personal example, Walker offered the citizenry a form of entertainment. He tended to follow his heart more often than his head, and his heart beat to the music of Broadway. In Shakespeare's genteel phrase, Jimmy liked to tread "the primrose path of dalliance."

Dalliance became personified, for the mayor, in the shape of a gorgeous brunette who sang and danced in Broadway musicals. Originally from the Isle of Wight, Betty Compton arrived in Canada with her ambitious stage mother, Mrs. Florence Halling Compton—Jimmy affectionately nicknamed her the Duchess—after studying singing and winning a beauty contest in Toronto. Inevitably, mother and daughter set their sights on the splendors of Broadway. Season after season in those years, hundreds of dramas, comedies, and musicals appeared on the New York boards.

With her incandescent smile, Betty stood in contrast to Jimmy's faithful, long-suffering, sweet, but dowdy wife, Allie. And the Walkers were childless.

Betty Compton was in her early twenties when Mayor Walker, an inveterate theatergoer, spotted her in the hit Broadway musical *Oh, Kay!* With her caplike hairdo and Chiclets smile, she was as smart-looking as any ingenue in the big-time theater. The play's opening night was at the Imperial Theatre on November 8, 1926. The sumptuous stage set was a Gatsbyesque Long Island estate used for rum-running; the audience cheered the lighthearted, mindless girl-meets-playboy theme. The critics admired the contemporary flavor of the words and music:

We'll hail each Prohibitionist a brother,
And sell a dozen cases to his mother!
When our ship comes sailing in—
Full of Haig and Haig and gin!

Oh, Kay! was loaded with talent in every department. The book was by Guy Bolton and P. G. Wodehouse, the music by George Gershwin, and the lyrics by his equally talented brother, Ira. The cast starred the suave comedienne Gertrude Lawrence (as the Kay of the title), in the role of an English duke's sister who is disguised as a housemaid, singing the sentimental hit song "Someone to Watch Over Me," and Victor Moore, one of the best double-take comedians in the business, playing a butler-bootlegger.

Oh, Kay! was one of those silly, happy, funny, singable shows that symbolized the carefree 1920s. The chorus boys wore tennis, anyone? sweaters and black-and-white shoes and their hair shone with brilliantine; the chorus girls wore big hats and flouncing skirts and showed a little leg, but otherwise they didn't expose much more than wide-eyed smiles.

Betty Compton was a featured player in *Oh, Kay!* By a coincidence, one of the songs she sang was addressed to her character's boyfriend, "Jimmy Winter." The real Jimmy in the audience must have listened with delight as he watched Betty sing:

Whoop it up! Tonight is the night!
For dear old Jimmy's coming home!
Clear the floor!
For Jimmy's a pal, that every gal
Must adore!

At the cast party afterward, Mayor Walker singled out the captivating young actress. He was immediately smitten and invited her to a supper party that he claimed to be giving that night. She politely declined.

Over the next few weeks, Betty continued to ignore Walker's overtures. But by avoiding his City Hall desk during his short working day and frequenting Manhattan's pleasure domes after dark, he showed Betty that she was more important to him than the dreary business of government.

In the meantime, following her husband's style of cost-free vacations, Mrs. James J. Walker, usually accompanied by her mother, was junketing around Europe. As a guest of the Hotel Owners Association, Allie met presidents and crowned heads and had an audience with Pope Pius XI in Vatican City. In 1927, she sailed to Germany, this time to christen the *New York,* a newly built transatlantic liner. In front of the clunky Speed Graphic cameramen with press passes stuck in their hatbands, Mayor Walker dutifully greeted Allie after the ship docked at its North German Lloyd berth on the Hudson. (Not long afterward, the same German liners would be proudly flying the Third Reich's swastikas.)

A half-year passed before Betty Compton succumbed to Jimmy Walker's celebrated charms. After serving as toastmaster at a fundraising event for Mrs. William Randolph Hearst's Free Milk Fund for Babies, he offered to give Betty a lift home through the crowded Times Square traffic. As they drove slowly, the mayor ordered his chauffeur to turn on the siren—something he seldom did. Betty immediately recognized what he was up to.

"All right," she said, smiling. "I'm impressed. Now you can stop the siren."

Several days later, Betty finally consented to have dinner with him. The owner of an expensive restaurant bowed and scraped before them. Their friendship blossomed. Jimmy nicknamed his new love Monk. It did not hurt the mayor's romantic cause that he had clout in the theatrical community. Once, during a rehearsal, Betty complained about her role and billing in the cast. With the help of his producer friends—some of whom needed real estate variances and tax abatements for their theaters—Walker was able to get her a larger dressing room at the drop of a hint and a wink.

Oh, Kay! ran for 256 performances on Broadway before moving on to His Majesty's Theatre in London for another 215 performances. Betty Compton did not go abroad with the company; Jimmy Walker preferred to keep her closer to home.

They were, in the gossip columnists' word, an "item." The liaison did no harm to Betty's career. Her photographs were regularly featured in the Sunday newspapers. But thanks to some of Mayor Walker's publisher friends, Betty was coyly shielded from unwanted photographs with him at public events. Allie loyally turned up at official ceremonies; unaware, she served as a beard for her philandering husband.

A certain chivalry prevailed among the hard-boiled newspapermen of that day. They agreed never to mention the indiscretions of any man—or woman—unless one party or the other was headed for the divorce court, according to Gene Fowler of the *Morning Telegraph,* a horse-racing sheet with literary pretensions. Even Walter Winchell abided by this unwritten code. The reporters tried to shield the mayor from himself, not wanting to penalize him for his lack of hypocrisy. Unlike others in public life, Jimmy Walker was quite open about his private affair.

To the dismay of Tammany Hall and the St. Patrick's Cathedral "powerhouse"—both equally influential in controlling the destinies of Democratic politicians in New York—this romance was not just another passing fancy but the real thing. Both groups pressured Walker to break off the relationship; they warned him that he had become an embarrassment not only to the church and the party but to the faithful electorate.

Governor Al Smith cautioned him: "The only thing that's worse for a public man than being funny is for him to chase women if he's married."

Jimmy responded: "Could you by any chance be thinking of one of the neighbors' children?"

Governor Smith: "Jim, I have a genuine deep-down affection for you. It's a shame you won't listen to reason."

Inevitably, the arrangement had its problems. Betty wanted marriage and a family. Jimmy's religion would not permit a divorce; he did not want to sever his ties to the Church. The valiant Allie kept up the pretense of a happy married life to the husband she cherished.

In 1928, two years after that fateful premiere of *Oh, Kay!,* Jimmy left his wife and home in St. Luke's Place in the Village and moved into a suite at the swank Ritz-Carlton Hotel overlooking Central Park. Betty Compton's apartment was on East seventy-sixth Street, a few minutes away. Walker's valet, Roberts, helped him carry his vast wardrobe into his elegant new quarters.

Before the Great Crash and the Depression, it seemed as if the good times would never end. In the sports, entertainment, and business worlds, New York could rightfully be called the capital of the United States.

If there was no joy in Mudville, the mighty New York Yankees delivered nothing but pleasure to the city's baseball-mad fans. Led by Babe Ruth, who hit a record-breaking sixty home runs, the Yankees won the World Series in 1927, beating the St. Louis Cardinals four games in a row. The powerful bat and winning personality of the "Sultan of Swat" helped fans forget the 1919 Black Sox scandal.

During many a long afternoon, Mayor Walker could be found at the newly inaugurated Yankee Stadium, watching the Bronx Bombers field the most memorable team in baseball history. On April 12, the opening day of the '27 season, the lineup of dangerous batters—"Murderers' Row"—led off with center fielder Earle Combs (.356), followed by shortstop Mark Koenig (.285), right fielder Babe Ruth (.356, with his 60 homers), first baseman Lou Gehrig (.373, not to mention *his* 47 homers), left fielder Bob Meusel (.337), second baseman Tony (Push 'Em Up Tony) Lazzeri (.309), third baseman Joe Dugan (.269), and catcher John Grabowski (.277). Nor was the pitching staff in the shadows of the ballpark that became known as the House That Ruth Built. The Yankee hurlers were brilliant that season: Waite Hoyt (22 wins), Wiley Moore (19), Herb Pennock (19) and a pitcher with the unlikely name of Urban Shocker (18), who was an ancient thirty-six years old.

In the same year that Jimmy Walker was flying high, Charles A. Lindbergh became the hero of the decade. After taking off from Roosevelt Field on Long Island in his single-engine *Spirit of St. Louis* on May 20, 1927, Lindy flew nonstop to Le Bourget, outside Paris, in thirty-three and a half hours. When he returned to New York, Mayor Walker and a million other people gave him an unforgettable reception. As the mayor and the aviator rode uptown from Lower Broadway, eighteen hundred tons of ticker tape, newspapers, and toilet paper rained down upon them from office buildings.

Introducing the "Lone Eagle" at a dinner at the Commodore Hotel, Jimmy Walker managed to put in a plug for his hometown. He called New York City the Gateway of America. The leading businessmen and politicians in the audience loved the phrase; they saw it as an inducement to move more of their merchandise and services. Turning to Lindbergh, Walker said, "So while you took the *Spirit of St. Louis* abroad, you found out something of the Spirit of New York before you left and after you returned. Thank God!"

(Lindbergh's heroic image was later tarnished after he visited Nazi Germany three times in the mid-1930s, accepted a medal from Hermann Goering, made anti-Semitic remarks, and became an outspoken advocate of American isolationism. In his final years, he partly redeemed himself by working for environmental causes.)

On Wall Street, the stock market was soaring. The economy seemed headed in the right direction, but there were warning signs. Cautious analysts believed that investments in the market were fueled by too much optimism and too much buying on margin. In some industries, wages were not keeping pace with profits. Small farmers were overextended on credit. Consumers bought durable goods in large quantities for the first time—on credit.

The Federal Reserve's attempt to raise interest rates to discourage speculation brought on an initial recession. President Hoover and his Treasury Department economists expected that recession to be self-limiting. Instead, prices fell and set off contractions in production. Investors panicked. The decline of prosperity in rural industries such as mining and farming and the unprecedented boom in consumer credit presaged the Great Crash of October 29, 1929. The overheated securities market collapsed; by mid-November $30 billion had been erased from the value of stocks. A famous headline written by Sime Silverman, editor of *Variety,* the show business weekly, summed up the situation:

WALL ST. LAYS AN EGG

A worldwide depression followed. The game of business as usual, as it was played during the reckless Roaring Twenties, no longer worked. Unemployment contributed to changed attitudes about the need for government intervention. There were no large-scale social insurance programs to cushion the shock for businessmen, workingpeople, and families. Tough federal measures to promote national recovery would have to await another presidential election and the Roosevelt administration in Washington.

In good times and bad, for Mayor Walker the focus of his free hours was the Great White Way. Jimmy was a habitual Broadway first-nighter, part of the show in the audience as well as during the revelries afterward. He believed in the world of entertainment for himself and the public. The producers and performers showed their gratitude by making sure that he had two on the aisle in the most visible orchestra seats.

During Walker's first term in office, the Broadway stage was alive with the sound of music. In 1927 Jerome Kern's *Show Boat* opened and influenced not only critics but other composers. George Gershwin wrote the score for George S. Kaufman's *Strike Up the Band,* a musical satire that portrayed the United States as a jingoistic country willing to go to war for the sake of big business. Ira Gershwin's lyrics underscored that theme:

> Whoops, what a charming war!
> Whoops, what a charming war!
> It keeps you out in the open air.
> Oh, this is such a charming war! etc.
> We're glad that we're over here over there,
> We sleep in downy feather beds, we never see a cot;
> Our contract calls for ice-cream soda

When the weather's hot;
And very good publicity if we ever get shot!
Oh, isn't this a charming war!

If the theme and lyrics sounded cynical even to New Yorkers, they exemplified the freedom of the post–World War I era. Kaufman, former drama editor of *The New York Times,* considered himself a newsman as well as a wit. He also happened to be a former colleague of Brooks Atkinson, in the newspaper's theater department. The Great War had ended only a decade before, and some veterans were offended by the tone of the musical. *Strike Up the Band* displeased so many people during its two-week road career that it was taken off the boards; America, said Atkinson, was "not yet ready for such acid iconoclasm." It was later rewritten by Morrie Ryskind, who softened Kaufman's book, and ran for 191 performances.

Gershwin, Ryskind, and Kaufman continued their brilliant collaboration with an acerbic, jeering musical comedy, *Of Thee I Sing,* that became emblematic of Calvin Coolidge's and Herbert Hoover's do-nothing tenure in Washington—and, by extension, of Jimmy Walker's mayoralty in New York. Indeed, the painted curtain read: "Put Love in the White House." The sign seemed to apply more to City Hall than to Washington.

In their time, the lyrics were outspoken but their underlying humor prevented the padlockers from closing the show. In fact, the Pulitzer judges gave a prize to *Of Thee I Sing,* saying that the musical was that year's best representative of "the educational value and power of the stage." The song "Wintergreen for President" included such lines as: "He's the man the people choose / Loves the Irish and the Jews." Another number, "Who's the Lucky Girl to Be?," went: "If a girl is sexy / She may be Mrs. Prexy." ("Prexy" meant "President," and, of course, rhymed with "sexy.") There was plenty of satire, but no nudity.

To avoid the bluenoses and the possibility of a police raid, there was an unwritten rule in the legitimate theater that the tall, motionless showgirls in the back row were allowed to give audiences a peek at their bosoms as long as they (the girls) didn't cause them (the bosoms) to jiggle. For $5.50 for the best seats in the house and 50 cents in the second balcony, the Broadway houses were filled with appreciative patrons who could afford to go to the theater regularly. Both musicals and straight plays flourished.

While Mayor Walker was in office, the public had between 200 and 250 productions a year to choose from. In one season, theatergoers could see Noël Coward in *The Vortex,* Marilyn Miller in *Sunny,* Ethel Barrymore and Walter Hampden in *The Merchant of Venice,* Lionel Barrymore in *The Piker,* and Humphrey Bogart in *The Cradle Snatchers.* Jimmy Walker was present at the creation when the movies first began to talk, at the Warner Theater in October 1927, as Al Jolson stunned audiences with his historic performance in *The Jazz Singer.*

Not everything in the sexy world of entertainment was without controversy. Some Broadway numbers were considered a little too raunchy for the general public. To show his power in the theatrical community, Mayor Walker once threatened managers with punitive action unless they cleaned up their acts. Some civic and religious leaders called Broadway "unchaste and lustful." (As Brooks Atkinson later observed, "Jimmy Walker himself was both of these things.")

The hypocrisy of certain public officials was exposed when a citizens' panel of three hundred members, appointed by Joab H. Banton, Mayor Walker's district attorney, passed judgment on the "moral content" of various theater productions. The panel denounced an insignificant revue that was aptly titled *Bunk of 1926.* But instead of closing it, as the district attorney advised, the management applied for a court injunction, which it got, and the revue kept on playing until the public wisely stopped buying tickets.

Next the district attorney handed the mayor a list of shows he regarded as "morally unacceptable." With a straight face, Jimmy Walker agreed that the shows were too sexy for the delicate sensibilities of New York theatergoers.

The condemned dramas included Philip Kearney's dramatization of Theodore Dreiser's classic novel *An American Tragedy; Lulu Belle,* by Edward Sheldon and Charles MacArthur (co-author with Ben Hecht, of *The Front Page*); Arthur Hornblow, Jr.'s adaptation of Edouard Bourdet's *The*

Captive (the story of a French diplomat's daughter seduced by another woman and finally involved in a permanent lesbian relationship); William Dugan's *The Virgin Man;* Roland Oliver's *Night Hawk,* which told the familiar tale of a noble prostitute, and *Sex* by Mae West and Jane Mast.

The producers of these shows refused to take any action, and the plays continued on stage without causing any noticeable physical or mental harm to their audiences. Frustrated, the district attorney raided three of the shows that he regarded as "socially degrading"— *Sex, The Captive,* and *The Virgin Man.* Mae "Goodness Had Nothing to Do with It" West paid a fine of $500 and actually spent ten days in the workhouse. The author and producer of *The Virgin Man* paid fines of $250 each and briefly languished in jail. *The Captive* played for 160 performances before police wagons backed up to the stage door of the Empire Theatre and carted off the actors and management. It was a carnival for photographers, reporters, policemen, and lawmen who enjoyed the offstage scandal. Rather than fight the case in the courts, Gilbert Miller, the producer, closed down the show.

In the 1927 season, Broadway suffered another blow when the state legislature passed a censorship act popularly called the Wales Padlock Law. By the district attorney's loose standards, the law allowed the cops to arrest any producers, actors, and playwrights they considered immoral and to padlock a theater if the courts brought in a guilty verdict. *Maya,* a philosophical drama about the dreams that a French prostitute induced in her patrons, was promptly closed. To avoid having the theater padlocked and everybody concerned arrested, the producers withdrew the play.

The Shuberts uncharacteristically spoofed the Wales Padlock Law by producing a revue called *Padlocks of 1927.* It starred Texas Guinan, the symbol of nightclub revelry, who always greeted her patrons with the trademark phrase "Hello, suckers!" Miss Guinan made her entrance on a white horse, sang some songs, and browbeat the audience with insulting remarks. A line of comely chorines backed up her star turn. The more Texas upbraided the customers, the more they loved her.

The thrice-married Miss Guinan, whose real name was Mary Louise Cecilia, was born in Waco, Texas, but much preferred Manhattan and the riches she accumulated as a nightclub hostess. Manhattan returned the compliment by patronizing her West Side speakeasies. Whenever the Feds padlocked one, she opened another, and another. There Jimmy rubbed elbows with athletes, socialites, Wall Street brokers, politicians, and mobsters who had grown semirespectable by "importing" Canadian whisky and even backing Broadway shows.

Collier's magazine reported that "three-quarters of the 2,500 dry agents in New York are wardheelers and sycophants named by politicians." Entering a speakeasy wasn't difficult for the better class of drinkers. The speakeasies, or simply "speaks," gained their name because the fancier establishments required a few whispered words of recognition at the entranceway's peephole to make sure the caller wasn't a Treasury agent.

Not surprisingly, the speakeasy world was closely tied to bootleggers, organized crime, and some Tammany politicians. Miss Guinan's partner, a Hell's Kitchen hood named Larry Fay, was linked to Owney Madden, the town's biggest bootlegger. Madden, who had friends in the Tammany clubs on the West Side, was not a man to be crossed. He usually found it sufficient to exercise only silent muscle against rival gangsters. It was rumored that he considered Legs Diamond— the Hotsy Totsy Club owner and Arnold Rothstein's former bodyguard—anathema because the flamboyant Legs called too much attention to his colleagues in the underworld. Whether Madden had anything to do with Legs's death will never be known.

"I would rather have a square inch of New York than all the rest of the world," said Miss Guinan, who lived hard and passed on at the age of forty-nine. The *New York Herald Tribune* offered this generous tribute: "She was a master showman and accomplished psychologist. She had ability, too, and would have been successful in any one of a dozen more conventional fields. To New York and the rest of the country, Texas was a flaming leader of a period which was a lot of fun while it lasted."

New Yorkers seeking racier entertainment than the hundreds of Broadway shows and thousands of speakeasies could always pull down their fedoras, pull up the collars of their raincoats, and duck into the Gaiety on Forty-sixth Street or one of the other five-shows-a-day "burleycue" houses. If they bought a watered lemonade drink, patrons could sit through two shows while eating a thick fifteen-cent hot pastrami club sandwich, with mustard and coleslaw, from the crowded Gaiety delicatessen next door.

The "burleycues" featured aspiring or retired Catskill Mountain comedians. Their standard jokes invariably included a fire hose spritzing a stream of water as the phallic punchline. The strippers shed their garments, piece by flimsy piece, to the beat of a five-piece pit band while an over-the-hill tenor in white tie and tails sang, "A Pretty Girl Is Like a Melody." One star performer on the burlesque circuit was known for her remarkable ability to jiggle the tassels on the nipples of her ample breasts in opposite directions at the same time.

But it wasn't all fun and games in the field of entertainment. New York was also the center of book and magazine publishing; bookstores, newsstands, and neighborhood public libraries offered a variety of works for new learners and serious readers—though there is no evidence that Mayor Walker was among them.

The 1920s saw the internationalization of American literature, partly the result of widening horizons after World War I. It was a decade that produced lasting literature. For his remarkable group of novels depicting the smugness and hypocrisy of American small-town life—*Main Street, Babbitt, Arrowsmith* (Pulitzer Prize, 1926, declined), *Elmer Gantry,* and *Dodsworth*—Sinclair Lewis received the 1930 Nobel Prize for Literature, the first American to be so honored (he accepted). Lewis said he refused the Pulitzer because the prize was awarded not for literary merit but for the best presentation of "the wholesome atmosphere of American life." By his standards, "wholesome" was a dirty word.

In the same decade, Pulitzer-winning novelists included Edith Wharton, for *The Age of Innocence;* Booth Tarkington, for *Alice Adams;* Willa Cather, for *One of Ours;* Edna Ferber, for *So Big;* and Thornton Wilder, for *the Bridge of San Luis Rey.* Novelists who were *passed over* for Pulitzers at the time included John Dos Passos, for *Manhattan Transfer;* William Faulkner, who published *Sartoris* and

The Sound and the Fury; Ernest Hemingway, for *The Sun Also Rises* and *A Farewell to Arms;* and F. Scott Fitzgerald, for *The Great Gatsby.*

Black writers came to the fore during the 1920s in the literary and artistic movement that became known as the Harlem Renaissance. The nucleus of the movement included Jean Toomer, Wallace Thurman, Arna Bontemps, Countee Cullen, and Zora Neale Hurston. Among the notable authors (and books) were Langston Hughes (*The Weary Blues*); James Weldon Johnson (*God's Trombones*), and Claude McKay (*Home to Harlem*). They offered a realistic portrayal of black life.

"The 1920s were the years of Manhattan's Black Renaissance," said Langston Hughes, linking music and literature. "It began with 'Shuffle Along,' 'Running Wild' and the 'Charleston.' It was the musical revue that gave a scintillating sendoff to that Negro vogue in Manhattan, which reached its peak just before the Crash of 1929, the Crash that sent Negroes, white folks, and all rolling down the hill toward [President Roosevelt's] Works Progress Administration. White people began to come to Harlem in droves. For several years they packed the expensive Cotton Club on Lenox Avenue. But I was never there, because the Cotton Club was a Jim Crow club for gangsters and monied whites. They were not cordial to Negro patronage, unless you were a celebrity."

Almost as soon as Walker entered City Hall, he found it necessary to preserve his health by leaving Manhattan as often as possible, winter and summer. After the strenuous campaign, he went to Palm Springs to rest up. Shortly after taking office, he attended the Kentucky Derby. The papers reported his wardrobe as well as the race results. Field glasses were formally draped over his double-breasted suit. His wide-brimmed light fedora was rakishly tilted to one side, Walker style. At the estates of his wealthy friends, he took vacations in Malibu and Palm Beach, wearing his special sports outfits.

Instead of reprimanding the mayor for his long absences in the better watering holes of Florida and California, the tabloids found him wonderful copy. He represented the people, living out their dreams. Irving Berlin found time to capture the mood of the public in another musical tribute to his dear friend that did not, however, endure in his catalogue of hit tunes:

> Who told Broadway not to be gay?
> Who gets his picture taken three times a day?
> Jimmy!
> We're glad to show,
> That we all know,
> That Jimmy's doing fine.
> Can't you hear those old New Yorkers hollering:
> Gimmie—gimmie—gimmie Jimmy for mine!

In his first year in office, the Honorable James J. Walker put on his top hat and tails and became a self-appointed ambassador to Europe, spending more time with the royalty than the peasantry. His entourage set sail on the *Berengaria,* a German ship that had become a Cunard liner after the Great War as part of reparations. The Walkers occupied the luxury liner's Imperial Suite, the cost to them unknown.

At a reception given the night before by the Grand Street Boys at their Fifty-fifth Street clubhouse, the mayor had been presented with a golden scroll of the Ten Commandments, written in Hebrew. Among those cheering him were Governor Alfred E. Smith, Patrick Cardinal Hayes, U.S. Senators Robert F. Wagner and Royal S. Copeland, a dozen state Supreme Court justices, Al Jolson and other theatrical personalities, and such "philanthropists" as Paul Block (who would later be heard of as one of the mayor's illicit financial sources).

In a sentimental speech, Walker said, "I love my city more than anything else in the world, unless it be my country and my God. I must, on my travels, earn the respect to which my city is entitled, and I promise you boys tonight, that I will think, look and act in terms of a public servant."

Hundreds of well-wishers came to the Hudson River pier to bid him bon voyage, the fire department band played and the police department glee club serenaded him with Irving Berlin tunes. Walker turned to his shipboard pals and said, "I never would have believed there were so many people glad to see me leave town. I hope they'll be just as glad to see me get back!"

The mayor's principal spear carrier, Hector Fuller, an advertising and publicity man who accompanied Jimmy, Allie, and their friends, put out the word that the mayor was taking a "hard-working vacation" in the "charming cities" of London, Dublin, Berlin, Munich, Baden-Baden, Venice and the Lido, Rome, Paris and Castlecomer, his father's hometown in County Kilkenny.

No newspaper dispatches exist about Allie Walker's clothes for the trip, but Jimmy's wardrobe included forty-eight suits, twelve sports jackets and matching striped pants, twenty white piqué vests, a dozen topcoats, morning coats, and top hats, and one hundred ties, and that was only the outerwear. The foreign press reported Jimmy's outfits more closely than his speeches.

The high point of the grand tour was his visit to Ireland. In the village of Castlecomer, Walker spoke emotionally:

"When a man comes from a far country back to the land of his fathers, back from Castle Garden where his sire entered to become an American citizen, to arrive at Castlecomer whence in the years gone by his father came, who shall find words adequately to express his emotions? Mine own people! How truly now can I use that phrase about Americans on one side of the Atlantic and the Irish on this. To have looked into the eyes of villagers who knew my dear father and have shaken his hand; to stand in their hearts as a symbol of the great opportunity that America offers! This has been a privilege of which a much humbler man than I might well be proud."

In Rome, Mayor Walker proved a dangerous amateur as an envoy for the United States. His blarney did not do him—or his country—proud when he met Benito Mussolini, the Fascist dictator. After a private talk with Il Duce (Hector Fuller boasted that it was the longest interview Mussolini had given since coming to power), Walker gave a press conference at the Excelsior Hotel before forty newspapermen.

Confidently but witlessly, Walker said:

"I told Mussolini that it has been one of the greatest honors of my European tour to meet him. I told him that I really believed he was the greatest figure in modern times and that I have long admired him. I can understand, without difficulty, after talking with Mussolini for forty-six minutes, why he has been the wonderfully successful man that the world recognizes. I found him a man of great personal attraction. Like all great men, a man of great mental strength and at the same time a man of deep sympathy. His one outstanding success lies in the fact that he is a genuine humanitarian."

Il Duce issued this statement to the world press:

"Mayor Walker is young, not only in appearance but also in spirit. He is a man of great talent, an idealist, and a practical man at the same time. Therefore, he is highly fit to govern the great metropolis where millions of Italians live and whom the New York Mayor has praised, saying they were upright, hardworking and obedient to American laws. Mayor Walker has left me with a feeling of greatest sympathy."

It was an exchange that Walker's sympathetic biographers have chosen to forget.

After six weeks, the mayor's entourage returned to New York on the *Ile de France*. In honor of its distinguished passenger, boasted Hector Fuller, the flag of the City of New York flew from the liner's foremast for the first time in its history. When the ship docked, the police department band vied with the Boys' Band from the Greenwich Village Post of the American Legion in playing such popular tunes as "Maggie Murphy's Home" and "Sidewalks of New York."

As cameras clicked and flashbulbs went off, Walker made a brief speech to the welcoming newspaper reporters on the pier: "Boys, primarily I'm glad to get back in New York for a vacation. I went abroad for a rest, but the constant round of hospitality and courtesy shown me had us on the go constantly. To detail everything would take hours and days. But I come back joyful to know the great esteem in which Europe holds New York. Wherever I went I heard nothing but admiration for our city and it made me proud to be a New Yorker."

Most of the newspapers bought the line that the junket was a success, comparing Jimmy Walker to the Prince of Wales, England's own dandy. An editorial writer in the *New York Evening World,* reaching for elegant words to match the mayor's dashing wardrobe, wrote:

"Whether he receives a French committee in his pajamas, or strolls into the smart Mayfair Hotel in London, dapper and smartly garbed in a double-breasted suit, panama hat, soft-collared grey shirt and blue scarf, he exudes geniality and goodwill and sells America. Verily, the Prince of Wales may be a good salesman for the British Empire, but he will find the going hard after Jimmy Walker has smiled upon his customers, sung them a song, and sold little old New York."

A new round of official receptions, led by the businessmen of the Advertising Club, greeted Jimmy as a conquering hero. At a luncheon in the Grand Ballroom of the Hotel Astor in the heart of Broadway, three thousand people were somehow accommodated. Walker was presented with a portfolio, bound in morocco, that included photographs of every city and resort he had visited.

Responding to the welcome-home speeches by his friends and benefactors in the business community, the Night Mayor said, "You can find some comfort from the fact that in my every waking hour I love New York. There is not anything in the world I would not do for this great city, nor anything that I would not give for it."

Referring to his visit to Mussolini's Rome, he added, "Your Mayor, if you please, took off his hat to the statue of Christopher Columbus who made it possible for you and me to live in a place where we could be on the level with ourselves and all the world."

Rising to their feet, the businessmen, churchmen, and public officials applauded every one of Jimmy Walker's sincere platitudes.

It was now the autumn of 1927. Walker was at the height of his popularity. His life and the city's life were filled with sunshine and prosperity. The darkening clouds were barely visible.

SIX

Hares and Hounds

Arnold Rothstein's murder was still "unsolved," and reformers knew that New York's police and courts (not to mention prosecutors) were on the take or simply looking the other way. But where to begin an investigation? The Appellate Division of the New York State Supreme Court finally started the ball rolling after an incident involving Magistrate Albert H. Vitale, a Tammany hack, who was used to line up votes for Jimmy Walker in the Bronx. Magistrate Vitale had been a friend of Arnie Rothstein. Some time before the gangster was gunned down, Vitale had borrowed nearly $20,000 from him.

A seriocomic incident took place that proved Magistrate Vitale's underworld connections to be of the finest. It happened at a testimonial dinner and fund-raiser held by the Tepecano Democratic Club at the Roman Gardens in the Bronx. (Italian members of the club altered the club's name; it derived from the nickname—"Old Tippecanoe"—of General William H. Harrison, hero of the battle of Tippecanoe, who was the ninth American president.) Most of the members were lawyers and bail bondsmen doing business in Vitale's courtroom. The guest of honor was none other than the Honorable Albert H. Vitale himself.

With a wave and a hearty salute, he stood up to acknowledge the plaudits of his fellow Democrats and financial contributors. They included various gentlemen with police records, including Ciro Terranova, the "Artichoke King." Terranova, who monopolized the sale of vegetables in the city's Italian neighborhoods, arrived at the affair in his armored limousine, which had bulletproof windows.

Suddenly, six masked men, pistols drawn, entered the private dining room and lined up the guests against the wall. A city detective handed his revolver to the robbers without attempting to use it. Magistrate Vitale slipped off his diamond ring and hid it in his pants; a former magistrate, Michael Dilagi, stuffed *his* diamond ring in his shoe. The six masked robbers took thousands of dollars from the guests, quickly dashed outside, and disappeared into waiting getaway cars driven by experienced wheelmen.

Naturally, this unscheduled entertainment embarrassed Vitale, the honorary president for life of the Tepecano Democrats. He left the Roman Gardens at two o'clock in the morning and immediately drove to his own Democratic clubhouse. With a few well-placed telephone calls in the next two hours, he rounded up all the cash, gold cuff links, and star sapphire pinky rings that had been stolen at his party, restored the loot to the surprised guests, and saw that the police detective's stolen gun was returned.

On August 27, 1930, Edward R. Finch, the acting presiding justice of the Appellate Division's First Department, which covered Manhattan and the Bronx, ordered an investigation of the Magistrates' Courts.

At the same time, with the national Democratic convention two years away, some of Governor Roosevelt's political intimates were already working for his presidential nomination. They did not want to arouse anti–New York sentiment that might damage F.D.R.'s chances around the country. The full depth of corruption in the city could not be anticipated by Roosevelt or his advisers. Tammany Hall was still in a position of influence in city, state, and national elections. Its leaders had contributed to F.D.R.'s gubernatorial victory. It was not yet time for Roosevelt to put on his armor and challenge the Hall and its designated officials.

The New York Times sensed that the contagion ran deeper than bail bondsmen, payoffs, and light sentences for the city's second-level criminals. It expressed the belief that major departments in the city were infected by the virus of corruption. But the newspaper, at least at this initial stage, failed to say that Mayor Walker had a measure of responsibility for what was taking place on his watch:

"Till now nothing has come from City Hall to indicate that Mr. Walker is aware of the discredit brought by his associates and subordinates upon his own record," *The Times* commented. "When so many cracks show in the structure, there is lowered resistance to stress. The hour has come for the Mayor to summon both the demolition and reconstruction crews. It is not too late for Mr. Walker, who has in no personal way been even slightly connected with any of these scandals, to voice the indignation of the community which has twice elected him."

But Mayor Walker had no time to pay attention to ivory-tower editorial writers. Hadn't the electorate reaffirmed its support of his administration at the polls?

The irony of the moment was pointed up by a news item that appeared the same day in *The East Hampton Star.* It announced with pride that a local resident, Judge Samuel Seabury, "who is very popular with both the summer colony and the permanent village," had received an investigative appointment from the Appellate Division and that "East Hampton will watch the proceedings with great interest." The appointment had been made with Governor Roosevelt's approval; Seabury would carry the city investigation forward for the next two years, finally passing on the evidence to the governor for a final judgment.

The retired Judge Seabury had begun his legal career as a crusading lawyer for the poor and for labor unions. With the approval of the Citizens Union and the bar associations, he was first elected to the city court and in 1907, at the age of thirty-three, he became the youngest justice of the state Supreme Court. In 1914, he was elected on both the Democratic and Progressive party tickets to the Court of Appeals. Two years later he resigned to run for governor on the Democratic ticket, lost, and returned to private practice. But he still nurtured an ambition to hold high political office—governor of New York or even (rather foolishly, since he had no political machine) president of the United States.

On the surface, Seabury appeared to be the patrician lawyer and Walker the man of the people. In their private law practice, the opposite was true. Walker's minor legal career had not been devoted to aiding society's underprivileged. As a state senator, he brought some clout to his clients because of his name and visibility. Occasionally, he served as a court-appointed attorney in homicide cases. The law was a place for him to hang his hat and pick up some extra money, but he devoted his main energies to his political career and his personal wanderings.

As a young labor lawyer, Seabury worked for enactment of legislation recognizing employers' responsibility for the welfare and protection of their workingmen during the time they were on the job—a fairly new concept. He was a firm believer in labor education and labor lobbying.

Seabury was also an advocate of public ownership of city transportation facilities. Corruption was bipartisan. Franchises for privately owned street railways were a source of graft. What shakedowns of whorehouse madams brought in was only pin money for the politicians and police; the railways brought in fortunes for the Tammany bosses themselves.

In one respect, Walker and Seabury had common New York backgrounds. They were both born on the Lower West Side of Manhattan, not far from the Hudson River—Jimmy in a flat on Leroy Street and Sam in the rectory of the Church of the Annunciation on West Fourteenth Street.

But they inhabited two different worlds, and fate would make them rancorous enemies. The two men were opposites, and not only in religious upbringing. Jimmy Walker's father was a carpenter who became commissioner of public buildings in New York City at a time when Irish Catholics ruled Tammany Hall. Seabury's father, a professor of canon law at the General Theological Seminary, named his son after their ancestor, the first Episcopal bishop in the United States.

Seabury was usually called Judge even though he had left the Court of Appeals in 1916. His pince-nez glasses, center-parted white hair, and starched look gave him an aloof, superior air. He was a knightly crusader who carried a banner of righteousness as his main weapon.

Unknown to all but his closest friends and family, he harbored a grudge against Tammany for not helping him to become governor.

Yet he enjoyed the good life. At the height of his career after he left
the bench, Seabury had a flourishing general law practice at 120
Broadway and owned a spacious six-story mansion on Sixty-third
Street on the Upper East Side of Manhattan, as well as six hundred
acres of land surrounding his large farmhouse in East Hampton. He
was a self-made millionaire and lived like one.

Seabury's serenity was interrupted by the arrival of an urgent
cable informing him that he had been appointed the referee to conduct an investigation of the Magistrates' Courts.

After the Appellate Division assured Seabury that he would have
full authority to look into any and all dark and hidden corners, he
agreed to take the job. He envisioned his role as that of an independent prosecutor. Indeed, that was how he would conduct the public office for the next two years while his private practice faded away. The
newspapers were uniformly pleased with his decision.

As a faithful New Yorker, Seabury was aware of the magnitude of
the job he was undertaking—perhaps more so than the mayor who
devoted so little time to his day job. In the early 1930s, New York was
a big city to play with. Its population was seven million. There was $20
billion worth of taxable real estate; this private property annually
brought $535.5 million in revenue. Still, the city was in constant finan-
cial trouble, trying to meet its bonded indebtedness.

Six hundred million dollars a year went to run the city government; $286 million was paid to the 148,000 men and women holding
city jobs. Thousands of these appointed jobs came directly under the
purview of the mayor and Tammany Hall. At best, even for men of real
ability and dedication, running New York City was a superhuman task.

The revelations about the corrupt magistrates and his own talks with
the Appellate Division justices immediately caused Seabury to broaden
the scope of the inquiry. He insisted that not only the magistrates but
the attorneys practicing in the lower criminal courts be investigated for
"corrupt, fraudulent, unlawful or unprofessional" conduct.

After he was authorized to enlarge the investigation, Seabury appointed Isidor Jacob Kresel as his chief counsel. Kresel, who later became the target of Tammany's counterattack, was a highly respected member of the New York Bar. A Jewish immigrant from Galicia, who had put himself through college from a crowded Stanton Street tenement by helping to tutor less gifted men at Columbia Law School, he had lifted himself to the top of his profession.

At the age of twenty-three in 1901, Kresel was appointed a Manhattan assistant district attorney; in 1913, he was counsel to the New York State Assembly during the impeachment trial of Governor William Sulzer, a Tammany faithful from the Upper East Side's Silk Stocking District, who had played the stock market with falsified campaign funds. Sulzer was convicted and removed from office—the only time a New York governor has been impeached. Kresel also had served as a special assistant attorney general in federal antitrust and bankruptcy cases. A year before joining the Seabury staff, he had prosecuted and caused to be disbarred dozens of lawyers for the crime of barratry (stirring up litigation, by, among other means, ambulance-chasing).

The lofty Seabury and the diminutive Kresel—it was said that "he could run under a table wearing a high hat"—made a formidable combination. Kresel, more experienced in a prosecutorial role, set the pattern for the investigation. He didn't depend on confessions. His technique was to perform the unspectacular job of researching income tax returns, bank deposit slips, records of savings accounts belonging to members of a witness's family, real estate documents, and brokerage account statements. It was nearly impossible for a big or little fish to slip through such a tight net.

At the same time, Judge Seabury obtained the assistance of Professor Raymond Moley of Columbia University as a consultant. Moley was an expert in the field of government and economics. Among other tasks, he supervised the editorial reports that Judge Seabury prepared for Governor Roosevelt about the progress of the investigation. It was a wise appointment for political reasons as well; Seabury realized that he had to protect himself from backstabbing by political enemies in Tammany Hall. Moley was destined to become a leading figure in the group of academic advisers who would later serve Roosevelt in the White House.

One of the first things that Seabury did was to assemble a dedicated staff of tireless young legal sleuths like those who worked on the investigations that would dominate late-twentieth-century politics, from Watergate to Whitewater. Most of them were in their twenties or early thirties; some were barely out of law school. All were hungry and, not incidentally, eager to build their own reputations. Several would go on to become state and federal judges. Oren Herwitz, George B. Levy, and Harold Melniker all joined the staff before they were admitted to the bar. When James H. Goodier, a former U.S. consul to Tahiti, returned to private practice, he found it lacked adventure. He barged into Seabury's office, proved his enthusiasm, and was hired on the spot.

Seabury liked to call his young staff "my boys." Speaking to them, he appeared almost Edwardian in manner. "I will not be exceeded in courtesy" was one of his favorite expressions. Rarely would he order one of his lawyers to perform an assignment. He would call him in for a "discussion." When he wanted something done, the phrase he used was "I would suggest." When he insisted that it be done, the command took the mild form "I think it might be done this way."

The young men with whom he labored in his office often were invited to join him at the Bankers Club, where they observed him order his usual roast beef and cigar. When a case carried over into the evening, Seabury and his colleagues went home to dine with Mrs. Seabury. The Seabury "boys" remembered that dinner was usually preceded by one rather mild drink (Prohibition was still in force).

Seabury was aware that both he and his staff would themselves be challenged by Tammany and even by some of the newspapermen who were drinking buddies of Jimmy Walker. Since Walker and a number of other officials under investigation were Catholics and of Celtic origin, Seabury didn't want it to appear that their religious or ethnic backgrounds had anything to do with the investigation. The staff of lawyers he chose included Protestants, Catholics, and Jews.

One of the legal sleuths, Philip Haberman, would be remembered for his ability to unearth Mayor Walker's hidden bank and brokerage accounts. It was Haberman who would discover a letter of credit given to Mayor Walker by a group of businessmen and politicians—and who played a leading role in cracking the meaning of certain secretive code words that identified Jimmy Walker as the "BOY FRIEND."

Irving Ben Cooper, a future federal District Court judge, was another young lawyer with street smarts. Lunching on malteds and dime sandwiches, he pursued suspects and developed his own cases, riding in police cars when a witness was sought to make sure that nobody would be tipped off by the cops. It was a dangerous job. When Cooper applied for life insurance, he was turned down as a poor risk.

The investigators made a special effort to appear to be above politics. Seabury was aware that he had to strike a balance between Democrats and Republicans in order to obtain the support of independents as well as the major party voters in the city. Jacob Gould Schurman, Jr., son of the former ambassador to Germany, and a former assistant district attorney, was a Republican; so was Harland B. Tibbetts, who had been a member of Kresel's law firm. Both were added to the staff.

William Mulligan joined Judge Seabury right out of Harvard Law School, where he had been one of Professor Felix Frankfurter's brightest students. During the hearings, the silver-tongued mayor turned on the grinning Mulligan and, accusingly, demanded to know his name. The request boomeranged. Mulligan's Irish name startled Walker and made the spectators and reporters in the courthouse break out in laughter.

Seabury's boys now covered a cross-section of the city's legal talent.

At the first meeting of his full staff, Judge Seabury passed along the experience he had gained on both sides of the bench:

"The public will not be aroused to an awareness of conditions in the Magistrates' courts through a series of graphs, charts and reports. We must divorce this investigation, as far as is possible, from legalistic machinery. There is more eloquence in the testimony of a single illiterate witness telling of oppression suffered from legal processes than in the greatest sermon, editorial or address ever written. Where preachers, editors and lawyers have failed in arousing the public to a consciousness of unjust conditions these simple, unlearned witnesses will succeed.

"Let's attack this subject man-fashion. Do not be discouraged—the facts we bring out are going to sink into the public's mind long after Jimmy Walker's wisecracks are forgotten."

Then he uttered a slogan that they all took to heart: "Old heads for counsel—young heads for war."

That was to be their watchword for the next two years.

The Depression had weakened President Hoover and his chances for reelection. Judge Seabury dreamed that the national attention he gained from what became known as the Seabury investigations would make lightning strike—and even lead to his nomination for president at the 1932 Democratic convention. He hoped to overcome ex-Governor Smith's effort to win the nomination a second time and even thought he might, miraculously, beat out Roosevelt, whose political operatives had begun to work behind the scenes almost from the moment he became governor.

Seabury knew that he would need the public's acceptance and support during the investigation. A little over a month after his appointment, on September 29, 1930, he addressed a meeting of leaders of the bar and members of the press in the New York County Courthouse. Anyone expecting spectacular revelations was disappointed.

"There are two paramount questions," Seabury said, defining the scope of the inquiry. "What are the conditions in the Magistrates' courts? Is justice being done? The essential facts can be ascertained only by laborious investigation. They do not lie patent upon the surface—they must be brought to light."

The newspapers played the story on the inside pages; no fireworks. But not long afterward, the investigation would produce page-one banner headlines all over the country.

Just as the investigation was about to begin, a strange voice from the past was heard. Lincoln Steffens attempted to help calm the storm clouds gathering over New York. His crusading reporting in *McClure's* magazine and in *The Shame of the Cities* was a quarter of a century behind him; his personal reputation was linked to the muckraking years of the early 1900s. But now, at age sixty-four, he was behind the times.

"The thing to do," Steffens told the Citizens Union, "is to have a frank talk with Jimmy Walker, and say, 'This won't do. Of course, we know that vice, lawlessness and civic corruption cannot be eliminated but at least it should be kept under control. After all, the people will be satisfied with nothing less than the outward appearance of decency, no matter how bad things are beneath the surface.'"

Unfortunately, it would not be that simple. Steffens was as wrong about Jimmy Walker and the need for the Seabury investigation as he would be in his 1931 book, *The Autobiography of Lincoln Steffens,* where he famously said about Russia, "I have been over into the future, and it works."

For after observing the tough methods employed by Seabury and his sleuths in their game of hares and hounds, Walter Lippmann, the influential *New York Herald Tribune* columnist—who at the time thought much less of Governor Roosevelt than he did of Judge Seabury—wrote:

"Samuel Seabury is the most terrifying biographer that Tammany has had in modern times."

SEVEN

The Tin Box Brigade

During the autumn of 1931, in the county courthouse in Lower Manhattan, the Honorable Thomas M. Farley, sheriff of New York County, president of the Thomas M. Farley Association, leader of the Fourteenth Assembly District, and Tammany Hall Sachem, sat on the witness stand. The Seabury investigation had already spread from the magistrates themselves to the police, the sheriffs, and almost everyone connected to the judicial system and the affairs of the City of New York.

Farley was trying to explain how he accumulated nearly a half-million dollars in six years on an annual salary of $8,500. His interrogator was Judge Seabury. Their dialogue would go down in American musical (*Fiorello!*) and municipal history:

SEABURY: Where did you keep these moneys that you had saved?

FARLEY: In a safe-deposit box at home in the house.

SEABURY: Whereabouts at home in the house did you keep this money that you had saved?

FARLEY: In the safe.

SEABURY: In a safe?

FARLEY: Yes.

SEABURY: In a little box in a safe?

FARLEY: A big safe.

SEABURY: But a little box in a big safe?

FARLEY: In a big box in a big safe.

SEABURY: Was the big box in the big safe fairly full or crowded when you withdrew this money?

FARLEY: I didn't withdraw it all at once. That is money that was in the safe-deposit box—

SEABURY: When you first drew it, Sheriff, was the box then crowded or very full?

FARLEY: Well, it was full and plenty in it.

SEABURY: More and plenty?

FARLEY: Yes.

SEABURY: And, Sheriff, was this big box that was safely kept in the big safe a tin box or a wooden box?

FARLEY: A tin box.

SEABURY: Is it the type of tin boxes that are specially manufactured and designed to serve as a receptacle for cash?

FARLEY: It is.

SEABURY: Giving you the benefit of every doubt on sums from your official vocation and other gainful pursuits, the $83,000 extra you deposited in 1929 came from the same source that the other money came from?

FARLEY: Yes.

SEABURY: Same tin box, is that right?

FARLEY: That is right.

SEABURY: Now, in 1930, where did the extra cash come from, Sheriff?

FARLEY: Well, that is—. My salary check is in there.

SEABURY: No, Sheriff, your salary checks are exclusive of the cash deposits which during the year you deposited in those three banks.

FARLEY: Well, that came from the good box I had. [*Laughter*]

SEABURY: Kind of a magic box.

FARLEY: It was a wonderful box.

SEABURY: A wonderful box. [*Laughter*] What did you have to do—rub the lock with a little gold, and open it in order to find more money?

FARLEY: I wish I could.

Spurred by Judge Seabury, Governor Roosevelt personally summoned Sheriff Farley to Albany to give him a last chance to explain the sources of his mysterious fortune. The Tammany Sachem arrived in morning coat and stand-up collar, looking more like Jeeves than an arresting officer, but his formal attire couldn't help him. He had become a figure of public ridicule. Governor Roosevelt used the sheriff's appearance before him to establish an unofficial code of conduct (with the help of Samuel I. Rosenman, his legal adviser and frequent speechwriter in Albany and later in Washington, where he was familiarly known as Sammy the Rose) for all government officials in the state:

"As a matter of general sound public policy, I am very certain that there is a requirement that where a public official is under inquiry or investigation, especially an elected official, and it appears that his scale of living or the total of his bank deposits far exceeds the public salary which he is known to receive, he, the elected public official, owes a positive public duty to the community to give a reasonable or credible explanation of the sources of the deposits, or the source which enables him to maintain a scale of livng beyond the amount of his salary."

Roosevelt removed the dishonored sheriff from his shrievalty. The fact that Farley had once contributed $20,000 to Roosevelt's political campaign fund didn't save him. There was too much evidence against him to let him off easily; it was all out in the open and Roosevelt had no other choice.

Because of the Tammany links between the discredited sheriff and City Hall, Jimmy Walker decided to mount a counterattack against Judge Seabury. Through his assistant, Charles F. Kerrigan, he claimed that the Seabury investigation was concerned only with the "private affairs" of city officials and not with their public service. (The newspapers, which had covered up his own private affairs of the heart, were beginning to be a little bolder in discussing the mayor's relationship with Betty Compton). In a communication to the Republican leaders who dominated the state legislature, Kerrigan said that the Seabury hearings were "a futile waste of the money of the taxpayers."

Tammany and the town's Democratic bigwigs made an effort to cut off the funds to Judge Seabury and his staff. They claimed that the investigation was harming the city's credit rating, the banks, and the stock market. Irwin Steingut, an influential assemblyman from Brooklyn, claimed that Judge Seabury sought another $150,000 for his investigation and "that does not include his personal fee, which is expected to be at least another $150,000." Although Seabury himself was a longtime Democrat, Assemblyman Steingut said that "the Republicans are attempting through the investigation to collect propaganda material at the expense of the State."

Another Tammany hack, Assemblyman Louis Cuvillier, a minority member of the legislature's investigative committee, protested: "It has dawned upon the millions who live in New York and love New York that their city, the greatest in the world, is getting a daily black eye from the counsel to the committee. The conviction is growing among the people that there is something sinister, something cruelly unfair, about this investigation. Let us stop this criminal waste of funds and end the dismal failure of this committee."

Next, Jimmy Walker's corporation counsel took the bold step of refusing to honor the salary vouchers of Seabury's staff of lawyers and accountants. The trick didn't work; it only infuriated the reformers and investigators. Judge Seabury brought a writ of mandamus against Mayor Walker and Comptroller Charles W. Berry. The state Supreme Court issued an order to force the corporation counsel to release the money.

As the investigation continued, a "tin box" brigade of corrupt officials paraded through the courtroom. In addition to the Tammany sheriffs, registers, and county clerks, one of the more colorful witnesses to appear before Judge Seabury was a woman: Miss Polly Adler, a self-described "student of the human condition." As Arnold Rothstein was the gambling czar of New York, Miss Adler could lay claim to being the czarina of prostitution. Everybody knew that when you winked and said you were going to one of Polly Adler's places for a good time, you weren't going there to say your paternoster. The public wanted to know "who's who after the sun goes down," as the *New York World-Telegram* put it, "and what connection if any exists between the police and the profession of which Miss Adler is the acknowledged chatelaine."

Delicately, Judge Seabury asked her if it was not true that a number of Tammany leaders—including the mayor himself—had "celebrated" important events in her house-that-was-not-a-home. Miss Adler's recollection failed her a number of times. Confronted with a check that she had made out to a vice squad cop to protect her winsome young ladies from arrest, she feebly denied that the signature was hers.

In words and pictures, the *New York Daily News* covered Miss Adler's appearance as a scandal that besmirched the good name of the city of New York. Even *The New York Times* reported the questioning of the city's leading "vice entrepreneuse." Her raunchy business, the editors rationalized, deserved to be recounted in the columns of the family newspaper as a cautionary tale. For the delicate sensibilities of its readers, *The Times* didn't call Miss Adler's places whorehouses but, more politely, "houses of ill-repute."

Before Miss Adler testified publicly, she made an appearance before Seabury and his assistants at their offices in the state building at 80 Centre Street. That was the key to the Seabury-Kresel investigative method: to get witnesses to spill their guts privately without courtroom rules of evidence or objections from defense lawyers.

There was a little unspoken trickery involved here. The Seabury-Kresel team's usual procedure was to tender witnesses a "request" subpoena that began "You are hereby requested . . . " (rather than "commanded" or "ordered"). A "request" didn't require a court order. Few witnesses were aware that they had a choice in the matter. Some witnesses were tipped off that they were about to be grilled at 80 Centre Street and avoided process servers or disappeared. In such cases,

Seabury used the press to flush them out. Friendly reporters who tracked down missing witnesses received special treatment from the Seabury staff.

(In future investigations of alleged misconduct in Washington—involving officials up to and including the president of the United States—a "special counsel" under the attorney general would use a similar technique, leaking information to favored columnists and broadcasters. This investigatory style became known as trying your case in the press.)

During her private session, Miss Adler said that Irving Ben Cooper's "piercing eyes never left my face and his silence was like an attack." Cooper, one of Seabury's toughest "boys," had copies of her bank and brokerage accounts in front of him to see if there were payoffs to police and public officials.

"Cooper wasted no time on the amenities and began firing questions at me the moment I came into the room," the enterprising whorehouse madam recalled. "Did I know a certain man? No. Had I been at a certain place at a certain time? I didn't remember. For what seemed hours he continued to throw names at me, and I continued to deny knowing all except those who could not possibly be hurt by our acquaintanceship. At the end of the long afternoon, Cooper glared at me out of sharp blue eyes that seemed to bite into me: 'You are positive you don't know these men?' 'Positive.' 'You understand, Miss Adler, that everything you say is being taken down by a court stenographer?' You're telling me, brother, I thought to myself. But aloud I said demurely, 'Yes, I understand.'"

The investigation made no effort to prosecute Miss Adler. For a while, the low-level police payoffs stopped. Ironically, traffic in Miss Adler's houses became even more profitable as their existence became better known to the citizenry.

Seabury's staff discovered that three methods were used by police making arrests of women charged with prostitution. The first was known as the direct case: the arresting officer obtained entrance to the premises and collected evidence. The second, the indirect case, arose when neighbors complained about the proximity of the whorehouses. The third, most prevalent method was to use "the unknown man"—a stool pigeon.

Under the one-sided law, the sex act itself was no misdemeanor, but when the woman accepted money for the purpose of prostitution, she committed a crime. Even though the officer entered the room while the act was in progress, the stoolie could not be held. He was usually on the vice squad's payroll as an informant rather than a participant.

As the referee rooting out corruption in the magistrates' hearings, Judge Seabury and his boys examined 1,059 witnesses at 80 Centre Street. The minutes covered 15,356 pages. "Some of this testimony seemed to me, in view of the public interest involved, to require presentation at public hearings," Seabury told the Appellate Division justices. Beginning in September of 1930 and continuing for eight months, open hearings were held in which 299 witnesses were interrogated. Their testimony covered 4,596 pages.

During the hearings, a Runyonesque character appeared on the witness stand who captured the town's bawdy imagination, as much for his name as for his activities. Chile Mapocha Acuna, thereafter the subject of wisecracks in which he was called the "Human Spitoona," was a stool pigeon employed by the police vice squad. He joined other stoolies with such colorful nicknames as "The Dove," "Pinto," "Chico," and "Harry the Greek."

Acuna, a diminutive thirty-one-year-old native of Santiago, Chile, had been betrayed by the vice squad on grounds of "extortion" and had spent a year in the penitentiary. He walked into the Seabury offices during the first week of the investigation and joined a score of other witnesses, both voluntary and subpoenaed, who were sitting on a bench waiting to be examined by the lawyers. When Acuna was called in, he confessed that he knew a number of policemen who had committed perjury to obtain the conviction of innocent women.

"Is this thing on the level?" Acuna asked. Having been double-crossed by the vice squad, he knew that his life wouldn't be worth more than the cost of a bullet if he testified openly. Seabury and Kresel assured him that the investigation was indeed on the level and that he would be protected. At Seabury's request, Police Commissioner Edward P. Mulrooney assigned six police lieutenants to guard Acuna around the clock. Mulrooney warned them that they would never make captain if Acuna was "accidentally" killed. After three days of hesitation, Acuna said he was willing to go public.

"He became a witness without parallel in the history of American jurisprudence," Seabury declared.

On the witness stand for four days, Acuna told his story to Kresel. While serving as a waiter in Reuben's, a Broadway restaurant frequented by actors, he became acquainted with two detectives who often ate the famous heavyweight sandwiches, on the house. They suggested that he inform them of any crimes he might hear of, either in talks with patrons or among his friends in the Latin-American community. As a stool pigeon for two years, Acuna averaged about $100 a week—twice what he made as a waiter. In addition, the detectives sometimes paid him a share of the shakedowns after raids on houses of prostitution.

"This is how it worked," Acuna told Kresel before a packed courtroom. "I went into a whorehouse. The vice cops and I set our watches together. They would give me a five- or a ten-dollar bill in marked money, whatever it cost. I went into the house and had a woman or girl, whoever was available. I'd go into a room so that when the officers came in I would be in a compromising position with the girl. I would also see if she had any marks on her body, so that if the officers arrived late, and we were already dressed, they could identify her in court and say that they had seen her undressed and that they had seen those marks on her body. Then they arrested her, shook down the house, and brought the girl to court the next day. The magistrate asked me if I gave her any money. I said, 'Five dollars, your Honor, marked. I found the money under her pillow.'"

In a more sophisticated operation, which Acuna called the doctor's racket, the stool pigeon, posing as a patient, entered an office while the doctor was away and demanded treatment for some made-up ailment. Despite the protests of the nurse, he would place money in a conspicuous place in the office and begin to undress. Just as he dropped his pants, the cops would break in and arrest the nurse for prostitution. This would be followed by more payoffs to drop the phony case. Unless there was a protest by the doctor, the ruse worked.

The "landlady racket" was another kind of shakedown. After renting a room in a boardinghouse and paying for it in marked money, the stoolie brought a woman he called his wife to the room. Soon after, the police broke into the boardinghouse, arrested the girl for offering herself as a prostitute, and arrested the landlady for running a house of prostitution. The vice squad officers thus obtained double graft, from the unsuspecting woman *and* the entirely innocent landlady.

When business was slack, the vice squad swooped down upon Harlem, broke into people's apartments, and made arrests at random. The magistrates believed the cops rather than the innocent women accused as prostitutes. Sometimes, Acuna said, false arrests were made to keep up the monthly averages for the precinct houses. In this way, some women languished in jail for as much as a hundred days. If the vice squad members didn't maintain cash flow, their captain would reduce them in rank and assign them to pound a beat on Staten Island.

Acuna gave the names of fifty policemen and numerous other stool pigeons who were involved in the schemes. Some of the houses of prostitution were connected to saloons. Acuna had collected thousands of dollars a month from speakeasy owners. He shared these payoffs with police officers and vice detectives from the West Sixty-eighth Street precinct station in Manhattan. The ex-stoolie was able to identify them all by name.

Police Commissioner Mulrooney suspended every policeman, from patrol officer to deputy inspector, who was identified by Chile Mapocha Acuna. For the first time, Mayor Walker half-apologized for the crimes: "I will confess that I have been more or less shocked by the framing of innocent women," he said. "However, we must not look upon conditions with an eye to the past. We do not want to break down the morale of the police department."

Seabury's boys began to accumulate testimony showing that scores of people who worked in and around the lower criminal courts—clubhouse lawyers, bondsmen, clerks, court attendants, assistant district attorneys—were receiving a share of the payoffs in vice cases as well as in matters resulting from gambling arrests and convictions.

"The ring operating mainly in the women's court is a shocking example of the lengths to which distortion of law to illegal ends was carried in the magistrates' courts," Seabury reported. "It was made up of interlocking halves, the lawyers, the bondsmen and the fixers, on the one hand, and members of the so-called vice squad and their stool pigeons, on the other. The magistrates sat back and permitted this outrageous spectacle to be enacted before them day in and day out. What I am criticizing is the supineness of the magistrates in the face of palpably perjurious testimony by police officers."

The honor of being the first police officer during the Seabury hearings to claim the existence of a magical tin box kept in a bank went to Lieutenant Peter J. Pfeiffer. A check showed that he made five visits a month to the bank vault. He explained that he did so not to put in cash but to inspect, over and over, his insurance papers. A police lieutenant who also had a tin box in a bank vault said that he didn't keep cash there, either: he visited the vault once a week only to put in and take out his wife's earrings.

A police officer named James Quinlivan said that he kept his money at home in a box as well as in a large trunk. He claimed he had won $9,000 on a horse named Flora Belle, on a tip given to him by a drunken jockey. Pressed for details during his cross-examination, he couldn't remember the jockey's name. For that matter, nobody could find a horse named Flora Belle.

Another police officer, Robert E. Morris, explained to Kresel that he had a wonderful "Uncle George" who handed him forty $1,000 bills one day on a street in California. The next thing that happened was that Uncle George dropped dead. "Where did you keep the $40,000?" Kresel asked him. "Right in the house," Officer Morris replied. "Where in the house?" "I had it in a box."

The Seabury-Kresel team decided that their mandate required them to investigate every magistrate in New York City. One by one, they called in the lower-court judges to see if they were fit to hold office. The first interrogations were held in private; then some judges were asked to repeat their testimony in public. Suddenly there was a wave of resignations.

In one case, the departure of Magistrate Francis X. McQuade "obviated the necessity for a trial." Through a dummy, Magistrate McQuade was a stockholder in the Polo Grounds Athletic Club, a corporation organized to sponsor boxing matches in New York. He had also served as treasurer of the New York Giants before his services were dispensed with by the National League team's owners. The sports-minded magistrate also had a piece of the Havana Casino, a gambling establishment in Cuba; he received 5 percent of the casino's income.

Magistrate Albert H. Vitale was removed by the Appellate Division because of his friendship and business dealings with Arnold Rothstein. Magistrate Jean H. Norris, the first woman judge in New York City history, was a Tammany loyalist who had received her appointment through Boss Murphy. From Harlem Court to Women's Court, she had a reputation for harshness against prostitutes. It was revealed that she had convicted some women on uncorroborated testimony and then destroyed court records.

As Judge Seabury walked down the courthouse steps after word got out that Magistrate Norris's judicial career was over, several hundred young women from nearby offices, standing outside during the lunch hour, cheered and applauded him.

Louis B. Brodsky, a real estate operator buying and selling city-owned parcels of land, was the wealthiest magistrate in New York. He was also a stock market speculator whose margin operations while on the bench amounted to $7 million. Judge Seabury wanted to know the sources of his income. During Brodsky's time on the stand, he refused to produce any financial records—but it emerged that he, too, had a tin box. When Referee Seabury turned over his evidence to the Appellate Division, three trials followed, with Seabury and Kresel acting as prosecutors.

During his trial, Magistrate Brodsky defended himself by reading a corny prose tribute to dogs: "A man's reputation may be sacrificed in a moment of ill-considered action, but a dog stands by him in prosperity and in poverty, in health and in sickness," etc. Apparently,

Brodsky's dog act worked. The majority of the Appellate Division judges ruled that Brodsky's financial speculations were not sufficient cause to remove him from the bench. It was a setback for the investigation, and Tammany rejoiced—momentarily.

While more and more revelations came out about the ineptitude and corruption of a dozen city magistrates, Jimmy Walker decided to spend a few weeks taking a "sun bath treatment" at the desert estate of Samuel Untermyer in Palm Springs, California. Untermyer, a prominent New York lawyer, was a self-described public-spirited citizen and an old Tammany stalwart.

A delegation of Indians from a nearby reservation arrived at the Untermyer estate to greet the mayor. The Indian chief stepped forward and offered him a free thermal mud bath.

Mayor Walker replied, "Thank you, no. I've been in one constantly during the past eighteen months."

Walker held a daily morning front-porch press conference during which he wore black and orange pajamas. Mr. Untermyer, a publicity hound who liked to try his cases in public, stood at his side. Walker's face was feverishly flushed. When asked if he had received bad news from New York City, Walker abandoned his usual cool and gruffly replied:

"No, politics has nothing to do with my health now. I think I got a little too much of this blistering sun. I don't think I'll even put my clothes on today."

Walker told the reporters that in fifteen years this was the only vacation during which he could completely relax and rest. "Ever since I let down from the tension of my Wild West reception here, I've had wonderful rest and enjoyed myself immensely," he said. To one of his friends, a gossip columnist, he confided, "I'm like a burlesque theater—a lot of ballyhoo outside, but not such a good show inside."

When asked about the Seabury investigation going on in his hometown on the other side of the continent, Walker disclaimed official responsibility for any of the conditions under examination.

"While the mayor has power to appoint magistrates," he said, "he does not have power to fire them. A promising candidate may be selected and appointed in all good faith, but if he later turns out to be a lemon, the mayor is powerless to rectify the error."

Walker repeated his previous statements in Palm Springs that New York's police department was the finest in the world, with "only a normal percentage of weak spots" that existed in any organization.

"If John Q. Citizen will quit bribing weak officials for this, that and the other thing that he wants, most of the trouble will be eliminated," he declared. "Then when something blows up this bribing citizen is the first and loudest squawker."

But not every journalist in New York was overwhelmed by Jimmy Walker's charm and excuses. Heywood Broun, the liberal *World-Telegram* columnist who became the founding president of the American Newspaper Guild, observed:

"Though I grant that James Joseph Walker is sick, it seems to me unlikely that his health can be as precarious as that of the City of New York at the present moment. It is a pity that the mayor cannot take the metropolis with him on the trip. The city stands in need of scathing sunlight, fresh air and a fine rousing wind to cleanse its lungs and vitals. In Palm Springs, I trust, the palms will be straighter and itch less than those of Tammany."

Just as Arnold Rothstein's murder in 1928 had helped ignite the initial investigation, now another brutal murder set off a new chain reaction of accusations against the Walker administration's laxity in law enforcement.

The body of an important Seabury witness, Mrs. Vivian Gordon, was found in Van Cortlandt Park in the Bronx. The red-haired, thirty-two-year-old divorcée had been strangled with a clothesline. Only a few days before, Mrs. Gordon had been questioned in private and testified that she had been framed by a member of the police department's vice squad. She was scheduled to appear again before Irving Ben Cooper and provide even more damaging evidence about the police who had falsely arrested her for prostitution. When Mrs. Gordon's body was discovered, her distraught sixteen-year-old daughter committed suicide.

From Albany, Governor Roosevelt declared that the murder of a witness put the police on trial. Mrs. Gordon's death made headlines across the country. Police Commissioner Mulrooney said there would be "a stain on the shield of every policeman in New York" until the murder was solved. The fact that the murder had been committed in a neighborhood park, the reformers said, was a horrifying example of the cavalier attitude of criminals toward the Walker administration's law-enforcement machinery.

Because of his close supervision of the corruption cases and how they affected the state, Governor Roosevelt was mentioned more often in the national press as a presidential contender. He was beginning to fill the vacuum left by Mayor Walker in pursuing criminal justice in New York.

As usual, the tabloids had a field day. They claimed that Mrs. Gordon had "five hundred sugar daddies." More kindly, the broadsheets described her as "a misled woman who followed the tinsel path." The phone number of Polly Adler, the town's leading "vice entrepreneuse," was found in the murdered woman's address book. "She was just another attractive woman out to feather her own nest," said Miss Adler.

With the heat on to solve the murder, a taxicab driver piped up who told of driving the car in which "underworld friends" of Vivian Gordon strangled her. It was a story the police were pleased to believe, since it removed the possibility that one of their own had done the deed. The police arrested one Harry Stein; his record included strangling and robbing a woman. There was some evidence that he had tried to sell Mrs. Gordon's jewelry and a fur coat. But a jury of twelve men acquitted him and an accomplice. The case against them was so thin that it sounded like a cover-up.

All eyes turned toward Andrew G. McLaughlin, the vice squad cop who had arrested Vivian Gordon for soliciting and caused her to be convicted of prostitution. At first, McLaughlin could not be reached because

he was on a cruise to Bermuda. When he returned, McLaughlin noncha-
lantly denied any complicity in the murder. He smilingly told newspaper
reporters that the whole Seabury investigation was a farce; that he
would willingly take the stand and justify the vice squad's tactics.

When called before Referee Seabury, McLaughlin suddenly suffered memory loss. He couldn't recall his arrest of the Gordon
woman. He couldn't even remember "if she was black or white." Then
the Seabury-Kresel technique of "following the money" pinned
McLaughlin to the mat:

How, investigators asked, did you manage to bank $35,800.51 in
two years despite the fact that your pay as a member of the vice squad
was only $3,000 a year?

McLaughlin refused to answer on the ground that the Appellate
Division was exceeding its authority and infringing on his constitutional rights.

After a departmental trial, Police Commissioner Mulrooney dismissed McLaughlin from the force for two reasons: he had arrested
women as prostitutes with insufficient evidence and he had failed to
answer the Seabury inquiry's questions.

That was all the punishment anyone received for the crime. Vivian
Gordon joined Arnold Rothstein as an officially unsolved mystery that
pointed to a rotten core in the city.

Following the resignations of the magistrates and the vice cops, Referee Seabury submitted a 70,000-word report to the Appellate Division and Governor Roosevelt that called for reforms in the lower
courts to rid them of politics and graft. In what looked like a direct
slap at Jimmy Walker, Seabury proposed that in the future no mayor
be allowed to name any judges.

The reforms proposed in the Seabury report included consolidation of the existing criminal courts, which would be supervised by a
presiding justice with strong administrative powers; passage of a state
constitutional amendment to permit the appointment of lower-court

judges by the Appellate Division instead of by the mayor; the tightening of civil service regulations for court officers to eliminate political influence in appointments; higher bail for felons and persons charged with minor offenses; a law permitting the immediate arraignment of arrested persons before a judge, eliminating the booking at police precinct station houses, where most of the corruption was found to originate; elimination of the homicide courts, and the creation of a special court for all felony cases; a new law defining the circumstances under which a police officer could make an arrest; a public defender system, with attorneys designated by the Legal Aid Society, to represent poor defendants in the lower courts.

Many of these reforms would slowly be adopted—not without a struggle in the city and state legislatures—over the next fifty years. They did not eliminate politics from the bar and bench, but they weakened the grip of the mayor and Tammany Hall on the judiciary.

To back up his recommendations, Seabury offered evidence to underscore what he and his boys had discovered about the politicized judicial system:

"What we have seen is a hideous caricature which parades as justice," he said. "The insidious auspices under which the magistrates, the clerks, the assistant clerks and attendants are appointed is bad enough; the conditions under which they retain their appointments are infinitely worse because they involve the subserviency in office to district leaders and other politicians.

"It is a byword in the corridors of the courts of this city that the intervention of a friend in the district political club is much more potent than the merits of the cause or the services of the best lawyer. Unfortunately, the truth of this statement alone prevents it from being a slander upon the good name of the city."

In a conclusion to his lengthy report, Judge Seabury sounded like the crusader of his early years, when he was a lawyer representing the trade unions. He emphasized that the abuses didn't strike at people of wealth and power; they oppressed those who were poor and helpless, while the oppressor enjoyed practical immunity. There could be no remedy for these abuses, he concluded, unless the courts were entirely freed of political control.

Long afterward, the thievery of Sheriff Farley and the other members of the citywide tin-box brigade contributed to the creation of the 1959 Broadway musical comedy *Fiorello!* The brilliant lyrics (copyright, by Sheldon M. Harnick) to a song titled "Little Tin Box" included these lines, slightly abridged here:

> Mr. X, may we ask you a question?
> It's amazing is it not
> That the city pays you slightly less
> Than fifty bucks a week
> Yet you've purchased a private yacht?
>
> I am positive Your Honor must be joking,
> Any working man can do what I have done.
> For a month or two I simply gave up smoking
> And I put my extra pennies one by one
> Into a little tin box,
> A little tin box
> That a little tin key unlocks.
> There is nothing unorthodox
> About a little tin box.
> Mr. Y, we've been told you don't feel well
> And we know you've lost your voice.
> But we wondered how you managed on the salary you make
> To acquire a Rolls Royce?
> You're implying I'm a crook and I say No Sir,
> There is nothing in my past I care to hide.
> I've been taking empty bottles to the grocer
> And each nickel that I got was put aside . . .
> Into a little tin box,
> All aglitter with blue chip stocks
> There is something delectable,
> Almost respectable
> In a little tin box,
> In a little tin box!

EIGHT

Ring Around the Rackets

New York's crooked magistrates, cops, sheriffs, and low-level court officers were just the tip of the iceberg. Now attention turned to the District Attorney's Office. As a direct result of the brazen murder of Vivian Gordon in Van Cortlandt Park, reform groups began to wonder if the Walker administration's lackadaisical D.A., Thomas C. T. Crain, was one of the main reasons for the rampant crime problem in New York City.

Crain had a string of failures behind him, indictments that were never brought or that collapsed. The public remembered that he had bungled the notorious murder case of gambling czar Arnold Rothstein, foolishly promising to solve the crime within two weeks. Everybody on the street seemed to know who had pulled the trigger on Big Arnie except the D.A. himself.

The influential City Club of New York petitioned Governor Roosevelt to remove the seventy-year-old Crain. He was an elected official in New York County—that is, the borough of Manhattan. Under the state constitution, counties were subdivisions of the state, not of the city. Thus the governor had the power to discipline and discharge the D.A. (By the same token, under the city charter Mayor Walker could appoint magistrates in all five boroughs, but only the Appellate Division had the power to remove a magistrate.) The City Club charged that Crain's office was "incompetent, inefficient and futile"; that he had failed to conduct prosecutions for "crimes and offenses cognizable by the courts"; that even when he initiated investigations he conducted them "inadequately and ineffectively."

Furthermore, the reformers maintained that Crain had made misleading statements about how he handled frauds concerning the "delivery business and dock racketeers"; that he failed to expose graft in the "Department of Purchase and crimes connected with the Board of Standards and Appeals"—centers of Tammany influence; and that he never bothered to investigate white-collar crime and "various stock frauds." The corruption net was cast wider.

Heywood Broun cracked: "The crane is mightier than the Crain and much more stalwart. The crane stands on at least one leg."

Confronted with the need to respond to these accusations, Governor Roosevelt asked his closest advisers: Who, *other* than Judge Seabury, could investigate the charges and, sustaining or dismissing them, still retain public confidence? Their answer: only Samuel Seabury.

At the same time, Tammany insiders spread the story that Roosevelt had deliberately encouraged the City Club and other leading citizens to petition him to remove Crain. They believed that Roosevelt wished to prove he was a strong governor and to gain public favor for his presidential ambitions. The D.A. had been sponsored by John Francis Curry, the Tammany chieftain, and supported by Mayor Walker; both preferred a tame prosecutor to one who would look too closely at the patronage system. To serve as Crain's lawyer, Tammany enlisted the support of none other than Samuel Untermyer, Jimmy Walker's Palm Springs host.

Governor Roosevelt retaliated by inviting Judge Seabury as his personal commissioner to look into Crain's office. At first, Seabury declined. As an Appellate Division referee, he was still wrapped up in exposing the crooked magistrates and cops and all they had done to discredit the courts and the police force. But Roosevelt knew how to touch a vulnerable spot in the Seabury psyche: he appealed to his sense of honor.

In formal legal language, lawyer to lawyer, Roosevelt wrote Seabury: "I have decided to appoint you commissioner under Section 34 of the public officers' law to hear and investigate formal charges which have been filed with me against the district attorney of the County of New York, and to take evidence relative thereto. I sincerely hope that you will be willing to accept this appointment in addition to the other public service you are rendering.

"I shall be glad to have you start your duties as commissioner at the earliest possible moment; and, as you are in the very strict sense, acting as the commissioner of the Governor in this matter, I shall be glad to confer with you at any time. I am very confident that your fine reputation for fairness and justice peculiarly qualifies you.

"You will, of course, note that the charges made do not in any way involve the personal integrity of Justice Crain, but relate solely to his competency to fulfill the office which he holds."

Crain, who had once served quietly on the Court of General Sessions and the state Supreme Court, had inherited millions of dollars and attended the Episcopal church regularly. In the past, Crain had been a Tammany Sachem for many years. His main service to the Hall was giving a Monday night lecture, "On the Merits of Democracy," to young recruits for his Tammany club on the Upper West Side of Manhattan. As Roosevelt pointed out, he was never accused of dishonesty, only of incompetence.

Judge Seabury decided he couldn't turn down the Governor's offer.

Defending Crain, Samuel Untermyer immediately mounted an attack against Seabury. He called the City Club's charges "preposterous," demanded a bill of particulars, and said that Seabury was too full of "bias and prejudice" to serve as commissioner. People in the political know were aware why Untermyer was so stalwart in his defense of the sleepy D.A. and, by implication, of his good friend Jimmy Walker: the year before, Untermyer's son, Irwin, had been elected a Supreme Court justice.

While Manhattan's D.A. was being examined during that Depression summer of 1931, and New York's millions cooled off at Coney Island and the other crowded beaches on the fringes of the concrete city, Jimmy Walker also decided it was time to get away from the burdensome heat. He went to Monte Carlo.

Accompanied by Maurice Chevalier, the French film star and boulevardier, Mayor Walker attended a boxing match in Monaco for the featherweight championship of Europe. Jose Girones of Spain, the reigning champ, scored a technical knockout over Guy Bonagure of France in the eighth round. The challenger's seconds threw in a sponge when they saw their man was outclassed. As the crowd cheered, Walker congratulated the winner.

There was a flurry among members of the principality's police force when it was rumored that the mayor had lost some of his personal jewelry. A hurried investigation disclosed that one of the members of the Walker party had dropped some of her jewelry on the beach as she stepped from the speedboat that brought them from Cannes. A private detective employed by the casino recovered it.

By "special cable," *The New York Times* reported this breathless international news: "Mayor Walker appeared to enjoy himself very much." Perhaps one reason is that he was a nonpaying guest of the new Monte Carlo casino management.

After a few days at the gambling resort, the junketing Mayor departed for Paris.

The investigation of District Attorney Crain's office led to the discovery of unprosecuted or poorly prosecuted "racketeering" cases in a score of businesses, including garment manufacturers, florists, funeral parlor owners, kosher butchers, milliners, master barbers, paper box makers, window cleaners, launderers, furriers, and wholesalers in the Fulton Fish Market—touching almost every aspect of life in the city.

To manufacture, sell or move anything in New York during the 1920s and early 1930s, somebody had to be paid off.

On the witness stand, Crain admitted that racketeering had him bewildered. The frail, thin-faced D.A. seemed more pathetic than villainous. By contrast, Mr. Untermyer, his defender, appeared to be trying out for the role of a busker outside a Broadway theater. Sitting at the counsel table, Untermyer continually mumbled at witnesses,

"Louder, please!" Nearly every day, he came into the courtroom be-decked in a new tailor's creation, with an orchid in his lapel to match his tie. It was a sartorial effect that would not be matched until Beau James himself took the witness stand.

The D.A. testified that his method of combating crime was to form a Committee on Public Safety made up of seventy influential citizens to "wage a war on racketeering." He even provided them with a room where they could receive complaints from merchants who had been shaken down. "I had an appropriate sign made and directed that it be placed outside the room," he said. Judge Seabury asked Crain if any merchants appeared, knowing that they might risk their lives by com-ing forward and going public. Crain couldn't understand why nobody had showed up.

SEABURY: Then the net result of your committee was nothing, wasn't it?

CRAIN: That is a fair statement.

One of the centerpieces of Seabury's investigation was the D.A.'s fail-ure to stop the shakedowns in the Fulton Fish Market. (More than a half-century later, efforts were still being made to eliminate payoffs to racketeers there.) The Fulton Fish Market in lower Manhattan sup-plied seafood to most New Yorkers and to many towns along the At-lantic seaboard. It was the underworld domain of Joseph "Socks" Lanza, the muscleman in charge of protection for the fish dealers and truckers; unsurprisingly, the protection paid to Socks was to protect the merchants against Socks himself.

Street legend had it that Socks got his nickname not because of his sharp clothing but because he was so good with his fists. Socks, who was born on the Lower East Side, had spent his early life as a ju-venile delinquent, a fish handler, and a political worker for Tammany. He was a friend and contemporary of Lucky Luciano, Joe Adonis, and Frank Costello, the Italo-American dons who ruled the rackets in the

Northeast. His brother-in-law was Prosper Viggiano, secretary to a Supreme Court judge and a Tammany district leader.

Socks Lanza was the official delegate representing Local 16975 of the United Sea Food Workers. He also had held interests in a waste-fish rendering plant and in a can factory. Lanza was shaking down the Middle Atlantic Fisheries Association. When a management representative told Lanza that the employers couldn't afford to pay steeper wages, he suggested that an under-the-table payment be made to him to ensure a sweetheart contract. Thus he undercut his own union.

"I guess we can fix it," said Socks.

Certain fish firms made annual payments to Lanza to keep their plants nonunion. The six hundred retailers trading in the Fulton Fish Market each paid a "tax" to Lanza or one of the other gangsters in Local 16975 to get their deliveries. Socks was a racketeer who worked both sides of the street. As a result, fish prices were kept artificially high.

None of these facts came from D.A. Crain or his assistants; they were uncovered by Seabury and his boys.

One of Crain's deputies, Charles C. Pilatsky, was asked what he did to investigate racketeering in the Fulton Fish Market and in other businesses.

"Well, we had an office on the same floor that was almost as big as the D.A.'s and we had a sign painted on the door," the deputy replied. "The sign read: RACKETEERING COMPLAINTS HERE. I investigated 150 complaints."

"How many indictments came out of your investigation?"

"Two."

"And how many of those were dismissed without trial?"

"I understand both of them."

Looking at racketeering in the millinery trade in New York, Seabury's investigators exposed a pair of underworld characters—"Little Augie," who was gunned down after extorting money to prevent unionization, and "Tough Jake" Kurzman, his successor in the same anti-union racket. When a warrant was issued for his arrest, Tough Jake fled the jurisdiction, but during his career he had received $10,000 a year from various hat manufacturers. They carried the payoffs on their books as "protection."

Similarly, in the cloth-shrinking trade, a racketeer named Joseph Mezzacapo dissolved the Cloth Shrinkers Union and set up his own union to replace it. No one could work who was not a member of Mezzacapo's personal union. He levied tribute on the cloth-shrinking industry, getting money both from union members and from the manufacturers. The investigators found that Mezzacapo had made deposits in excess of $332,000 in a single account with the Federation Bank and Trust Company.

Sounding like a premature New Dealer, the Seabury of old, not the wealthy lawyer serving as a state commissioner, reported to Governor Roosevelt:

"The trade union accomplishes a useful and necessary purpose when it is honestly administered. The system by which a blackleg labor leader is permitted to extort money as the price of non-enforcement of union requirements not only strikes a direct blow at the whole trade union movement, but is clearly illegal. Furthermore, it permits employers to buy immunity and subjects them to the necessity of entering into contracts, the terms of which are not prescribed by market conditions but are fixed and determined by the amount which may be extorted from them by an unscrupulous labor union delegate."

Surprisingly, when Commissioner Seabury filed his final report to Governor Roosevelt on August 31, 1931, he recommended that the City Club's charges against D.A. Crain be dismissed, despite all the evidence that he and his staff had turned up revealing the old Tammany Sachem's incompetence:

"Truth compels the conclusion that in many instances he busied himself ineffectively, and that he did not grasp or act upon opportunities for high public service which some of the matters referred to presented to him," Seabury reported to Roosevelt. "I am satisfied that wherever he failed, and I think he did fail in many cases to do all that he should have done, his failure was not due to any lack of personal effort or any ignoble motive."

Governor Roosevelt agreed, and dropped the charges.

In the view of the citizenry, both Commissioner Seabury and Governor Roosevelt behaved like gentlemen toward District Attorney

Crain. To be sure, some disappointed reformers said under their breaths that what saved the D.A. from a reprimand and dismissal is that he was a prominent Episcopalian; he shared this religious affiliation with Roosevelt and Seabury. Yet even so prominent a reformer-in-opposition as Norman Thomas agreed with Seabury's dismissal of the charges against Crain. "I believe the decision is warranted," he told *The New York Times.* "In a democracy, you have to lean over backwards not to remove an elected official short of clearly proven corruption or gross incompetency. I do think that Crain's inquiry into the magistrates' courts was incompetent in such a way as to protect Tammany, but not so grossly incompetent as to warrant removal. The trouble is not with one particular district attorney but with the system."

Long afterward, a more sophisticated political interpretation was given by George Trosk, Seabury's chief of staff. He said that there was no question that the investigators could have gone the other way and recommended that the D.A. be thrown out of office. But Seabury and his aides realized that Tammany's leaders were going to nominate Crain for the office again, no matter what the report recommended, and in Tammany-controlled Manhattan he was sure to win.

"We knew we would be left looking silly—that it would look like a repudiation of our efforts," Trosk said. "So we decided to do the practical thing, set out all the damaging evidence that we uncovered but not recommend removal. We knew that there was much more to be gained by continuing the investigation into the whole city's affairs."

With the district attorney remaining in office, many New Yorkers heaved a sigh of relief, hoping that the turmoil in their city would quiet down. Although Jimmy Walker was still popular, and his D.A. was regarded as a nice old gentleman, a growing number of New York businessmen began to realize that they stood to gain from the elimination of municipal corruption. The investigative machine was running on sixteen cylinders and the engine couldn't be suddenly turned off.

First, Judge Seabury had been named referee to examine the

Magistrates' Courts; next, commissioner to look into the district attorney's conduct; now, he received a third mandate with a new title: counsel for "the investigation of the departments of the government of the City of New York." At last, by a joint resolution of the New York State Senate and Assembly, on March 23, 1931, Seabury was given carte blanche to look into every office and every official in the city—including Jimmy Walker's mayoralty. Albany had unsheathed all its daggers and given Seabury license to flail in any direction he chose. His mission was to investigate in order to bring charges where warranted. Once charges were brought, then normal due process would begin.

It was a prosecutorial opportunity that no single individual had ever been handed in the history of New York, not even in the Tweed Ring years. Fresh evidence of corruption was emerging nearly every day, yet the resolution authorizing a citywide investigation appeared to be a direct assault by the Republican-dominated state legislature upon the Democrats who ran the city.

As a Democrat who was already campaigning for the presidential nomination in 1932, where did Governor Roosevelt stand? How would he handle the touchy issue of investigating his own party? If the Republicans had thought that the third stage of investigation would help F.D.R.'s run for the presidency, perhaps they would have been content to let New York City fester quietly.

A year before, Roosevelt had opposed a broad-gauged investigation, declaring that it would set a precedent for future governors to meddle in the affairs of every city and county. But now the heat was on from various constituencies whose help he would need to gain national support. On behalf of the City Affairs Committee, Rabbi Stephen S. Wise of the Free Synagogue and John Haynes Holmes of the Community Church brought charges against Mayor Walker, questioning his ethics.

Tammany and its subalterns cried foul. "Stop this criminal waste of funds," said the Tammany minority on the legislative investigative committee, which was chaired by Senator Samuel Hofstadter, a Manhattan Republican. "Mr. Seabury has only succeeded in besmirching the character of 130,000 city employes by innuendoes and undermining the goodwill and financial standing of the City of New York."

For Governor Roosevelt, the investigation was both a caution and an opportunity. He approved a $250,000 appropriation for the legislative committee. Seabury's official title was that of counsel, yet in all practical respects he was now exercising the duties of a "special prosecutor."

The citywide investigation—eventually, it cost half a million dollars—ran from April 8, 1931, until the end of December 8, 1932, a month after Franklin D. Roosevelt was elected to his first term as president of the United States. Seabury's staff examined 2,260 persons in private; this testimony covered 47,000 pages. Another 175 witnessses appeared in public hearings; their testimony added 5,000 mimeographed pages to the record.

Once again, the tabloids had a field day. They first went to town with a certain gentleman known as Horse Doctor Doyle. Dr. William F. Doyle, who represented private businessmen before the Board of Standards and Appeals, was indeed a doctor—a veterinarian. The board handled not horses but two-legged real estate operators with lots of cash. In its discretion, the board could permit variances in the height of buildings, setbacks, the location of garages and gasoline stations, and the occupancy of homes and factories. Five men sat on this board—four appointed by Mayor Walker and one by the fire commissioner, himself a Walker appointee.

Horse Doctor Doyle got into the lucrative rackets in the early 1900s, when he was named chief veterinarian of the fire department in the days of horse-drawn wagons. The records failed to show any complaints from his first patients, the fire horses. But then Doyle was named chief of the bureau of fire prevention; he was indicted for malfeasance when a building he failed to check went up in flames.

Forced to retire, he began a private practice before the board, representing landlords, builders, and contractors. In one good year during Walker's first term, Horse Doctor Doyle put over $243,000 into his bank accounts, which held a total of a million dollars.

"Doctor," Judge Seabury said, "there's only one thing I would like you to tell me. Would you kindly tell me with whom you split your fees?"

"I'd like to but my lawyer tells me that to do so would incriminate me," Dr. Doyle replied.

"When you appeared before the board, wasn't it your practice to take part of your fee in cash and part by check?"

"I refuse to answer that question because it might tend to incriminate me."

"Did you ever bribe any political leader in the County of New York?"

Again Doyle refused to answer on grounds of possible self-incrimination.

Chairman Hofstader cited Horse Doctor Doyle for contempt and he was sentenced to thirty days in jail by Justice William H. Black. Boss Curry, Tammany's Chief Sachem, immediately put through a call to a more sympathetic judge, Henry L. Sherman of the Appellate Division, who granted a stay of the order jailing Dr. Doyle. When Seabury learned that Boss Curry had interfered in the case, he called upon the Tammany boss to explain his actions on the witness stand before the Hofstadter committee.

SEABURY: Is it fair and accurate to say that you *reached* Judge Sherman?

CURRY: Wait a minute, I don't like that word *reach*.

SEABURY, smiling: Very well, Mr. Curry, I don't want to injure your sensibilities.

Curry frowned at the sarcasm.

SEABURY: What was the purpose of your interfering in a judicial proceeding?

CURRY: I wanted to have the powers of the committee tested with regard to the immunity clause. I want to tell you, Judge Seabury, I did not try to influence justice. I tried to get a judge to hear a case.

SEABURY: You thought it was part of your political duty as leader of the Democratic organization of this city to interfere in a case. Did you do it as a personal favor?

CURRY: Yes, but that was only secondary. I resent Judge Seabury's statements about obstruction. I, as representative of the Democratic organization of the City of New York, was expecting someone to test the constitutionality of this committee's powers to grant immunity, and therefore when the request came for my aid, I was glad to be of service.

Seabury again demanded to know why Boss Curry telephoned the appellate justice. Curry replied, "Because this is a crucification, if it can be done, of the Democratic party of the City of New York."

Praising Boss Curry, Jimmy Walker compared him to such previous Tammany Hall leaders as Boss Murphy, Boss Kelly, and Boss Croker. Curry gratefully responded, "It is fiction, this so-called New Tammany. I will carry out the politics in which I grew up."

Horse Doctor Doyle's refusal to rat, which was based on his fear of being convicted, threatened to undermine the investigators' tried-and-true tactic of turning little targets against bigger ones. But the Hofstadter committee was made up of legislators, and Seabury was only a temporary commissioner. Could they protect the Doyles they needed?

The question of immunity for witnesses went up to the Court of Appeals, the state's highest court. None other than Benjamin N. Cardozo, who would later be appointed to the Supreme Court of the United States by President Hoover, delivered the opinion that the legislative committee did not have the power to grant such immunity, except by statute, which he recommended. Judge Seabury then drafted a bill giving the committee that power, the legislature enacted the bill, and Governor Roosevelt signed it.

Gleefully, the anti-Tammany reformers summed up the situation in a ditty:

> Tammany Hall's a patriotic outfit,
> Tammany Hall's a great society,
> Fourth of July they always wave the flag, boys,
> But they never, never waive immunity!

More tin boxes now came to light as Seabury's lawyers and accountants reached beyond Manhattan to show how the boodle machine operated all over the city.

The chief clerk of the Queens County Surrogate's Court was John Theofel, the borough's Democratic leader. During his six years in office, his net worth jumped from $28,650 to $201,300. Theofel couldn't remember whether he kept his money in "a closet, in a shoe, in a sock or in a box." Seabury enlightened him by producing bank slips showing deposits of large sums of cash.

Seabury wondered what Theofel's duties were as the court's chief clerk. Scratching his head, the witness finally came up with an answer: "Walk through, keep around on the job."

By a strange coincidence, all the official cars purchased in Queens were Pierce-Arrows. When an assistant D.A. tried to buy a less expensive Packard for himself, Theofel told him that he had better buy a Pierce-Arrow from Wilson Bros., Inc., where all the other official cars came from. Dudley Wilson, it so happened, was Theofel's son-in-law, and Theofel owned most of the stock in the auto dealership. With a straight face, the Tammany leader testified that the reason Queens officials were only allowed to own and drive Pierce-Arrows was to uphold the dignity of the borough.

Not to be outshone, Brooklyn graft was demonstrated by three Tammany stalwarts: McCooey, McQuade, and McGuinness. "Uncle John" H. McCooey, the borough's Democratic leader, held an official job as clerk of the Surrogate's Court. From this sinecure, he was able to handpick judges for the state Supreme Court and approve dozens of courthouse jobs—with the usual kickback to the clubhouse.

One of the new judges had a name that sounded familiar: John H. McCooey, Jr. Seabury asked McCooey how his inexperienced thirty-year-old son had received a $25,000-a-year Supreme Court job. "Oh," said the elder McCooey, "nearly every leader in the party urged me very strongly to nominate Jack. I had no idea there was such a unanimity of opinion." The notoriously corrupt Brooklyn Bar Association endorsed Junior's nomination to become a Supreme Court justice because he had "poise and character."

The Honorable James A. McQuade held down the no-show job of

county register in Brooklyn. And how, Judge Seabury inquired, did he succeed in accumulating $510,000 in six years on a salary of $12,000 a year? McQuade's dissembling response invoked traditional family values:

"It's money that I borrowed. If you want me to get to the start of it, I will have to take and go over the family in its entirety, without feeling that I am humiliated in the least or am not humiliating the other thirty-four McQuades. If this committee can take the time, I will go over it from the start. I, unfortunately, went into politics. I say that cautiously."

Addressing him as "Mr. Register," Seabury asked McQuade if the $510,000 he had deposited came only from the mysteriously borrowed money.

In a laughable explanation—the newspapers called it the story of "the thirty-four starving McQuades"—he testified that a family business had failed after an unnamed person had stolen money from his company, causing McQuade Brothers to be liquidated.

> McQUADE: The thirty-four McQuades were placed on my back, I being the only breadwinner, and after that it was necessary to keep life in their body, sustenance, to go out and borrow money. I felt it my duty, being that they were my flesh and blood, part and parcel of me, to help them. I am getting along in fairly good shape when my mother, Lord have mercy on her, dropped dead. I am going along nicely when my brother, Lord have mercy on him, dropped dead. But doing nicely, when I have two other brothers, and when my brother died, he willed me his family, which I am still taking care of, thank God. The extra money that you see in this year or any year from that year on has been money that I borrowed, and not ashamed of it.
>
> SEABURY [politely]: Well, now, Mr. Register, will you be good enough to indicate from whom you borrowed the money?
>
> McQUADE: Oh, Judge, offhand I could not.

Judge Seabury continued to press McQuade, getting the figures from his various bank accounts into the committee's record. The indomitable Brooklyn register finally attempted to sound penurious and wealthy simultaneously.

McQUADE: I would, for instance, borrow a thousand dollars off John Brown. In two weeks time John wanted that thousand dollars, and I would borrow a thousand dollars off John Jones. Another, maybe two weeks he would want that. I would get it off John Smith, where in reality there would be possibly ten thousand dollars deposited for the thousand dollars that was actually working.

SEABURY: Mr. Register, do you have any records of the sums you borrowed or paid off?

McQUADE: As the money was paid, it was off my mind, and I thanked God for it and destroyed anything that I might have.

McQuade grew indignant when Seabury told him not to cry because he was getting the hearing he wanted to clear his good name.

McQUADE: You never heard me cry. With all my trouble, and I had plenty of that, I never cried. My name was McQuade. There are very few McQuades that do any crying.

When McQuade finally left the stand, none the poorer, he grinned and asked the reporters, "How did my story go over?"

In the opinion of his Brooklyn political colleagues, obviously well. Uncle John McCooey rewarded McQuade by nominating him for a job with a higher salary to take care of all those McQuades. In the fall election of 1931, the Democratic Brooklynites dutifully voted Register McQuade into office as Sheriff McQuade of Kings County.

The investigation of the Honorable Peter J. McGuinness, assistant commissioner of public works, showed Seabury capable of low theater.

At one point, Seabury asked, "Who suggested you to become assistant commissioner of public works?"

McGuinness replied, "Well, as leader of the Greenpernt [so he pronounced Greenpoint] People's Regular Organization of the Fifteenth Assembly District, I couldn't pick a more better person to suggest for this job than myself. I drove nine gypsy bands out of Greenpernt, as well as three hundred Chinese coolies, and all the cats and dogs that used to run down the streets. I got Greenpernt three playgrounds, the subway, the one-and-a-half-million bridge on Greenpernt Avenue, and two million dollars' worth of paving. . . . I done good. I thank you."

Judge Seabury reminded Commissioner McGuinness that gambling and bookmaking—two sources of the money he kept in his office safe—went on in his Greenpoint clubhouse.

McGuinness replied that he couldn't be held responsible for everything that went on there. In fact, he said, he had once watched his own club members gambling and warned them about a police raid. Seabury expressed surprise that McGuiness would do so.

> McGUINNESS: Yes, I will spy on them, too. They were doing things there they shouldn't do.
>
> SEABURY: Did you have any agreement with the raiding police?
>
> McGUINNESS: Judge, in my public life, me and the police never agreed.
>
> SEABURY: But you said, "Here comes the police" or "Cheese it, the police"?
>
> McGUINNESS: No, "Cheese it, here comes the *cops.*"
>
> SEABURY [bowing]: I stand corrected.

It was now April 1932, two months before the Democratic national convention in Chicago. Governor Roosevelt's political operatives put his name forward as the presidential nominee in all forty-eight states. Among the heavy hitters on his team were Jim Farley, Basil O'Connor, Sam Rosenman, Raymond Moley, Rexford Tugwell, and Louis Howe— a mixture of brainy advisers, canny idealists, seasoned politicians, and, above all, loyalists.

Actually, the campaign for the nomination was already under way. It had officially started in January when F.D.R. entered his first primary in North Dakota. By March a majority of the delegates in other states had been corralled but, by an old rule, it would take two-thirds to nominate, a proportion not yet attainable.

Governor Roosevelt's early bid for the nomination did not sit well with Al Smith. Roosevelt had developed a sense of independence in Albany; a coolness had developed between them. As the 1928 candidate, Smith still considered himself the head of the Democratic party—and the deserving contender for the nomination. What's more, he was much closer to the still-powerful Tammany machine than Roosevelt. Behind the scenes, the Happy Warrior expressed his unhappiness with Roosevelt's ambition, especially because President Hoover now seemed vulnerable.

In his annual message to the state legislature in 1932, Roosevelt seemed to be talking to a national audience: "We know now from bitter experience that the theory that the nation could lift itself by its own bootstraps was not sound," he said. "The mistakes of the past among men and among nations call for leadership broad enough to understand the problems not only of our nation but of their relationship to other nations, the problems not of New York alone but of all the other forty-seven states."

During the spring of 1932, Roosevelt's campaign for the presidency was widely reported in the national press. At the same time, the newspapers were paying greater attention to the most colorful mayor in the country. Jimmy Walker still walked and talked with confidence; he was not abandoning his Tammany friends and appointees in the municipal departments. The clownish behavior of the sheriffs and other city officials questioned about their mysterious riches kept the country entertained; yet people were beginning to wonder about the efficacy of Mayor Walker's administration.

In the upcoming presidential nomination and election, delegates and voters from New York City and New York State would be of crucial importance. A duel between Governor Roosevelt and Mayor Walker appeared inevitable.

NINE

Little Boy Blue Blows His Horn

"Let them come," said Jimmy Walker defiantly.

He spoke to a claque of friendly reporters while vacationing at the estate of Samuel Untermyer in Palm Springs, California. "I shall answer them in good time when I get back home."

That was the mayor's only reaction on learning that Governor Franklin D. Roosevelt had airmailed copies of charges against him to his temporary refuge in the far west. Editorial writers at the newspapers and constitutional scholars in the law schools reminded the public that under the state constitution, the governor of New York had the power to remove public officials—including mayors—for good cause. Tammany Hall quaked at the news that the investigation had finally reached City Hall itself.

On that spring day in 1932, Mayor Walker arrived at the New York County Courthouse in Foley Square, immaculately dressed in a blue shirt, blue tie, blue pocket handkerchief, blue socks. His haberdashery was carefully (if a bit ostentatiously) coordinated with his blue one-button, double-breasted suit. A close observer could notice that the ring on his pinky finger had a blue stone.

Walker turned to his valet and, half in jest, said, "Little Boy Blue is about to blow his horn—or his top."

He carried with him a subpoena duces tecum calling for the production of all the records of his personal financial transactions from January 1, 1926, to May 25, 1932. It was a staggeringly far-reaching request.

Still none of his intimates thought the worst could happen, not to Jimmy Walker, not to their *Jimsie*.

The most notorious scandal in Gotham's history wasn't supposed to soil the elegant and popular mayor himself. Aware of Walker's quick wit, his admirers reassured each other: Wait'll he gets on the witness stand, he'll make mincemeat out of that starched Seabury character.

After all—as Jimmy Walker often reminded his doubters and accusers—the people had voted overwhelmingly to make him their mayor two times running. He had even defeated Congressman Fiorello H. La Guardia, who was no slouch as a campaigner and could outtalk him in a half-dozen languages.

"Seabury doesn't dare call Mayor Walker, because he knows he has no case against the greatest city in the world." So declared Brooklyn's Irwin Steingut, a Tammany operative who was minority leader of the New York State Assembly and a member of Republican senator Samuel Hofstadter's joint legislative committee.

As a prelude to the interrogation, Red-baiting of Seabury and his staff began immediately. Steingut and the other Tammany wheelhorses said that the investigators and reformers were only "an annex of the Socialist party—a bunch of agitators and Soviet sympathizers."

Even before mounting the witness stand, Walker publicly denied any responsibility for the graft taken by Tammany's exposed tin-boxers. Instead, the mayor used the old technique of blaming the messenger(s): certain journalists on the broadsheet newspapers who were not his favorite drinking buddies.

One writer who surely couldn't be counted among Walker's admirers was Heywood Broun:

"I seem to see a willingness on Mayor Walker's part to shift responsibility. He expressed grave concern over the failure of civic organizations and great newspapers." (In a speech, Walker had said that any corruption should have been disclosed long ago—if only the press had been alert!) "In other words, the press has held out on James Joseph Walker. Apparently no reporter took the trouble to tell the Mayor the facts of life in a great city. Somebody should blurt out to him that there is no Santa Claus within the ranks of Tammany. At least, only for a very restricted set of good little boys and girls."

Before Walker's first appearance began that morning, readers in New York and Washington carefully studied the lead editorial in *The New York Times*. Suddenly, the trial of Jimmy Walker, taking place only weeks before the Democratic presidential convention, had attained national meaning. Mayor Walker was a symbol of big-city machine politics; if nominated, Governor Roosevelt needed the machines for success at the 1932 convention and in the election.

The unsigned *Times* editorial, titled "Not Even Standing Room," said in part:

"Much more than local concern is involved. The whole nation is watching the inquiry. At stake is the fate of more than one personality—even when it is such a flashing and brilliant personality as that of the Mayor of New York. The affair now branches out into national politics.

"Everybody is wondering what Governor Roosevelt will do when a transcript of the evidence is laid before him by Judge Seabury. Even college undergraduates are eagerly debating the question whether Governor Roosevelt as an educated man of a favored social class will rise to the great opportunity to strike a powerful blow for honest government.

"Today, in what may prove to be an exciting and dramatic clash between two strong characters, the public should not forget what is really to be decided. It is not whether the Mayor, under great stress, is able to maintain his reputation for mental alertness, ready wit and sharp sayings. What the city wants to know is whether Mr. Walker is able to meet and dispel the grave charges with the gravity and force of evidence and weight of character which befit the Chief Executive of this metropolis.

"Our whole citizenship will be breathless spectators of the duel between Judge Seabury and Mayor Walker."

Walker was directed to produce not only his personal papers but also whatever data he had regarding business transactions with seven businessmen interested in bus franchises and taxicab ownership in the city.

All seven had links to Jimmy Walker.

Among them was State Senator John A. Hastings of Brooklyn, who was a silent partner in the Equitable Coach Company, an employee of the Terminal Taxicab Company, and a stockholder in a company seeking to sell tiles to contractors building city subways. It was the senator who had arranged and paid for Mayor Walker's trips around the United States.

Another was Russell T. Sherwood, whose business affairs with the mayor were so entangled that it was hard to tell where the interests of one left off and those of the other began. Sherwood, who was the mayor's financial agent, fled New York when he received a subpoena. In spite of a $50,000 fine imposed upon him for contempt, he defied a Supreme Court order to return.

Three backers of the Equitable Coach Company, whose political contact man was Senator Hastings, were also named in the subpoena. They were Frank R. Fageol, president of the Twin Coach Company of Ohio; William O'Neil, head of the General Tire and Rubber Company, and J. Allen Smith, who was brought back from Europe under court order to explain why he'd bought Mayor Walker a $10,000 letter of credit for use on his European trip in the summer of 1927.

The two others named were J. A. Sisto, a taxicab financier whose great admiration for Walker moved him to make the mayor a gift of $26,500 worth of bonds, and John J. McKeon, who delivered the securities to the mayor in a sealed envelope one day when he rode uptown with him.

Of the businessmen linked to Mayor Walker, only one, J. Allen Smith, was not called to be an early witness. It was Smith, in reporting to his superiors on the progress of negotiations for a city franchise,

who referred to Jimmy Walker—in a secret telegram that was un-
earthed and decoded by Seabury's staff—as THE BOY FRIEND and to
Tammany Hall as THE WAR BOARD.

Five thousand spectators were outside the courthouse and another
seven hundred inside when Judge Seabury and eight of his associate
and assistant counsel arrived, laden with briefcases and exhibits. They
were greeted by scattered applause and a sibilant undertone of hisses. In
a courtly gesture, Judge Seabury responded by tipping his soft gray hat
to the crowd.

When Mayor Walker arrived and slowly ascended the courthouse
steps, the same crowd cheered and whistled. The man beneath the wide-
brimmed fedora, rolled down on one side Broadway sharpie–style, was
in no hurry to leave his admirers. He grinned and waved his arms overhead like a gladiator as they shouted, "Good luck, Jimmy!" "Atta boy,
Jimmy!" "You tell 'em, Jimmy!" As a reminder that Prohibition was still
the law and should be repealed, several of his fans wore neckties that advocated "Beer for Prosperity." Some had already imbibed that morning.

A police inspector suggested that Walker enter by a side door, but
he replied—throwing the reporters in his wake a colorful quote for tomorrow's feature stories—"I'm used to traveling in crowds." One gentleman managed to break through the police escort to ask the mayor
to use his influence and get him a seat inside the courthouse. Walker
quipped, "I'd be most happy to give you *my* seat."

There were squads of cops inside and outside the courthouse.
Among the parentless rumors that went the rounds was that a large
delegation of Reds was coming to demonstrate for their own political
purposes. Five members of the police department's Radical Squad
quickly arrived and took up their task of mingling and scrutinizing the
crowd. (The Reds failed to materialize.)

Among the "vital statistics" reported in the *New York Daily News*,
the straphanger's newspaper, which had the largest circulation in the
city, was that the first man trying to get into the courtroom arrived

three hours before the doors opened. Unemployed at the moment, this man, one Max Shardinsky, told the guards that, after looking at the meager employment ads and finding nothing, he decided to attend the hearing without one of the necessary passes. He was turned away.

A second unemployed man arrived five minutes later. Asked to identify himself, he declined, saying that one couldn't be too careful these days, with investigations going on all over the city. "You'll have to see my lawyer," he exclaimed.

It was Uptown rather than Downtown that held the passes to get in. The pass holders and well-dressed crashers who knew someone who knew someone spread themselves on benches and camp stools— seven hundred people in a room for three hundred. Some of the spectators brought lunch. Before the hearing started, a pass from a district leader was enough for a seat. The Democratic—or pro-mayor—spectators were a clear majority.

When Jimmy Walker entered the courtroom, Judge Seabury and his aides were already seated at the counsel table. The two sides did not acknowledge each other. Applause and cheers broke out for the mayor. The Hofstadter committeemen moved to their elevated judicial chairs behind a varnished oak railing.

With a confident air, Jimmy Walker sat down in an armchair to the right of the committee.

Judge Seabury had been given rather unusual advice by some of the experienced litigators on his staff: "Don't look Walker straight in the eye when he's on the witness stand. He has an uncanny ability to stare you down. Once he's eyed you, you're liable to be stunned and confused, like a deer caught in a car's headlights." Apparently Seabury kept the warning in mind. Front-page pictures in newspapers all over the United States later showed him staring at Walker, but most of the time he seemed to be glancing at the mayor sideways.

Mayor Walker put on his horn-rimmed spectacles, looked at a waiver of immunity, and signed it. But in response to the subpoena, he

Arnold Rothstein as he appeared in New York State Supreme Court in Manhattan, fighting a bankruptcy receiver's attempt to collect $366,000 from him in July 1928. At one time, that was only "walking-around money" to the politically connected gambling czar of New York. Several months later, on November 4, 1928, the 46-year-old gambler was gunned down in the Park Central Hotel on Seventh Avenue and Fifty-sixth Street by an "unknown" assailant. His "unsolved" murder touched off a crisis in the Tammany circles around Mayor Jimmy Walker. (UPI/Corbis/Bettmann)

Governor-elect Roosevelt and Mayor Walker in the conference room of the Roosevelt home in New York City in December 1928. The two Democratic officials had known each other since before World War I when both served as state senators in Albany. They discussed transit, harbor development, and traffic legislation. Walker is wearing spats; Roosevelt is wearing braces on both legs. (Franklin D. Roosevelt Library)

Tammany Sachems at the dedication of the new Wigwam on Union Square in 1929. Left to right: New York Surrogate James A. Foley (son-in-law of the late Tammany boss Charles Murphy); Mayor Walker; John Voorhis, Grand Sachem of the Tammany Society at age 100; former governor Alfred E. Smith; John F. Curry, the Manhattan Tammany leader. (*New York Daily Mirror*)

Governor-elect Franklin D. Roosevelt in December 1928, drawn from life by S. J. Woolf. (*New York Times Magazine*)

Three New York State governors in 1930: Franklin D. Roosevelt, two years before he interrogated Jimmy Walker and was nominated for president; Herbert H. Lehman, then the lieutenant governor, who succeeded Roosevelt in Albany in 1933; Alfred E. Smith, who served four terms beginning in 1919, before becoming the first Catholic to run for president, in 1928. With Jimmy Walker's support, Smith unsuccessfully sought the nomination again in 1932, but it was Roosevelt's turn. (New York Public Library Picture Collection)

Jimmy Walker, running for his first term as mayor in 1925, was a protégé of Governor Alfred E. Smith. Left to right: Allie, Walker's first wife; Smith's daugher, Emily; and Mrs. Smith. (*New York Daily Mirror*)

In 1927, at the age of the twenty-three, Betty Compton (left) appeared in the musical *Funny Face* with Fred Astaire, his sister, Adele (center), and an unknown actress. That year she began to be courted by Mayor Walker. (New York Public Library Picture Collection)

"Will You Love Me in December as You Do in May," Jimmy Walker's most popular song, which he wrote before entering politics, found an attentive audience in Betty Compton, the second Mrs. Walker. The lyrics foretold their relationship. (New York Public Library Picture Collection)

Mayor Walker and Police
Commissioner Edward P.
Mulrooney leading a police
department parade in 1931.
(Associated Press)

Like a winner at the racetrack,
Jimmy Walker poses inside a floral
horseshoe during a dinner honor-
ing him, given by the Jewish
Theatrical Guild at the Hotel
Commodore in 1931. (New York
Public Library Picture Collection)

Two mayors: During a
pleasure trip to Berlin in
1928, Jimmy Walker poses
in the garden of Herr
Ober-Burgermeister Boess.
(New York Public Library
Picture Collection)

Gene Tunney, the heavy-weight boxing champion who defeated Jack Dempsey in 1926, gets the Walker-Whalen treatment on the sidewalks of New York before an assembly of U.S. Marines. (Culver Pictures)

Charles Lindbergh got his ticker-tape parade in 1927 after flying from Long Island to Paris solo in *The Spirit of St. Louis.* Grover Whalen, the city's official greeter (in top hat), sits in front of Lindbergh and Jimmy Walker. (New York Public Library Picture Collection)

Allie Walker with Mayor Walker in 1930, before their marriage broke up, receiving a bouquet of roses at their home in Greenwich Village. (*New York Daily Mirror*)

Mayor Walker's last hurrah on Fifth Avenue—the "beer parade" to repeal Prohibition in 1932. Not long afterward, he appeared before Governor Roosevelt to answer charges about his sources of income. (International News Service)

Governor Roosevelt surrounded by members of his engineering staff in August 1932, when Mayor Walker was "on trial" before him during the hearings in the Executive Chamber in Albany. (Franklin D. Roosevelt Library)

A portfolio of five newspaper cartoons drawn in August 1932 during the Albany hearings, with Mayor Walker on the witness stand before Governor Roosevelt—at the same time that Roosevelt was the Democratic nominee for president. (Franklin D. Roosevelt Library)

Carefully Weighed.
(*New York Mirror*)

The Carriage Awaits Without.
(*Brooklyn Eagle*)

Just in Time.
(*Washington Post*)

Plenty of Fuss.
(*New York Post*)

All in the Game.
(*New York Post*)

Mayor Walker in the witness chair in the spring of 1932 at the New York County Courthouse to answer charges about his sources of income, including a secret brokerage account. Here he is interrogated by Samuel Seabury, counsel, before a joint state legislative committee, during the citywide investigation of corruption. (*New York Daily News*)

Judge Samuel Seabury— Jimmy Walker's nemesis—relaxes in 1933, a year after the end of the citywide "Seabury investigation" that exposed corruption in the mayor's tin-box administration. Seabury, a retired jurist, was invited by Governor Roosevelt to present the evidence that led to Walker's resignation. (New York Public Library Picture Collection)

Tammany Hall stalwarts representing New York at the 1932 Democratic convention in Chicago, which nominated Governor Roosevelt to be president: Brooklyn's John H. McCooey, Manhattan's John F. Curry, and Mayor Walker, who backed an embittered Alfred E. Smith for the nomination. (*New York Daily Mirror*)

Whistle-Stop Campaign: On October 18, 1932, Governor Roosevelt boarded "The Roosevelt Special" for a campaign swing around the country, beginning in Albany. No believer in a back-porch campaign, F.D.R. insisted on speaking in towns large and small before he was elected president. (Franklin D. Roosevelt Library)

The Republican-Fusion mayor Fiorello H. La Guardia in 1937, during his second term of office. (New York Public Library Picture Collection)

Reunion of old foes and friends: Mayor La Guardia, ex-Mayor Walker, and James Farley at a dinner in 1937. La Guardia appointed Walker impartial arbitrator of the garment industry, while Farley was President Roosevelt's postmaster general. (Franklin D. Roosevelt Library)

Close allies in New York and Washington: President Roosevelt, Eleanor Roosevelt, and Mayor La Guardia campaigning in Manhattan (1940) for F.D.R.'s third term. (Franklin D. Roosevelt Library)

During the Second World War, when Mayor La Guardia was named head of the Office of Civil Defense (1942), Eleanor Roosevelt served as his assistant. (Franklin D. Roosevelt Library)

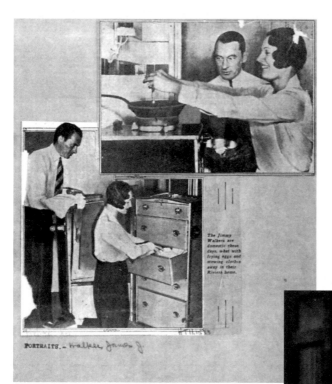

Domestic relations: Ex-Mayor Walker and Betty Compton were married by the mayor of Cannes on April 19, 1933, while they were living in Europe. The rotogravure pictures of the Walkers in their Riviera home appeared in the *New York Herald Tribune* in November 1933. (*New York Herald Tribune*)

Jimmy Walker, private citizen, in self-imposed exile, 1934. He lived with Betty in England, making frequent trips to the Continent, before returning to the United States in 1935, after he was cleared of his tax woes. (Private Collection)

In 1936, after they had returned from Europe, Betty and Jimmy adopted a daughter, Mary Ann, and lived quietly in an apartment on the Upper East Side of Manhattan. (Private Collection)

After Walker returned to New York in 1935, he frequently served as a toastmaster at charitable events. Here he is at a fund-raiser for the Disabled American Veterans, with Frank T. Hines, administrator of veteran's affairs, and Vice Admiral Ross T. McIntire, the Navy surgeon general. (Disabled American Veterans)

After the death of President Roosevelt in 1945, former Mayor Walker attended a dinner of the International Ladies Garment Workers Union with union head David Dubinsky, Eleanor Roosevelt, and Harry Hopkins, F.D.R.'s closest adviser. Walker served as impartial arbitrator in the garment industry in New York. (ILGWU photograph)

Mayor La Guardia, snow-sprinkled, chased fires to show his concern for the firemen and the fire victims. In 1942, when he had already been in office for nearly ten years, he turned up at a fire on the Hudson River pier at Forty-third Street. (*New York Daily Mirror*)

failed to produce any records of his savings accounts, brokerage accounts, or safe-deposit boxes.

Seabury pressed him on the Equitable Coach deal that had led to the $10,000 letter of credit for his European junket. There had been a second application from Service Bus, a competing company, to sell the city surface transportation. Walker favored Equitable, which owned no buses, over Service, which had a large fleet.

Walker's memory failed him about the details but enabled him to get his first applause—and the chairman's gavel. "Any petitioner for bus service would have to have, say, 1,000 buses," he said. "Now, if they had 5,000 besides, they would probably keep 4,000 in a garage." (*Laughter.*)

Seabury informed him that the Equitable Coach Company had offered only promises, while the Service Bus Company already had buses up and running.

Walker replied, "I would not know about that. That is evidently a matter of communication. Why, the best offer that the city ever had came from a company on Long Island, and upon investigation it turned out they were in the hay feed business [*laughter—gavel*] and yet in their communication, it was the most attractive offer."

Walker was a reluctant witness, looking at Seabury and refusing to make things easy—mostly to the applause of the crowd. At one point he became indignant and told Seabury, "Remember, I am still the mayor of the City of New York."

When one of the Democratic assemblymen protested that the committee had no right to concern itself with "a man's private life," Walker broke in, "Oh, run for mayor and you will read all about your private life in the newspapers."

As the grilling intensified, Walker complained to Chairman Hofstadter: "I don't believe that your counsel or you have any legal right to inquire into the operations of an executive's mind or to cross-examine him about why he reaches his conclusions, any more than I have a right or you have a right to examine the Governor as to why he makes an appointment or why the President of the United States vetoes a bill." (*Laughter—applause.*)

Walker and his cronies on the state legislative committee branded the entire investigation a "Red plot."

One of Walker's strongest Tammany supporters, Senator John J. McNaboe, muttered: "You have Reds and Communists in here! I want you people to go on record as approving prying into a person's private affairs, particularly his wife. I want a ruling to find out whether this is Russia or the United States!"

Assemblyman Steingut added, "Why, in the darkest days of Russia nothing like this would ever take place."

As the proceedings continued into late afternoon of the muggy May day, Jimmy Walker began to show his irritation. Out of earshot of the stenographers, he muttered something under his breath directly at Judge Seabury: "You and Frank Roosevelt are not going to hoist yourself to the Presidency over my dead body!"

Walker's insolent remark did not appear in the hearing transcript or, in fact, in any of the newspapers. But Louis Molloy, one of Seabury's assistant counsel, told his colleagues that he had clearly heard Walker half-whisper the angry words, not once but several times.

In his best thespian manner, the mayor alternated between humor and indignation. He turned to Seabury and the committeemen and said, "The Mayor of the City of New York has a great many things to do. Will you please not keep me in this room any longer than you have to, away from the duties I have to perform?" This was the first time anyone had ever heard Jimmy Walker complain that he had to leave center stage to go to work.

Judge Seabury began to hit pay dirt when he queried the mayor about the $10,000 letter of credit, which Walker had obtained from J. Allen Smith, the influence peddler, the day before Equitable Coach was granted its franchise. The mayor brushed off the gift as an innocent transaction to help a friend.

But the $10,000 was pocket change compared with the hundreds of thousands in stock profits Walker received—he called the money a "beneficence"—without putting up a nickel of his own.

With a shrug of his shoulders, Walker admitted that Paul Block, a newspaper publisher and wealthy investor, gave him $246,692.76, minus income-tax payments, between February 10, 1927, and August 5, 1929. This sum represented his share of profits from a secret joint brokerage account labeled "Paul Block and J. J. WALKER."

At a later point, to conceal Jimmy Walker's ownership of the account, his name was dropped and Paul Block substituted the name of his brother, Max Block.

Why was Block so charitable? Evidence dug up by Seabury's staff revealed that the publisher-investor was heavily interested in a company seeking to sell tiles to contractors building city subways.

New Yorkers chuckled when they heard Paul Block's fantastic story of the reason why he had been so generous to Jimmy Walker. Even the Tammany members of the committee, who shouted themselves hoarse with objections while the mayor squirmed under the cross-examination, settled back with smiles of mild amusement when the newspaper publisher related what led him to "try to make a little money for Jimmy."

Almost shyly, Block said he was a little reluctant to discuss the reason for his kindness. He was afraid it might sound "silly" and "semi-sentimental," but Judge Seabury coaxed him into telling.

Modestly, Block said that his ten-year-old son, Billy, who was fond of Uncle Jimmy Walker, gave him the idea. It seemed that the bright young lad was solicitous about the mayor's ability to support his wife and himself on the $25,000 a year the city paid him.

The subject came up while Billy and his father were walking up and down in front of their spacious home on Fifth Avenue and seventy-fourth Street, overlooking Central Park's model-sailboat pond, while waiting for the mayor to come and take them for a ride.

"Naturally," said Block, "our minds were on the mayor. Billy wondered aloud, 'How much salary does the mayor get?' I told him it was $25,000, which was his salary at that time. 'Does the city give him a home?' 'No, they don't,' I said. He asked me, 'Does it give him an automobile?' I said, 'Yes, but not one for Mrs. Walker.'

"'Can he live on what he gets?' Billy asked, and I told him, 'Well, I suppose he can, but it probably is a difficult problem.' And so, Judge, I want you to believe me that it entered my mind then and there that I was going to try and make a little money for him."

(*Laughter—Gavel*)

Judge Seabury produced an accountant's statistical analysis of the bank and brokerage accounts of Walker and his fugitive agent, Russell T. Sherwood. Sherwood, a $10,000-a-year accountant, had drawn $263,838.36 from a secret safe-deposit account in 1927, the day before Mayor Walker sailed for Europe. The application for the box had been cosigned by Walker.

Seabury entered into evidence a detailed analysis of Sherwood's deposits and withdrawals. Tens of thousands of dollars' worth of checks were made out either to Mrs. Walker or to "Cash" or "Bearer." One check read: "For expenses of yacht 'Mary W' in service of Mrs. James J. Walker—$6,034."

As Seabury unfolded the facts about the Sherwood-Walker secret account, the mayor retorted: "I hope he proves it is mine. I will try to collect it." Walker kept insisting that Sherwood was not his "agent," while the hard evidence of the checks bearing his or his wife's name proved otherwise.

"I want the privilege of adding one word," Walker said, after a long wrangle. "I showed that I was willing to cooperate, but there is no doubt in my mind but this is nothing but an examination before trial, else the papers are further from the truth than they ever were. This is preliminary to preferring charges to the Governor, and no one is fooled by this fact."

After his second and final day before the joint legislative committee, Jimmy Walker had his say for the benefit of the press—and of the politicos in New York City and Albany who, his instincts correctly told him, would eventually determine his fate:

"I hope with the close of the two national conventions in Chicago, we will be through with some of the politics."

This was a reference not only to Governor Roosevelt's expected nomination for president but also to the possibility that Judge Seabury would run for high office—perhaps for governor of New York.

Then, with a crack against Seabury as someone "who didn't know the difference between uptown and downtown," Walker left the courthouse to more cheering crowds.

He was greeted by a shower of roses. A dozen young women had stationed themselves on either side of the main doorway and threw flowers at him as he emerged. Before descending the steps, he greeted each woman. Jimmy Walker still had the people with him; their approval had always been his greatest tonic.

No roses greeted Judge Seabury and his staff as they left the courthouse. One of his boys dryly noted, "Well, at least there are fewer boos and hisses now than on the first day." They read the ten daily papers to see which way the public wind was blowing. The news was not encouraging; a headline in *The New York Times* read:

MANY PLEASED BY WALKER SHOWING
Friends Hold He Came Off Better
Than Even Against Seabury in
His Two Days on Stand

A few days later, Walker lashed back before an audience of 18,000 men and women at Madison Square Garden. The *Times*'s headline read:

OVATION FOR WALKER AT GARDEN
Wave of Applause Rolls after
Him as He Reviews Class–
Called 'Loved by All'

The news article went on to say that while reviewing the graduation exercises of the Police College's class of May 1932, Walker proudly maintained: "I am still Mayor of New York." He said bitter things about "criticism predicated on individual ambition; criticism arising out of political jealousy; criticism sometimes emanating from vindictiveness."

He was introduced by Police Commissioner Mulrooney as "the man loved by all the people of the city, His Honor the Mayor of New York." When he finished his inspiring talk to the new police officers, their families and foreign dignitaries, "[the] Garden shook with applause."

When he was told about the mayor's tumultuous reception, Seabury wryly declared, "They gave one to Tweed, too."

Of all the press coverage, the most amusing portrait of Jimmy Walker turned up in *The Nation,* the venerable political weekly. It was written by none other than George S. Kaufman, former *New York Times* drama editor turned playwright of such satirical hits as *Once in a Lifetime.* A week after Walker's testimony, he wrote *Jimmy the Well-dressed Man,* which he described as a "vaudeville act with music." The two-character playlet featured Walker and Seabury; their loosely rhymed exchange differed from the official transcript, and lightened the town's mood. It went:

MR. SEABURY

Your Honor, this committee
Has some questions it would hand
To the Mayor of New York City
Who is sitting on the stand.

MR. WALKER

I promise not to halt or pause
I'm famous for my wit
I'm sitting on the stand because
I can't stand on the sit.
[*He dances*]

MR. SEABURY

Now, to you it's old and hoary
But it's very new to us
So we'd like to hear the story
Of the Equitable bus.

MR. WALKER

I remember! Why, the driver
Sees a woman grab her knee
And he says, "Not worth a fiver!
Legs they ain't no treat to me!"
[*He cuts a caper. He offers half of it to Mr. Seabury, who
refuses because he has just had his lunch*]

MR. SEABURY

Now, to open matters wider
(I guess this is where we clash)
Did Samuel Ungerleider
Ever slip you any cash?

MR. WALKER

Say, here's the greatest yarn on earth
The one about the dame
That got into the Pullman berth
But I'll never tell her name.
[*He throws his hat into the air. It comes down with
$263,000 in it*]

After Mr. Seabury asks several more questions about the sources
of Mr. Walker's magical income, the mayor concludes:

MR. WALKER

Fee, fi, fo, fum!
Whoops-a-daisy, and ho hum!
The whole committee is on the bum—
Where do you get your questions from?
Hey, diddle, doodle!
The cash and the boodle—
It's ten to one they'll win again!
So what do I care
If you give me the air—

They'll only vote me in again!
In again!
In again!
They'll only vote me in—a-gain!
[*He dances. The rest of the committee comes down off
the bench and joins in the dance. At this point the piper
comes on the scene. The public pays him*]
CURTAIN

A far more serious comment came from Arthur Krock, the most influential columnist in the nation. As the Washington bureau chief of *The New York Times,* he was a confidant of presidents and aspiring presidents. Like Walter Lippmann of the *New York Herald Tribune,* he offered free advice to key officials in the power centers of the federal government; in return, he was given inside information. One of Krock's sources was Joseph P. Kennedy, a businessman and strong financial backer of Governor Roosevelt and the Democratic party. (Roosevelt later named Kennedy head of the Securities and Exchange Commission, then made him ambassador to the Court of St. James. The latter was a disastrous appointment; the ambassador was removed because of his Anglophobia. Joe Kennedy would later use his influence and money to help elect his son John Fitzgerald Kennedy president of the United States.)

In his turgid writing style, the estimable Krock made sure to underscore for his national readership that what had happened in a New York courtroom would affect the 1932 presidential election because, in effect, the legislative committee was acting like a grand jury:

"Regardless of what Judge Seabury does about the testimony, the Governor of New York, especially because he is a candidate for Presidential nomination next month, faces a perplexing problem in Jimmy Walker. If Judge Seabury files the charges, Mr. Roosevelt, unless he dismisses the Mayor or rejects the charges at once, an unlikely proceeding, must give Mr. Walker time to make a defense or he must appoint the Attorney General to conduct a hearing of the charges. This would carry a decision far beyond the adjournment date of the national conventions. If such be his course, the Governor, as a Presidential candidate, will be both helped and hurt by it.

"Helped, because Tammany will hesitate in the convention to make the Governor an enemy. Hurt, because there will be demands that he express indignation at the careless conduct of the Mayor of the country's greatest city. And there is the further complication that, if the Mayor is removed, and runs for 'vindication' in November, he will entirely muss up the Presidential contest. But, in spite of these imponderables, the life of a Presidential candidate must go on."

By contrast to what his colleagues on the newspaper considered to be Krock's patented boredom, the normally humorless *New York Times* decided that the mayor had been evasive and deserved a subtle lashing. An unnamed editorial writer, sounding as if he were trying to be E. B. White of *The New Yorker* (but not quite succeeding), wrote a pair of parodies of Jimmy Walker's answers to Judge Seabury's questions:

I.

Q: Your name, please?

A: George Washington.

Q: Business?

A: Commander-in-Chief of the Continental Army.

Q: I show you a document in which it is stated that on the night of December 25, 1776, you crossed the Delaware River. Is that correct?

A: Did I say that?

Q: Yes. Isn't it true?

A: Well, Judge, I really don't know. I'm a bit hazy about it.

Q: You admit that on Christmas Eve you were encamped on the Pennsylvania side of the river?

A: Yes.

Q: And that on December 26 you fought the Battle of Trenton on the Jersey side?

A: Yes.

Q: Then isn't it a fact that some time between those dates you crossed the river?

A: How do I know I crossed the river. I might have gone around it.

II.

Q: Please give the clerk your name.

A: Adam, your Honor.

Q: Business?

A: Horticulturist.

Q: In the Spring of the year 4000 B.C. where were you employed, and in what official capacity?

A: Head gardener in the Garden of Eden.

Q: Did you ever get in a jam in the Garden?

A: Oh, yes, your Honor! All those apple trees—that's what got Eve and me into so much trouble.

Q: What kind of trouble?

A: Well, the trees needed spraying every year, and I was contact man for the Eden Exterminator Company, makers of the Paradise Sprayer, and when we started in to draw up the specifications—

Q: Well, you needn't go into that now. All I want to get on the record is that as a result of yielding to this natural temptation to make a little money on the side you lost your job and had to leave the Garden on foot in the midst of the Depression—

A: Oh, no, your Honor, not on foot. Eve and I left the Garden in a covered wagon bought and paid for by a number of devoted friends.

The Democratic presidential convention was now only a few weeks away. Roosevelt already had 666 votes lined up; it would take 770 votes to gain the nomination. The other main players were far behind. They included Alfred E. Smith of New York, with some 201 votes, John Nance Garner of Texas, with 90, and George White of Ohio, with 52. Samuel Seabury, the dreamer, had no votes.

For reasons of his own, Seabury sat back and let the case against Walker simmer for several days after the hearings ended. He thought Governor Roosevelt should make the first move; Roosevelt thought Seabury, as counsel to the legislative committee, should do so. Neither wanted to take a step that might appear to be politically motivated. By this time, in fact, any extrajudicial statement by any of the parties was considered political. Tammany's Sachems waited in the wings, paralyzed into silence. The man in the middle, Jimmy Walker, turned up a little more often at his unfamiliar City Hall desk, not wishing to be perceived in his usual role as the Night Mayor of New York.

During the first week in June, Seabury gave no hint of his intentions. He went to Washington and Jefferson College in Pennsylvania, where he received an honorary doctor of laws degree. In the view of the Good Government forces in the city, he was riding high—talked about as a man on a white horse. Letters and telegrams poured into Albany and New York, praising Judge Seabury as an old-fashioned, hard-hitting counsel and demanding Mayor Walker's removal.

In a lead editorial, *The New York Times* summed up Governor Roosevelt's dilemma in the Walker matter, but without biting the bullet itself:

"To act on his own initiative now, the Governor's advisers have told him, would be to run the risk of being accused of political opportunism. The political effect of Mayor Walker's case on Governor Roosevelt's chances of winning his party's nomination for President cannot be minimized. Failure to act decisively if charges are filed with him might be interpreted as bowing to Tammany Hall, while precipitate action would alienate the local organization and cast doubt on Mr. Roosevelt's ability to carry his own state."

Pressed for a comment, if not for action, Governor Roosevelt issued a blunt statement from the Executive Mansion in Albany through Guernsey T. Cross, his personal secretary. It indicated that he was clearing the decks for action, if necessary; at the same time, he was taking a swipe at Judge Seabury:

"The only information before the Governor is in the form of very incomplete newspaper stories. It is not even clear from Judge Seabury's statement to Chairman Hofstadter whether he has fully completed his investigation. I act in each case definitely, positively and with due promptness. Get the law straight. It is the duty of the legislative committee and its counsel, if they believe they have sufficient cause, to present evidence to the proper authorities without waiting to make a formal report to next year's legislature. You cannot get away from that obvious public duty.

"In the case of Sheriff Farley, Judge Seabury asked the legislative committee to present the evidence to the Governor. The committee refused. Judge Seabury sent it himself. I acted. If the evidence in any case now before the legislative committee, in their judgment or that of their counsel, warrants, it is time for the legislative committee and their counsel to stop talking and do something. It is not the time for political sniping or buck passing."

In fact, the transcripts of the hearings had been sent to Governor Roosevelt right from the beginning. He did not have to rely on what he called "incomplete" news accounts for damaging information about Walker's shady sources of income. But he still needed an official recommendation to stay upright on his tightrope.

There was another way in which Roosevelt's bluntness was meant to be a subliminal message to Judge Seabury. Roosevelt's closest political aide, Louis Howe, had discovered a startling piece of news. He told Roosevelt that Seabury was making moves behind the scenes to capture the Democratic nomination for himself. Howe said that Seabury's friends had approached people on Capitol Hill to sound them out about his own candidacy in case the convention was deadlocked. Roosevelt and his operatives knew that despite Seabury's newborn fame, he had no delegates and didn't stand a chance of obtaining the nomination.

Yet Seabury began to believe his press clippings; they encouraged him to hope that lightning would strike in Chicago. One Connecticut newspaper said: "Seabury's probe of Tammany Makes National Sensation." A Michigan paper: "Tammany Foe to Be Candidate for Presidency." An Indiana paper: "Judge Seabury, Controlling Genius Behind New York Investigations, Does Not Deny Aspirations." Seabury's secretary, Dorothy Brenner, pasted all such clippings in a scrapbook labeled, rather prematurely, "President."

In a private letter to Colonel Edward House, one of his political advisers, Roosevelt wrote, "This fellow Seabury is merely trying to perpetrate another political play to embarrass me. His conduct has been a deep disappointment to people who honestly seek better government in New York City by stressing the fundamentals and eliminating political innuendoes."

Finally, with the convention a scant week away, Seabury sent Governor Roosevelt a copy of the transcript of the Walker testimony, together with his analysis. He filed the report in his own name because a majority of the members of the joint legislative committee refused to back him up.

"This record is presented to you by me in my individual capacity as a citizen of the State of New York," he wrote Roosevelt, "not as the counsel to the joint legislative committee. I submit the record to you not as formal charges but for your information so that you may determine what shall be done."

Judge Seabury's analysis of the evidence summarized the series of "beneficences" received by Mayor Walker from people doing business with the city, or hoping to. These moneys included Russell T. Sherwood's deposits of close to a million dollars in banking and brokerage accounts. Seabury concluded that Walker was guilty of malfeasance and nonfeasance, making him unfit to continue in office.

"I have no request or petition to make," Seabury concluded, although his intentions were obvious. "My only desire is that the matter may be dealt with solely upon its merits. In my judgment, the evidence presents matters of the gravest moment to the people of the City of New York. I therefore present it to Your Excellency, who alone, under the Constitution and the laws, is empowered to act."

Now the ball was finally in the governor's court. He and his legal advisers undertook a study of the transcript and an analysis of the evidence. Then Roosevelt forwarded the material to the mayor without comment, requesting that he answer Seabury's charges. It was now one week before the convention.

Jimmy Walker stalled, saying that he would reply *after* the convention.

Walker entertained the faint but not absurd hope that his mentor, Al Smith, might still be a contender. Even if Smith didn't get the nomination, Walker believed that, somehow, Smith would still be more influential than F.D.R. in New York State and more sympathetic to his plight. It was accepted wisdom that with the Depression on and unemployment high, almost any Democrat, even a Roman Catholic, could be elected in a contest against President Hoover.

Smith, however, was busy shooting himself in the foot. Strangely, the man who once boasted that he was a product of the sidewalks of New York now wore the mantle of a big businessman. While Governor Roosevelt, the one born into wealth, made speeches urging help for the "forgotten man," Smith in *his* speeches said that Roosevelt should "forget about the forgotten man" because such talk could only lead to class warfare: "Let us not stir up the bitterness of the rich against the poor, and the poor against the rich."

In his most truculent style, Smith referred to Roosevelt not by name but as a "prominent Democrat" who sounded like a "demagogue." Smith announced that he would attend the Chicago convention as a delegate; Roosevelt's close advisers feared that Smith might try to create a deadlock for his own benefit or to block Roosevelt.

So the investigation was at a temporary standstill as Walker, Seabury, and Smith prepared to entrain for Chicago. By tradition, Roosevelt, as the leading candidate, would not even appear.

In an installment of his "Today and Tomorrow" column that appeared before the convention, Walter Lippmann added more powder to his cannonades against Roosevelt by bringing up the Jimmy Walker case:

"There has been something distinctly queer in Franklin D. Roosevelt's mental processes throughout this affair. He seems to be mostly deeply irritated at the fact that the Seabury investigation has been producing testimony which compels him to choose between condoning corruption and striking it. He has displayed a singular petulance toward everybody who has had any part in putting him in a position where he might have to make a decisive choice between breaking with Tammany and surrendering to it.

"Governor Roosevelt has lost his moral freedom. He is so heavily mortgaged to Tammany that he must prove his independence of it. Yet at this late date there is no way of proving his independence except by a procedure which must outrage everyone's sense of justice.

For to try James J. Walker before a man who stands to profit enormously by convicting him is a revolting spectacle. But the problem is entirely a consequence of Governor Roosevelt's indecision during the last year."

As the convention opened at Chicago Stadium on June 27, 1932, Roosevelt was the clear front-runner. From his command post in Albany, where he waited to depart for Chicago at a time when he could make a triumphant entrance, he listened to the radio and consulted over a private telephone line with his Brain Trust (he also liked to call his group of wise men the Privy Council). In addition to Sam Rosenman, its first recruiting officer, the original Brain Trusters included five Columbia University professors—Raymond Moley, Adolf A. Berle, Jr., Joseph P. McGoldrick, Rexford Tugwell, and Lindsay Rogers. These experts in the social sciences and economics stood in sharp contrast to the Tammany hacks who occupied seats as Manhattan and Brooklyn delegates.

Al Smith sat with the New York delegation. The Tammany delegates were so hostile to Governor Roosevelt that Jim Farley, his campaign manager, had difficulty finding a seat during the roll calls.

"I do hope that Al Smith will not make a bitter or a mean fight," Roosevelt told a friend. "It does nobody any good and, though he may block the convention and raise Cain generally, it would be much better for the country if he would forget self and work primarily for the country itself."

After the nominating and seconding speeches and maneuvering over the voting rules by the state delegations, the first roll call was taken on July 1. Mayor Walker took his seat with the Tammany delegates from New York just before the official tally began. He then asked to be recognized.

"Who is the gentleman who addresses the chair?"

"Walker, a delegate from New York."

"For what purpose does he address the chair?"

"The delegate was not here when his name was called, and his alternate voted in his stead. The delegate requests permission to cast his own vote."

"The request is granted."

"I desire," said Walker dramatically, "that my vote be cast for Alfred E. Smith."

Suddenly, the faithful Smith delegates awoke from their torpor. Could it be 1928 again, but this time with a victory? They cheered and applauded and danced in the aisles. Many of them were aware that Walker's future rested in the hands of Governor Roosevelt.

Smith, his hopes raised, got caught up in the excitement. Even though he and Walker had their differences over the years, he exclaimed:

"Good old Jim! Blood is thicker than water!"

However, it was too little too late.

The main contenders stacked up just as had been expected, with Roosevelt immediately gaining a long lead, 666 votes against Smith's 201. John Nance Garner of Texas received his predicted 90 votes. Roosevelt was about a hundred votes short of the needed two-thirds. Jim Farley began working the floor; he had the vice-presidential nomination to offer.

On the second roll call, Roosevelt picked up only 11½ more votes. William Randolph Hearst now became a player. He had a big say in the California delegation, hated Smith and Tammany. (The reason for the Hearst-Smith animosity was that in 1922, when Smith was running for Governor, Hearst would have received the nomination for U.S. Senator from New York had Smith not refused to run with him.) That feud was another card in Farley's deck to deal votes toward Roosevelt.

As an isolationist, Hearst was in a quandary. He wasn't particularly a Roosevelt fan; he feared that F.D.R. would come under British influence. Furthermore, his isolationist editorials continually spread fears about the "yellow peril" of Asian immigration. Jim Farley called the San Simeon newspaper lord and reassured him that Roosevelt's "internationalism" was exaggerated.

A key figure at the convention was William Gibbs McAdoo, who had married President Wilson's daughter. He had emerged as a power in the western states. As a California resident and delegate, he served as Hearst's bargaining agent. Through McAdoo, Hearst helped swing the California delegation toward Roosevelt. F.D.R.'s tally edged up to 677¾ on the second ballot and to 683 on the third.

Texas, and "Cactus Jack" Garner, held the final key to a Roosevelt victory. Al Smith tried to reach Garner, who was in Washington, in an effort to keep him neutral for a few more ballots. But Garner, knowing the score, wouldn't take Smith's phone calls.

A deal was quickly made, supposedly with Hearst's approval: Roosevelt's running mate would be Garner. Now the Texans released their Garner votes and the Roosevelt avalanche began. The shift of Texas brought California around, too. Garner, Speaker of the House of Representatives, was Hearst's conservative choice; he would get the vice presidency if Hearst swung California and Texas to Roosevelt. When California was called on the fourth ballot, McAdoo got up and announced that his "sovereign state" (the sovereign being Hearst) had democratically decided to support Franklin Delano Roosevelt. Cheers and stamping broke out in the broiling convention hall.

"It's a kangaroo ticket," said a disappointed Texas delegate, still loyal to Garner. "Stronger in the hindquarter than in front."

While the Smith forces booed, Roosevelt made it on the fourth ballot as the delegations fell into line behind the certain winner. Roosevelt had 945 votes and Smith only 190¼. But Smith's diehard supporters—including Jimmy Walker—refused to make Roosevelt's nomination unanimous or to join in the victory parade.

Not every New York City newspaperman was happy about the outcome. Heywood Broun, an outspoken liberal, was a Smith man. He so far forgot his journalistic detachment as to grab a banner and march in a Smith demonstration. Broun thought of Smith as a martyred liberal; he began his post-convention column, "I'd rather be right than be Roosevelt." (Unsurprisingly, in the next presidential campaign, Broun recanted and came out in favor of Roosevelt's reelection.)

Defying those who advised a front-porch campaign, Governor Roosevelt flew from Albany to Chicago in a trimotored plane (it was buffeted by headwinds) to accept the nomination in person. With him were Eleanor Roosevelt, their son, John, and F.D.R.'s close confidant and favorite phrasemaker, Sam Rosenman. During the flight Roosevelt polished his acceptance speech, then fell asleep. The political scientist and respected Roosevelt biographer James MacGregor Burns later wrote that the long and rambling speech was essentially an appeal for an experimental program of recovery that would steer "between radicalism and reaction" and would "benefit all the people."

In Chicago the band greeted the nominee with "Happy Days Are Here Again." Cheerfully addressing the delegates on July 2, 1932, Governor Roosevelt said:

"I appreciate your willingness after these six arduous days to remain here, for I know full well the sleepless hours which you and I have had. I regret that I am late, but I have no control over the winds of Heaven and could only be thankful for my Navy training."

It was in winding up this speech that Roosevelt first used the phrase "new deal": "I pledge you, I pledge myself, to a new deal for the American people. Let us all here assembled constitute ourselves prophets of a new order of competence and courage. This is more than a political campaign; it is a call to arms. Give me your help, not to win votes alone, but to win this crusade to restore America to its own people."

Afterward, Al Smith became an embittered, unhappy warrior. When he was asked by reporters if he would support Roosevelt during the presidential campaign, Smith famously remarked: "Don't you know what Senator David B. Hill said after Grover Cleveland won the nomination? *'I'm a Democrat still.'* But the rest of that quotation from Hill, which some of you reporters may not have remembered, was *'Very still.'*"

Now, in the months before election day, a fundamental fact remained: Walker could only lose the mayoralty; but if how he handled the scandal became *the* issue in the campaign, Roosevelt stood a chance of losing the presidency. Facing Walker, F.D.R. was on trial, too.

TEN

F. D. R. vs. the Boy Friend

The packed Executive Chamber in the Hall of Governors in Albany, buzzing with excitement, suddenly fell silent. At 1:40 P.M., there was a rap on the door of the governor's office. A hush fell over the chamber as the tall, erect figure of Governor Roosevelt appeared, framed in the doorway. Hovering behind him was his secretary, Guernsey Cross. Roosevelt looked around the room, his chin in the air, confident. Then, on his secretary's arm, he began what seemed an interminable walk of only a few feet toward his desk.

As he moved through the dead silence, the creak of his leg braces could be distinctly heard. After years of practice, he had mastered what his physiotherapist called a two-point walk—right cane thrown forward and left foot forward together, lift right leg and left arm comes down with pressure. To the breathless onlookers, every step seemed a strained, endless effort.

When he finally reached the desk, his powerful hands gripped the arms of the high-backed leather chair. He tried to lower himself quietly, but his frail limbs, encased in the braces that were concealed beneath his trousers, demanded a long moment's adjustment so he could unsnap the knee locks and get into a seated position. At last, he dropped into the armchair and raised his eyes, studying the familiar faces in the crowded chamber. The nervous tension in the chamber eased. A faint smile crossed Roosevelt's face. In the true-life drama that was about to unfold, the most important Democratic figure in the nation had now taken his place at center stage.

The date was August 11, 1932. In his capacity as the chief executive of the Empire State, Roosevelt had called a "trial" to hear Seabury's charges and Walker's defense. Under the charter of the City of New York, the governor had the power to remove the mayor, but only after charges had been examined at a hearing. Pending the disposition of such accusations, the governor could suspend the mayor "for a period not exceeding thirty days." If that were ever to happen, of course, the mayor's administration would be weakened by his absence and his future political prospects would be dimmed.

The whole country was watching. For not only was Roosevelt the governor; he was now also the Democratic nominee for president of the United States.

Franklin Delano Roosevelt was running for president. James John Walker was running for his way of life.

Accompanied by his lawyers, Walker quietly entered the Executive Chamber of the Hall of Governors in the Capitol. For once, he was on time—and sartorially subdued, in a blue suit, white shirt, quiet cravat, black shoes. Judge Seabury and his assistants were already at the long counsel's table. Seabury sat quietly, looking out across the elm-shaded lawns leading down toward the Hudson River. A state trooper stood at either side of the governor's chair.

During the late mornings and afternoons, sunlight streaked across the tables; in the evening, chandeliers cast a pale light over the room, intensifying the deep maroon of the carpeting.

The chamber opened off Roosevelt's private office on the second floor of the statehouse. Here, he and his predecessors had heard appeals for executive clemency in pardon cases and presided over cabinet meetings. Upon the chamber's cherry-paneled walls hung paintings of all the governors of the Empire State, forgotten and famous; among them were two former presidents, Grover Cleveland and Theodore Roosevelt.

On the east side of the chamber, before cathedral windows that ran from floor to ceiling like castle doors of glass, there was a great desk where the governor and his legal advisers sat. To the left, facing the governor, were the tables and chairs for the accused and his defense counsel; to the right, a table and chairs for the accuser and his assistants.

A waist-high brass rail, borrowed from the Assembly chamber, separated those at center stage from the audience. Looking at the rail, Walker offered an aside: "I hope that they're not preparing to ride me out of town on it." Sixty newspapermen sat at press tables on the south end of the room. Along the north and west sides, there was a double row of folding chairs for friends and partisans of the parties involved in the hearing.

Earlier, at the end of July 1932, Jimmy Walker had finally responded to the charges brought by his nemesis Seabury. In a letter to Governor Roosevelt calling for Walker's removal from office, the intrepid anti-Tammany prosecutor had made these accusations:

- That the mayor had been guilty of "gross improprieties" and had given explanations of his acts "unworthy of credence."

- That Russell T. Sherwood, the mayor's agent, had received $22,000 more than the market price for certain stock from a concern interested in taxicab securities.

- That the mayor caused his financial transactions to be conducted through Sherwood, now missing; that Sherwood deposited nearly a million dollars, of which $700,000 was cash, in a secret safe-deposit box, and that the mayor failed to explain the source of this money.

- That the mayor accepted $26,000 in securities from brokers interested in taxicab legislation.

- That the mayor used his influence to obtain the award of a bus franchise to benefit his friends, including State Senator John A. Hastings of Brooklyn, and that he received a $10,000 letter of credit from the bus company.

• That the mayor accepted substantial "beneficences" from Paul Block, newspaper publisher and businessman.

• That the mayor failed to produce financial records and failed to testify frankly before the legislative committee.

Addressing "His Excellency Franklin D. Roosevelt," Mayor Walker offered a 27,000-word answer to Seabury's bill of particulars. The mayor maintained that Seabury's entire investigation was politically motivated—"conceived, born and fostered in politics." He attributed it to "the desperation growing out of the necessity to offset the failures of the present Republican organization." He explained that the administration was designed "to divert public attention from those responsible for the dreadful condition of affairs throughout the nation."

"I have been the special target of this hostility and misrepresentation," Walker replied. "Malice and slander and rancorous ill-will took the place of proof. Throughout the investigation, the counsel and his staff sought out and obtained all sorts of information on my personal and private life as well as my official acts. I was quizzed about my personal affairs and about the private affairs of others. I was asked very little, and only incidentally, about my conduct of the government of New York City."

These were Walker's main responses to Seabury's charges:

• That ten of the fifteen allegations of misconduct should be "outlawed" because they involved his "previous term of office."

• That the mayor "never accepted rewards" in return for "favorable taxicab legislation."

• That the mayor "never profited" from the Equitable Bus franchise, but acted only "in the interests of keeping the five-cent fare." (In campaign speeches, Walker had opposed raising subway and bus fares.)

- That the mayor "knew nothing" of the bank account of Russell T. Sherwood, the missing auditor, who was wrongly called his "financial agent."

- That the "beneficences" he received in the form of stock account profits from Paul Block "were not given for an improper consideration."

- That the mayor "testified fully" before the Hofstadter committee.

Walker underscored his popularity and criticized Judge Seabury's own electoral campaigns in the past. He was a master at talking directly to the emotions of the average New Yorker and—in a presidential election year—to an even wider constituency, if possible.

"Mr. Seabury would set up his opinion of my fitness for the office of Mayor as against the decision of 867,522 citizens who did me the honor of voting for me in the last City election, representing a plurality victory of 499,847 votes. Judge Seabury's own repudiation at the polls in 1916, when a candidate for Governor, probably explains his loss of confidence in popular elections. This distrust that he manifests for popular government he wants you to assume and, in spite of the votes of the people who supported me, to remove me from office."

In his finest heartfelt style, Walker concluded:

"Since the day of my birth, I have lived my life in the open. Whatever shortcomings I have are known to everyone—but disloyalty to my native city, official dishonesty or corruption, form no part of those shortcomings. It is sound American doctrine that the will of the people as expressed by their votes is not brushed aside to satisfy prejudice, a craving for publicity, or personal dislike, of political complainants. I respectfully submit that all the charges herein should be dismissed on the merits."

The next morning, July 30, 1932, *The New York Times* editorialized:

"Mayor Walker's answer to Governor Roosevelt consists, like all Gaul, of three parts. One is a stump speech about the Republican 'plot' to remove him from office and about the malevolence and dishonesty of Judge Seabury. This is irrelevant surplusage and may be ignored.

Another part is the impressive array of official precedents assembled by his lawyers to show that even if the Mayor were guilty of offenses in his first term, they would be invalid as grounds for removal in his second term. The third part, his denial of various charges, is so one-sided as to recall the story of the penitent who felt assured that his good deeds were such that the Almighty was heavily in his debt.

"No one doubts Mayor Walker's alert mind and ready grasp of affairs—when he can bring himself to give them his attention. His adroitness and lightning-like seizure of every point in his favor appear on almost every page of his reply to the Seabury charges. But it raises many questions with regard to the actual evidence, which Governor Roosevelt will have to consider carefully and judicially."

The tenor of editorial comment around the country was similarly unfavorable. The *Baltimore Sun* said that the mayor's effort to blame his troubles on partisan motives was "irrelevant." The *Richmond Times-Dispatch* branded the mayor's reply "slightly hysterical" because he tried to prove "his life was an open book." The *Buffalo Evening News* sarcastically said: "Perhaps if the Mayor's official reply fails to keep him in office, he can offer it as the season's best novel. Certainly it has all the appropriate characters, incident and plot."

Then Walker got an important lucky break. The federal government dropped nearly all of its income-tax investigations of city officials with large bank deposits, "for lack of evidence on which prosecutions could be based." The mayor's hefty "beneficences" from Paul Block were cited as an example of untaxable income, since gifts were not subject to a tax levy. Incredibly, former Sheriff Thomas Farley and others in the "tin box" brigade avoided scrutiny by the tax collector.

Reporting on the reasoning behind the government's decision, *The New York Times* said that George Medalie, U.S. attorney for the Southern District of New York, refused to comment on the action by the Internal Revenue Service. However, "other sources in the Federal building" said that the government could not find "present proof of the original source of the money." These sources said that "transfer of funds to a bank from savings accumulated earlier blocked the government from taking action" without starting grand jury proceedings. The explanation sounded deliberately vague and muddled.

In a cynical time, some New Yorkers assumed that someone high up at the IRS had been "reached." Medalie himself was a respected prosecutor with a clean reputation. After two years of legislative and judicial hearings, with thousands of pages of testimony and no "tin box" convictions of city or state officials, it is more likely that the federals simply didn't care to open this can of worms all over again.

So as F.D.R. settled into the governor's chair, the entire citywide corruption investigation had narrowed down to the trial of Jimmy Walker. People all over the United States were focused on the room where the Democratic presidential nominee challenged New York's still-beloved mayor.

During Roosevelt's presidential bid, other matters of importance were happening at home and abroad. It was a time that poet W. H. Auden labeled "a low dishonest decade" and philosopher Isaiah Berlin called "the dark and leaden 'thirties."

In that tenebrous summer of 1932, the world was spinning perilously. All over the United States, the chiffon sounds of the Jazz Age were being drowned out by the death rattle of the Depression's tin cups. Pundits said the outcome of the confrontation between Roosevelt and Walker might well determine who would be the next president. The trial's first day was the lead story in *The Times*. But the adjacent page-one articles on the same day dominated the columns even if they received less play than the Walker trial in the newspaper of record:

HITLER IS EXPECTED TO BE CHANCELLOR IN CABINET SHAKE-UP

ROME OFFICIALS WELCOME REPORT THAT ITALY MAY QUIT THE LEAGUE [OF NATIONS]

SPAIN QUELLS REVOLT
OF ARMY ROYALISTS

Three fascist dictators—Hitler, Mussolini, Franco—for the price of one paper (*The Times* then cost 2 cents). As for the authoritarian Soviet Union, Stalinism was also represented on page one:

RUSSIA TO SELL BONDS HERE;
TRADE INCREASE FORECAST,
WITH RECOGNITION NEARER

The subject of another story, one buried on an inside page of *The Times,* would change the world of energy and warfare, but hardly anyone realized its perilous significance then. It was headlined:

NOBEL PRIZE WINNER
MAKES ATOM 'TALK'

The unsigned story said that Dr. Arthur H. Compton, winner of the Nobel Prize for his work in physics, had told a rapt audience at the College of the City of New York that the tiny atom was "the ultimate unit of matter." Two thousand people watched as Dr. Compton produced, inside a tube the size of an ordinary lightbulb, a temperature equal to that of "the intense heat which rages on the surface of the sun."

The physicist concluded, "Man is high and mighty when compared to an electron but he sinks into insignificance when compared to the mighty cosmos. It takes as many atoms to make a man as it takes men to make up the sun. Chance controls the future and no one can predict what will take place in the future. . . ."

Compared to the lead story, these seemed little more than distractions. It was clear that the next president would simultaneously have to handle domestic instability and threats to American interests abroad. Was Roosevelt up to the job?

One of the European observers who sensed that Roosevelt had the required toughness was Isaiah Berlin. The British lecturer-diplomat wrote that, compared to Stalin, Hitler, Mussolini and Franco, F.D.R. had "all the character and energy and skill of the dictators, but he was on *our* side."

John Gunther, who came out of the tough Chicago school of journalism, had covered the American political landscape for many years. As a journalist and author, he was trusted and famous all over the country. Gunther saw the Roosevelt-Walker hearings as a contest between two vastly different heritages, personalities, and ways of life. He pointed out that Walker was a Catholic, a Tammany stalwart, an Al Smith devotee, and "a character who was full of the most fetching idiosyncrasies." In all fairness, he wondered if Jimmy Walker was plainly corrupt or simply "a gay dog having a wonderful fling."

The difference between the two antagonists amounted to the difference between two visions of responsible governance. One represented the spoils-system past, the other the social-minded vision of a New Deal for Americans.

Gunther pointed out that Roosevelt, an Episcopalian, bore a famous name as the fifth cousin of President Theodore Roosevelt. He was a blueblood who had gone to Groton and Harvard and to Columbia Law School, had become a New York state senator, served as assistant secretary of the Navy, and represented the Navy Department at the Versailles Peace Conference after World War I. After being struck down by infantile paralysis, polio, at the age of thirty-nine, he remained an invalid for the rest of his life. Gunther noted that Roosevelt conquered his physical tragedy by "a triumph of pure grit, the conquest of flesh by will and spirit."

Nevertheless, the standard-brand Walker supporters in New York City and in the state legislature did not think they had much to fear from Roosevelt's abilities as a jurist examining their man's financial affairs. They regarded Roosevelt as little more than a Hudson River Valley patrician. But they underestimated his record in Albany and what he stood for.

As a Democratic governor in a Republican-dominated legislature, Roosevelt had sponsored laws for the improvement of labor conditions, for old-age pensions, farm relief, and public works to employ the hungry and the poor. He had established the Temporary Emergency Relief Administration to assist the jobless and needy, making New York the first state to grant unemployment insurance. His state administration became the proving ground for the future National Recovery Act.

"Roosevelt found himself in a trying predicament," Gunther, a friend of both Eleanor and Franklin, declared. "Either he had to turn a blind eye to what was being revealed, or throw Walker out. To choose the latter course meant that he would mortally affront Tammany and prejudice his political power in the indispensable key stronghold of Manhattan. Tammany ran New York City; but Democrats elsewhere in the nation, particularly the dry South, hated Tammany.

"Many conservative Democrats had become bitterly anti-Roosevelt by this time and, along with the Republicans, they sought to smear him with the Walker mud. Roosevelt did not dislike Walker personally, and Walker has blamed himself for his churlish behavior to the Governor. In any case, this was one of the most ticklish tests F.D.R. ever had to face."

On the eve of the Albany hearings, suddenly the mood of the depressed country was diverted by another gloomy event: a clash between World War I veterans and the Hoover administration in Washington. The House of Representatives had approved an immediate $500 payment, in certificates or cash, to each of the 3.5 million ex-soldiers, -sailors, and -marines. But President Hoover threatened a veto, saying, "The urgent question today is the prompt balancing of the budget." The Senate refused to act.

Nearly ten thousand unemployed men—they came from Brooklyn and Atlanta, from Denver and San Francisco, from Tampa and Dallas and farms and towns in between—rode the rails, hitchhiked, and marched on Washington. They set up tents and soup kitchens in the open air off Pennsylvania Avenue and along the banks of the Potomac, within sight of the Capitol and the White House, demanding an immediate bonus for their service. To have fought in the war and returned home, only to see their wives and children near starvation during the Depression, was too much. The ragtag ex-soldiers became known as the Bonus Army, but they preferred to be called the Bonus Expeditionary Force, in a play on the American Expeditionary Force that had fought the Huns in the trenches of France.

In a communiqué addressed to their countrymen as much as to Congress, the BEF explained: "The crux of our fight for payment of adjusted service certificates may be summarized in a few words. We feel that the American veterans who offered their lives for their country are due the same consideration as the bankers and railroad owners whose property was protected during the late war. Through the Reconstruction Finance Corporation, this class has received billions of dollars of federal aid. All we ask is payment of a just debt."

The conservative American Legion denounced the bonus encampment, declaring that the veterans were inspired by Communists, a sentiment echoed and exaggerated in Washington by General Douglas A. MacArthur, the Army chief of staff. Responding to President Hoover's plan to call out the Army and remove the veterans, Congressman Fiorello La Guardia, a World War I major, sent an open telegram to Hoover: "Soup is cheaper than tear bombs and bread better than bullets in maintaining law and order in these times of Depression, unemployment and hunger."

President Hoover was not heartless; he ordered the Army to provide the veterans with tents, food and medicine. But General MacArthur, resplendent in full regalia as though directing a major military operation against a foreign enemy, waved his swagger stick and ordered his troops to lay down a gas barrage against the bedraggled veterans and burn down their tents. In doing so, he defied Hoover's explicit orders not to cross the Eleventh Street Bridge and attack the main Anacostia camp. The country shuddered at the sight of tanks, cavalrymen, and infantrymen with drawn bayonets moving against the unarmed veterans on Pennsylvania Avenue. The attack against his own countrymen was not the egotistical MacArthur's finest hour. (In a future war, a president with more spine, Harry S. Truman, was to fire him as commander in Korea for arrogance and exceeding his authority.) MacArthur's aide Major Dwight D. Eisenhower suggested to his boss that the action against the veterans was inappropiate, but was ordered to get into full dress uniform and join him.

After the veterans were routed, Governor Roosevelt concluded that General MacArthur and Huey Long, the demagogic Louisiana governor who resigned in 1932 to become a U.S. senator, were the two most dangerous men in America. Roosevelt was on record as advocating a state bonus for the World War veterans because relief was a matter of entitlement. "The time for platitudes is past," Roosevelt said. "The bonus money must be appropriated immediately."

The hearings in Albany were to last three weeks, until September 1, 1932. Thirty-four witnesses testified. Only Jimmy Walker really mattered.

"I wish to say one thing before leaving for Albany," said Walker. "I go with a clear conscience. Not one of the complaints contains the statement of any person that I have ever been false to the trust which the people bestowed upon me in two elections by overwhelming majorities. Those who are trying to bear false witness against me cannot prevail against the people of the City of New York. This is not the case of the joint legislative committee against James J. Walker. It is the case of disappointed but ambitious politicians who are trying to defeat the expressed will of the voters by the use of ouster proceedings instead of ballots."

A trial balloon was floated by the Walker camp: if he was removed by Governor Roosevelt, he himself would run for governor, with Tammany support. All the politicos knew that Roosevelt was supporting Herbert H. Lehman, his lieutenant Governor, to replace him, and that Tammany support was essential in New York City.

Another political move developed in the press to support the besieged mayor. The day before the hearings began, Walker was pleased to read an editorial in William Randolph Hearst's *New York American*. It was signed by "The Chief" himself. Hearst wrote that the removal of the mayor would be a violation of the home-rule principle and that New York City voters could very well decide at next year's election whether or not Mayor Walker should be retained in office.

There was a nuance here to be read between the lines. Hearst had contributed to Governor Roosevelt's nomination for president by helping to swing the ninety votes of California and Texas to him, after which Speaker Jack Garner was nominated for vice president. He now had influence with Roosevelt and was calling in one of his chips. Hearst felt that his own position in New York, where several of his newspapers and prosperous magazines were based, would be strengthened if he bridged the Democratic party's split and thus enhanced his role as a backroom political peacemaker.

At Grand Central Terminal, five thousand people showed up to see the mayor off and wish him well. A few scattered boos were mixed with the cheers. Fifty policemen cleared a path to Track 34, where a private car had been attached to the Ohio State Limited, departing at 4:05 P.M. for Albany and points west. With the mayor were his lawyers, John J. Curtin and John J. Glynn, and his City Hall aides. Curtin was the senior partner in the firm with Glynn, who was Al Smith's nephew.

Allie Walker, carrying her white poodle, Togo, arrived with her husband in his official limousine. They alighted on the Vanderbilt Avenue side of the station, where a crowd was collecting on the upper-level concourse.

"Atta boy, Jimmy!" "Get in there and fight!" "Give it to 'em, Mayor!" "Good luck, Jimmy!" As each wave of enthusiasm died down, an undertone of boos and hisses became audible, to be drowned out immediately by another surge of cheering. Time and again, Walker halted to pose for pictures and quick interviews by friendly reporters on the tabloids. His outfit did not disappoint; he was dressed in a gray business suit with matching gray shirt, tie, and collar. He carried a sailor-type straw hat, which he waved to the crowds.

Among the many persons who shook his hand while he waited for the train to pull out, five minutes late, was Joe Jacobs, the suspended manager of the German heavyweight Max Schmeling. Schmeling had lost the title to Jack Sharkey, on a close decision. After Jacobs wished him good luck, Walker replied:

"Thanks, Joe. I hope they don't hand me down the same kind of a decision you got."

Although they were no longer living together, Mrs. Walker decided to accompany her husband to Albany, to make it appear that they were reconciled. Nobody was fooled. He still lived in the suite at the Mayfair Hotel; she resided in the Walker house on St. Luke's Place. To the boys at Lindy's and the other hangouts where the Broadway crowd knew the score, it seemed like hypocrisy for the mayor to use Allie to gain sympathy for his plight. But the public admired her courage and devotion. Betty Compton was deliberately kept out of sight.

"I would rather be here beside my husband than sit at home and not know right away what was going on," Allie Walker said. "You know I feel that the Seabury investigation was very unfair and unjust to the Mayor. My name was mentioned in the testimony and I would have been glad to testify if I had been called. But I was never called. I will be at the hearing tomorrow, right beside my husband."

When the Walker party reached the Albany station at 6:45 P.M., it was met by the blare of a brass band and the boom of aerial bombs touched off in his honor. A crowd of about five hundred had turned out on orders of the Democratic overlords of Albany. Mayor Walker was driven to his headquarters at the Hotel Ten Eyck, where he clasped his hands overhead in a prizefighter's victory sign.

"I have no fear of removal," Walker told reporters. "I am prepared to meet any charge. I want to hear the testimony—the sworn evidence—which will give me an opportunity to cross-examine. If the kidnappers of the Lindbergh baby were to be discovered tomorrow they would receive a trial. They would have the opportunity to hear their accusers and to cross-examine. There is certainly no charge against me that is worse than kidnapping."

The mayor was clearly preparing the groundwork for a loud protest or a judicial appeal even before the hearings. He and his lawyers were aware that this was an investigation, not a courtroom proceeding, and that a different set of rules applied. In fact, the summons calling Mayor Walker before Governor Roosevelt on removal charges was the first of its kind ever served upon an incumbent of City Hall in New York State. A previous effort to remove Mayor Robert A. Van Wyck (because of a monopolistic city ice-supply trust in which Van Wyck and other Tammany cronies held stock) was dismissed without a hearing in 1899 by another Governor Roosevelt: Theodore.

By contrast to the cheers and bands rolled out for Jimmy Walker, Judge Seabury and his staff went quietly to Albany by automobile. He left his home at 154 East Sixty-third Street at 7:45 P.M., driven in the Lincoln by Nick Livingston, his longtime chauffeur. With him were Maud Seabury and two of his close aides, George Trosk and Louis Molloy. Long afterward, Trosk recalled that Seabury and Maud held hands during most of the trip.

Seabury's aides Phil Haberman, Harold Melniker, and Oren Herwitz piled into Bill Mulligan's Marmon for the trip north, loaded down with briefcases full of testimony and records. On Route 9W, not far from Roosevelt's Hyde Park home, a state trooper pulled them over. He looked suspiciously at the bundles blocking the back window and poked them to see if they were a cover for some illicit operation. Prohibition still existed. When they identified themselves and explained their mission, the trooper waved them on.

Actually, Seabury and his team were on their own. The state legislature was not compensating them; the young lawyers were contributing their services as private citizens. Judge Seabury picked up their expenses at the De Witt Clinton Hotel. He was never reimbursed by the state.

When they arrived in Albany that evening, Judge Seabury was informed that Jimmy Walker had received a great welcome. As he had done earlier, after the hearings in the New York County courthouse, Seabury dryly observed, "So did Tweed."

The Hofstadter committee had stepped aside, too divided along Democratic and Republican lines to take action against Walker. Here might have been another out for Roosevelt—if he wanted one. If the legislature was not opposed to Walker, why should he take the extra-ordinary step of interfering in city affairs? But Roosevelt pressed on. Actually, it was too late for him to take any other course. The national press was watching every move and recording every remark by the New York governor who was the Democratic candidate for President. Election day was only a few months away.

The responsibility for the investigation's rules and decisions—including the avoidance of pitfalls for F.D.R. in the unfamiliar role as a presiding judge, a role he was assuming for the first time in his life—had now shifted from Judge Seabury to Governor Roosevelt.

ELEVEN

F. D. R., Esq.— Judge and Jury

Governor Roosevelt immediately took command of his "courtroom"—much to the surprise of Walter Lippmann of the *Herald Tribune,* who, with his usual hauteur, wrote: "I continue to believe that the problem before Governer Roosevelt is that he must not only do justice as a judge but he must convince the people as a leader that justice has been done."

From the start, F. D. R. appeared judicious, yet firmly in control. To do so was a matter of professional pride even more than of politics. He had never made a great mark as a lawyer in private practice; now he was being challenged to show his abilities as a member of the bar in a new, untried role.

Perhaps to offset the punditocracy, which wrote from perches in Washington and New York, delivering its opinions at a distance without seeing him conduct the "trial" at the scene, Roosevelt had made an unusual request to the newspaper reporters: Your stories should carry an Albany dateline. The working press willingly complied.

The governor had been doing his homework for the past few weeks, preparing himself for the encounter by studying the record and transcripts with his counsel, Maldwin Fertig and Martin Conboy, and, behind the scenes, Samuel Rosenman. Fertig was Roosevelt's regular counsel. Conboy was added to the governor's staff especially for the trial; the fact that he was a prominent Catholic warded off any possible accusation of anti-Catholic bias. He stayed at the Governor's Mansion and briefed Roosevelt each night before the next morning's hearing.

The windy and combative John J. Curtin, Walker's lawyer, immediately acted as if he were appearing in front of a jury. He used an old criminal lawyer's familiar courtroom maneuver—shifting the bad-fellow image to himself and away from his client—because he was so outraged by the injustice. As an experienced litigator, he played not only to the court but to the "gallery"—the dozens of newspapermen in the chamber. His opening statement set the tone:

"I welcome at this time a hearing upon all the charges that have been submitted. Let us throw away the law books. Let's forget there ever was a written law in the statutes or in the decisions, and let's tackle this from a human, fair-minded standpoint. What is this thing we are doing here? What is it all about? My first proposal is to demonstrate to you that it is a matter of common fair play, and that idea of fair play should be backed up by decisions, and, if you please, because law is only a matter of common sense, after all."

Whereupon Curtin went into the familiar song-and-dance that Jimmy Walker had established as his main routine while tripping the light fantastic: the mayor of the City of New York led the largest municipality in the world. . . . He was the people's choice. . . . He had been elected twice to that office by an enormous plurality. . . . He was the man who for twenty-odd years, including in the state legislature, had submitted himself for approval to the voters successfully.

Roosevelt and Curtin quickly began to spar with each other about legal evidence and procedures. Curtin's main argument finally emerged as a request to be able to cross-examine every single witness that Seabury had questioned.

ROOSEVELT [consulting his notes]: As Governor, I wish to make it clear to the Mayor and to his counsel that if, in their judgment, the defense requires that any person who is available as a witness, whether he did or did not testify before the legislative committee, should be called before the Governor for examination, and the Mayor's counsel will give me the name or names of such witness or witnesses, together with a statement

showing the purpose for which the testimony is desired, I shall, upon due
consideration, require the attendance of such witnesses before me—and,
of course, a similar opportunity will be accorded to those who are pre-
senting the charges, which are the subject of this hearing.

While at first glance the governor's ruling seemed to be a victory
for Walker, it was nothing of the sort, and the Mayor and his counsel
knew it. Speaking carefully, Roosevelt said only that the mayor could
submit to him names of witnesses who might help him in his defense.
What Walker and Curtin wanted was to have the governor direct
Judge Seabury to recall all the witnesses who had testified against
him. But Governor Roosevelt had no intention of allowing Mayor
Walker's counsel to reexamine more than a hundred witnesses.

"I can be cross-examined but I can't cross-examine," the mayor
grumbled.

There was an obvious reason behind the open antagonism between Roosevelt and Curtin: Roosevelt had defeated Curtin's good
friend Al Smith at the Democratic convention in Chicago. When
Smith was governor, Curtin had been his legal adviser. Furthermore, Curtin looked upon the hearings as an opportunity to express
his dislike for Seabury, who had defaced the mottled image of Tammany for nearly two years and forced some of its thieving officehold-
ers to resign.

Soon enough, both Roosevelt and Curtin took off their gloves and
dropped the polite "Your Excellency" and "Counsel" talk. Walker, who
knew Roosevelt's temperament, had warned his lawyer in advance not
to get "Frank's Dutch up." Curtin ignored the advice.

At one point, Judge Seabury was called upon to read a letter giving
certain details about Walker's secret accounts, in which the mayor deposited large sums that he received from a friend who hoped to sell
his services to the City of New York. The questioning became a test of
the governor's judicial knowledge and pride.

CURTIN: One minute, I would like to know if that paper is in evidence that
Judge Seabury is going to read.

SEABURY: It is not in evidence.

CURTIN: Well, then, it cannot be used, I am sure of that. I don't know what it says but it can't be used.

ROOSEVELT: It can be marked for identification.

SEABURY: Yes, for identification.

CURTIN: Let someone say that they know something about it, through his own knowledge, and testify about it under oath.

ROOSEVELT: Mr. Curtin, I happen to be a lawyer, and remarks of that kind are wholly unnecessary to the Governor of this State.

CURTIN: I assume you do know that. Still, when a lawyer makes a statement as to what the—

ROOSEVELT: All right, don't try to instruct me about the difference between putting a thing into evidence and marking it for identification.

CURTIN: I am here to protect the rights of my client to the best of my ability, and that only.

The next day, news reports said that Curtin's face "flushed with color" when the governor put him down.

Curtin was not totally on his own. Walker was clearly guiding his lawyer's objections. In a voice that carried to the press tables, but did not appear in the official record, Walker said to Curtin, "If you waive the technical objections on one thing, you'll have to waive on something else."

Swaying back and forth in his chair, with his eyeglasses in one hand and their case in the other, the mayor parried the governor's searching questions. Occasionally, he glanced angrily toward the table where Seabury and his assistants consulted their records and busily took notes.

Every document mentioned in the "conclusions" against Walker was challenged by Curtin. He pointed his finger at Judge Seabury's staff and demanded to see what he called their "work sheets." Curtin said that "these gentlemen have been on the State payroll for months" and should be able to produce the papers for him. Seabury replied that he had given Curtin photostastic copies of every document in his possession relating to Walker's hidden banking accounts.

Roosevelt interrupted Curtin's demands. "I am a little fed up, talking about 'work sheets.' You don't need a work sheet. A bank statement is a bank statement. You have deposits, and withdrawals. Let us
stick to that."

Seabury and Trosk were permitted to read from the transcripts of
their own legislative hearings. As evidence or "marked for identification," most of the paper trail underlying the main charges was admitted into the governor's hearing.

"Perhaps you are right in not calling this law," Roosevelt said to
Curtin and Walker, "but you would also be right in calling it *my public
policy* in this state."

Again and again, Curtin interrupted Roosevelt with objections to
the admission of evidence, but he scored few points. Roosevelt, under
no compulsion to provide due process, nonetheless consistently won
the approval of the dozens of reporters in attendance. One amusing exchange between Roosevelt and Curtin involved knowledge not only of
the law but of the apocryphal thirteenth chapter of the Book of Daniel.

CURTIN: I dislike in some ways to refer to this, but perhaps it won't be
amiss. The earliest recorded—so far as I know—instance of the value of
cross-examination is contained in the Bible itself. You may recall one of the
Apocryphal books, the story of Susanna and the Elders; Susanna, a beautiful lady, and two of the Elders, enamored of her. She repulsed them,
whereupon, to get square, they accused her of impropriety with some
other third person. And these Elders were men of good standing in that
community, and they swore definitely before the counsel that this lady
committed this impropriety, and there was nobody to gainsay that, except
the lady herself, who met it with tears and denial. There is nothing dramatic about a denial. And she was condemned to death, under the laws of
Moses. And then Daniel arose and said, "Not so fast"—I am not quoting
accurately—"Not so fast. Let me examine these Elders." And he put them
both out, then brought in one of them and said, "You are sure this thing
happened?" "Yes." "Did you see this thing happen?" He said, "Yes, and I
am sure of it." "Where did it happen?" "Under the mastic tree." He was
sent away. And the other fellow was brought in. "You are sure this thing
happened?" "Yes." "You saw it with your own eyes?" "Yes, and I couldn't be

mistaken." "Where did it happen?" "It happened under the yew tree." Whereupon the committee put to death not Susanna but her accusers. I am talking thus bluntly to you as one lawyer to another.

ROOSEVELT: You have referred to the testimony before the legislative committee as "minutes." I consider it evidence. You have referred also to the interesting case of Susanna and the Elders. I think it is a very apt case. *You* are in the position of the Prophet Daniel. I will *not* say that His Honor is in the position of Susanna.

CURTIN: That isn't so.

WALKER: I certainly feel like it.

Everybody in the chamber broke out in laughter, including Seabury and his aides. The next morning the newspapers played the exchange as a small victory for Roosevelt. Curtin's biblical analogy had boomeranged on him and his client.

(The biblical tale of Susanna and the Elders is found in chapter 13 of the Book of Daniel in early versions of the Old Testament. Nowadays it appears in the Douay translation of the Latin Vulgate, but not in the King James version of the Bible. The biblical tale concludes: "And Daniel became great in the sight of the people from that day and thenceforward.")

Later, when the New Testament was referred to, Walker wisecracked, "This fellow Seabury would convict the Twelve Apostles if he could."

Governor Roosevelt soon discovered that Walker planned to continue what he had done with Seabury: address himself to the crowd instead of to the issues. Speaking directly to Roosevelt from the witness stand, Walker said:

"Now I must have my twenty-three years in public office snuffed out without an opportunity of looking into the faces of the men who would tear up my past, present and future. I can't be unlike every other human being in the world. I can't be so different than the rest of the human family."

And he dragged out the same red herring he had delivered when he was cross-examined in Manhattan:

"I haven't been transported back to Russia. I haven't been taken into other kingdoms and empires in Dark Ages and never to return again."

At another point, Walker openly spoke with bitterness to "Judge" Roosevelt about Seabury:

"Maybe I am wrong, maybe countless others are wrong, but there was a disposition to railroad me. Maybe, after all, they would like to have the comfort, the conscientious relief, maybe they would like to have the moral satisfaction of bringing to you and pouring into your own ear the testimony upon which they relied, which I never heard, which you never heard, and which was adduced in an ex parte proceeding."

In response, Governor Roosevelt patiently said, "It is to give you a square deal, Mayor, that I am going to ask the questions."

During this time, Allie Walker, smartly dressed in a brown silk ensemble with an enormous orchid corsage, watched her estranged husband being interrogated. She nodded with approval as he delivered his heartfelt speeches from the witness chair. Onlookers noticed that while sitting in her reserved seat, beneath a portrait of Governor Grover Cleveland, the diminutive Mrs. Walker continually adjusted her felt hat with bejeweled fingers. After the first day's hearing, she complained of fatigue and retired to the Walker suite at the Hotel Ten Eyck.

Following up the mayor's earlier testimony before the Hofstadter committee, Governor Roosevelt began to untangle several complex deals with businessmen seeking city franchises, deals in which the mayor had received a piece of the action. He pressed Walker to explain how he obtained $26,500 in bonds from J. A. Sisto, a financier and taxicab promoter. At a meeting in Atlantic City, the mayor had been "declared in" on a "pool" of Cosden Oil stock; its bonds were said to represent his "profit."

At first, the mayor denied that he knew until he received the "profit" money months later that there was any link between a taxicab deal and his bonds. He claimed he had no knowledge of the nature of Sisto's business, and that he had no idea he would be in a position to help Sisto bid for city contracts. A moment later Walker corrected himself, saying that he had known from the beginning that Sisto was the "operator" and banker of the money pool. He added that he had turned the securities over to Mrs. Walker.

An echo of the crash of the Bank of the United States was heard during the hearing. Governor Roosevelt tried to track some of the monies that had been given to Walker without any investment or responsibility for losses on his part. Referring to the Interstate Trust Company stock that was part of the Equitable Coach franchise deal— the deal for which the Mayor's indirect payoff was that $10,000 letter of credit—Governor Roosevelt asked him if he did not realize that the stock was valuable because it was oversubscribed.

"If it turns out to be a good thing," Walker replied, "I suppose the conclusion would be yes, but isn't that said by every promoter who sells a stock or promotes a stock? Is my standing and status as Mayor of the City of New York dependent upon my knowledge, my speculation or my reasoning or thinking of stock operations or whether they are valuable or not? Why, if that was so, and I was so completely familiar with the value of banks and condition of banks, I suppose I should have insisted on the City of New York withdrawing a million and a half dollars from the Bank of United States before it failed. But I can't be blamed for that, surely."

In an effort to link Roosevelt to big money interests, Walker subjected the Governor to what struck some listeners as an insulting remark: "Now, I won't argue finances with Your Excellency, *especially* Wall Street financing, but I don't know that that necessarily follows, because people fall all over themselves to buy something. That has been done with gold bricks for time out of mind."

The steady emergence of Roosevelt as the star of the hearing was echoed in the mainstream press. At the end of the initial testimony by Jimmy Walker, *The New York Times* editorialized:

"There is nothing but admiration, so far, for Governor Roosevelt's bearing in the Walker case at Albany. He has been firm but impartial, anxious to dispatch the business before him, and putting questions which show how closely and deeply he has studied the evidence laid before him with the charges. But what can be said of the methods of the defense? The Mayor himself has behaved well enough, but his counsel have been fighting on every technicality which they could conjure up, and threatening to carry the case to the Court of Appeals if it goes against them after the hearing.

"Every unbiased reader of the record made at Albany will infer that the tactics of the defense could come only from those who feel that their case is bad and that they must contest the law and the evidence at every point. Perhaps a little reflection over the weekend will induce the Mayor's lawyers to adopt a more reasonable course, and one less self-betraying, when the hearing is resumed."

As the hearings continued in the following days, the exchanges between Roosevelt and Walker's lawyer became more heated. It was clear that Curtin was getting Roosevelt's "Dutch" up by lecturing him about the law. In doing so, he was attempting to divert attention from the evidence amassed by Seabury and his sleuths.

The rancor and sarcasm between Curtin and Roosevelt don't appear in the mimeographed transcript, but press reports show that they were always present in the chamber. At one point, Roosevelt told Curtin, "Don't talk anymore. Proceed with the examination."

Curtin raised objections to the issuance of "request" subpoenas to witnesses and the admissibility of those witnesses' evidence.

ROOSEVELT: In other words, you are raising a technical objection.

CURTIN: No, it is not; and I haven't done that up to date.

ROOSEVELT: You have done it now; you have done it fifty times before.

CURTIN: I have not, and—

ROOSEVELT: It is dilatory tactics.

CURTIN: I beg your pardon; I disagree.

In an effort to make a record for an appeal about the way Governor Roosevelt was conducting the hearing, Curtin condemned the entire proceeding as unconstitutional. Occasionally, Roosevelt consulted his counsel, Messrs. Fertig and Conboy, who sat on either side of him, but he delivered the decisions of his "court" himself.

ROOSEVELT [to Curtin]: Counsel, I want to make just one comment, and that is I cannot agree in any shape, manner or form with the suggestion that this hearing is being conducted in any way differently from what hearings have been conducted by a long line of Governors for many decades. The historical record does not accord with the statement which you have made. This hearing is in line, so far as I have been able to find out, with all the proceedings of the past. Therefore, it is not exactly fair or right to give the impression that I am conducting this hearing in any way or manner different from any other hearing. Now, I don't think we need to argue this question further.

CURTIN: I realize you have the right to cross-examine any witness I bring on—

ROOSEVELT: I don't think I care to hear anything more along that line, counsel. This is a hearing by the Governor, and I will examine any witnesses that I want to, and I give you the privilege of examining any witnesses that you want to, and I shall cross-examine any witnesses that you bring on, as I want to. Now, I don't think we need clutter the record any more. Every ten or fifteen minutes you bring up the same point simply to create atmosphere, and I don't care to hear anything further along that line during the present course of this inquiry. I want that perfectly clearly understood by you."

CURTIN: As long as my position is clearly understood, I don't care.

ROOSEVELT: Right, and I shall have to insist that that shall not continue to go into the record. You have made your objection on the record about a half-dozen times along the same line. We will consider it made for the balance of this hearing, without making it again.

The Sherwood mystery remained. One of the charges against Walker was that "for the purposes of concealment he conducted his financial transactions through and in the name of Russell T. Sherwood," who had avoided questioning by leaving the jurisdiction and hiding in Mexico.

Walker could not explain how a $10,000-a-year accountant had accumulated nearly a million dollars in five and a half years. It was rumored that the mayor's putative agent, now missing almost a year, now would return in time to testify for the mayor.

"Ridiculous," Walker commented.

Of course, the governor wanted the mayor to explain the sources of the money in the Walker-Sherwood "tin box."

ROOSEVELT: Now, in regard to the safe-deposit box which was jointly in the name of Sherwood and yourself, do you know whether Sherwood had joint-name boxes with other members of your law firm?

WALKER: I do not. My name was added to that box or, rather, I had access to the box at that time, because of certain papers that I wanted to put in the box that were taken out, and I never was in the safe-deposit vault, never in the bank, never really knew where it was, never used it, directly or indirectly.

ROOSEVELT: Did you know after the removal of papers from that box that it was continued in your name?

WALKER: I did not. I don't know except whatever privilege I had in the beginning, I never paid for it, for instance. I had the right of access to it, in 1924, and I don't know that it was ever changed, and it never developed that I knew of it until the investigation opened. Certainly, then, I didn't go down and say, "Take my name off," in the middle of an investigation.

ROOSEVELT: Isn't it a curious thing for you, when a man with whom you had a safe-deposit box, and who looked after your personal affairs, disappears, and the whole town is looking for him, and he briefly turns up, not to communicate with him?

WALKER: There wasn't any opportunity to communicate with him that I know of after he was served with a subpoena, and I had no reason to believe he would disobey the subpoena.

ROOSEVELT: I wish he were here today.

WALKER: So do I wish he were here, and if there was any way for me to find him, he would be here.

Mayor Walker said he was willing to discuss the charges before the governor providing they were presented "innocently and unintentionally, if Your Excellency pleases." By contrast, Walker claimed, the Seabury investigation was conducted "by inferences, upon inferences, upon inferences."

In response to questions by Governor Roosevelt about why he awarded franchises to certain companies without necessarily accepting the lowest bid or any competitive bid at all, Mayor Walker advanced a rather ingenious theory about the independence of what he called "the executive mind." This is how Walker rationalized his solo decision-making power:

"I submit to Your Excellency that this cross-examination of the executive mind certainly has no foundation in law, any more than I have got a right to cross-examine *you* here about why you have arrived at decisions you made today. Mine was an executive administrative act for which I am responsible to the people, and I am going to waive it, and I am going to answer it, but I want to here give a close-up on the character and the aspect of the investigation we have had, which would not be obtained or permitted any other place. There are some prerogatives that an executive has, and his reasons for making up his mind."

Walker had a little more trouble when confronted with a document which showed his signature on a check that he used while junketing around Europe in 1927. The governor pointed out that the check read: "Pay to the order of the Equitable Trust Company of New York, $3,000; value received and charge the same to the account of James J. Walker."

In other words, Roosevelt pointed out, the check was drawn on a bank in which Walker didn't have an account, meaning someone else would make it good.

With two young women tossing roses in his path and Joe Quintano's eight-piece brass band playing "Hail, Hail, the Gang's All Here,"

Jimmy Walker returned to Grand Central Terminal at eight o'clock one evening, on a special train, after the first few days on the witness stand in Albany. Governor Roosevelt and Judge Seabury returned to their homes in Hyde Park and East Hampton.

Questioned by reporters about who had ordered them to greet Jimmy Walker triumphantly at Grand Central, the bandsmen claimed to be "friends of the Mayor," rather than musicians hired for the occasion. Quintano said that "someone," name unknown, had suggested that it would be nice if his band showed up to cheer the mayor. The flower baskets and flower girls were supplied by Peter Cappel, who was head of the New York Jewelers Exchange as well as the owner of a real estate company.

Five thousand people turned out to hear the band and greet Walker at the station as he emerged from the train with his lawyers, office assistants, and bodyguard, police captain Thomas O'Connor. A gray-haired woman, eluding fifty uniformed policemen, five sergeants, a captain, and an inspector, broke through the lines, flung her arms around the mayor, and kissed him three times. He was, as usual, carefully dressed for the crowds. Walker brushed off his single-breasted lightweight blue suit and black-and-gray-striped tie, waved his jaunty straw hat, and entered his waiting limousine.

The mayor spent the weekend resting at the Larchmont estate of A. C. "Blumey" Blumenthal, a California real estate operator, former movie magnate, and theatrical investor. Blumey, a social climber and celebrity chaser, used his palship with Walker to impress bankers and financiers. Walker often visited Blumey in his suite at the Ambassador Hotel in Manhattan, where the mayor performed marriage ceremonies for show-business personalities.

The atmosphere in Larchmont was relaxing. Blumenthal was married to Peggy Fears, a former Ziegfeld showgirl; their palatial home was usually papered with beautiful chorines, who lounged around the swimming pool, and name personalities who appeared between the dot-dot-dot items in gossip columns.

Blumenthal confirmed that he was ready to offer his friend Jimmy Walker a $100,000-a-year job should he be removed from office. "No, not in the movies," Blumenthal said. "The trouble with that figure of $100,000 is that I believe the Mayor could easily earn $500,000 a year if he returned to the practice of law. The man is brilliant. I don't know an attorney who can equal his oratory."

That skill could do little for him back in Albany. Returning for further grilling by Governor Roosevelt, Walker was closely questioned about the $246,000 he had received from the secret brokerage account set up for him by Paul Block, the publisher. (In Depression-era dollars, this was a fortune—close to ten times more than the mayor's $25,000 annual salary, before it was raised to $40,000.) A headline in *The New York Times,* above an article datelined Albany, explained:

WALKER SAYS HE USED WORD 'BENEFICENCE' WRONGLY; OBJECTS TO BEING PUT ON TRIAL FOR HIS ENGLISH

But there was far more to the story than the mayor's vocabulary. It involved a secret brokerage account, cash transactions, and influence peddling over a contract for subway tiles—the most incredible tale heard during the hearings.

Said Roosevelt, "The testimony is fairly clear that the Mayor received nearly $250,000 from Paul Block, less deductions for income taxes, up to the time of the closing of this account in August 1929. And, again, I think probably the easiest way would be to have you, Mr. Mayor, tell us the story about that account, its inception, and in general what was the result of it?"

Walker replied, "Well, that seems to be more important just at this time, if Your Excellency please. There is a cruel reference—Mr. Block's attitude—in the conclusions propounded by Mr. Seabury. When I used the word *'beneficent'* I didn't think I would be on trial for my selection of English. If I had been years ago I probably would have been convicted, as most men who speak that language. Evidently the word *beneficence* has been subjected by a very keen mind, with very subtle reasoning—coupled again with inference and innuendo.

"Now, Mr. Block never was interested, so far as I know, in any tile that was ever manufactured or sold to the City of New York. More than that, Mr. Block never attempted for himself, or on behalf of anyone else, to sell tile or anything else to the City of New York. That's a fact. So that the question becomes difficult to me—while that inference remains. It was gratuitous, and not predicated upon any testimony."

But under polite but steady prodding by Roosevelt, Mayor Walker admitted that he had actually visited the Beyer Tile Company plant with Paul Block, and there met Dr. Robert S. Beyer, a chemist. Walker's close friend State Senator Hastings was already on the tile company premises when the mayor and Block showed up; Hastings was arranging for approval of the tile by the city's Board of Transportation. The tile deal fell through, but it was discovered that Block, Hastings, and Beyer were the main stockholders in the company.

In an attempt to wiggle out of the original impression that he had meant to convey during the legislative hearings in Manhattan—that Block had given him financial aid and comfort out of the goodness of his heart—Jimmy Walker now put a new spin on the word, blaming himself rather than any dictionary for his grammatical slipup.

WALKER: Now, my word *'beneficence'* has all the shortcoming of a man who doesn't choose the proper word at the proper time. By *beneficence,* I meant good nature in managing this account—using his best judgment, with the judgment that followed. That is what I mean by the word *'beneficence'*—Block managed it, he handled it.

Regardless of what the account was called, Walker asserted, "There wasn't a dollar of a taxpayer's money in it."

The fact remained that Block was a shareholder in the tile company, and the Beyer Tile Company *was* hoping for a major contract with the city. About the money, Walker stubbornly maintained that "it had nothing to do with James J. Walker, the official, or with any official acts throughout his life. It was a private transaction between friends, which it seems difficult to have to argue about, that there is such a thing as friendship without an ulterior motive."

Roosevelt simply observed, "It's the most extraordinary business proposition I ever heard of."

Following the Seabury script, Governor Roosevelt now began to question Mayor Walker about his brother, Dr. William H. Walker, who served as medical examiner to the Department of Education and the City Pension Retirement Fund. Dr. Walker made a fortune splitting fees with a small group of doctors who monopolized the city's workmen's compensation cases. He received a kickback of one-half the fee, to the very cent, of every case the doctors handled.

At first, the mayor denied any knowledge of his brother's business. Then he added, "I don't know of itself that fee splitting is wrong. I have done it. I don't know if Your Excellency has done it in your law practice or not, but most lawyers have."

Governor Roosevelt's tone of voice changed; he did not appreciate the comparison of his old law practice to the practices of either of the Walker brothers.

ROOSEVELT: Wait a minute, do you consider that fee-splitting is a proper, ethical *medical* practice?

WALKER: If the city was not defrauded, I don't see anything unethical about that. I can't sit here and indict somebody of a crime when I have no knowledge of the commission of it.

ROOSEVELT: All right, I will put it in the form of a hypothetical question: Do you consider it to the interest of the City of New York to have doctors who are paid sums for specific compensation cases, pay a half of those sums to other doctors who have not treated in those cases?

CURTIN: Just a minute—

WALKER: I want to answer that. I wouldn't consider it ethical for any employe of the city—doctor, lawyer or otherwise—to give away any of his salary to anybody for any sinister or any illegal purpose. But I know of no law, no rule, or no ethics that permits the city to say to a man, when they pay for services rendered, what he shall do with his money.

To the end, Walker defended the Tammany system and insisted that money changed hands in the course of personal favors among friends, never as a quid pro quo.

After the mayor had been on the stand for more than a week, Governor Roosevelt invited Curtin to produce any witnesses.

"Not at this time," Walker's counsel said.

The same invitation was made to Judge Seabury. He, too, seemed satisfied that Roosevelt had covered the "conclusions" against Walker, and said, "Not as the record stands at present."

On the surface, all involved appeared to agree with the way that Roosevelt had conducted the hearings.

All, perhaps, but Jimmy Walker himself. This brief exchange took place between the governor and the mayor:

ROOSEVELT: I think that concludes the direct examination of the Mayor by me.

WALKER: What? *What* direct examination?

ROOSEVELT: Direct examination of the Mayor by me.

WALKER: I never want to be cross-examined if that was *direct.*

Support for Jimmy Walker came from several quarters, expected and unexpected. In a signed editorial in the *New York American,* the publisher William Randolph Hearst urged the mayor to resign and run for reelection in the autumn. Hearst declared that Governor Roosevelt should "recognize the democratic rights of the citizens of New York City to conduct their own political affairs" and avoid exercising "dictatorial powers" by removing the mayor.

Father Charles E. Coughlin, the anti-Semitic, fascist-minded firebrand from Detroit, who cloaked his raw ideas behind his priestly garb, had many admiring listeners. Coughlin wrote to Roosevelt that he should go the limit to give Mayor Walker his day in court. Because the so-called Radio Priest had a large following, Roosevelt responded cautiously: "I am, as you know, giving the defense every latitude and I am being scrupulously careful not to make up my mind in any way until their case is wholly in."

In his Washington column in *The New York Times,* Arthur Krock observed that the chastened mayor wisecracked while the governor conducted the difficult hearing with dignity and fairness. "Whatever the Governor's verdict," Krock wrote, "the political consequences will be enormous. If he removes the Mayor, he runs the risk of being knifed by the Democratic machine in New York City and faces resentment from Mr. Walker's Democratic admirers in New England and Illinois. If he does not remove the Mayor, the Republican orators will ascribe his negative act to Presidential politics and picture Mr. Roosevelt as a trimmer and low type of politician. It is unfortunate that the Mayor's judge is a candidate for the Presidency."

People west of the Hudson wanted a show of strength against New York corruption, and Roosevelt sensed that familiar anti–New York feeling. His mail ran overwhelmingly in favor of a tough but fair trial: "Your friends in Dutchess County and throughout the United States are proud of you." "You may lose a few Tammany votes but gain many independent votes." "Your cousin Theodore Roosevelt would do the courageous thing."

The Albany hearing went into evening sessions toward the end of August 1932. It was clear that the proceedings had exhausted all the parties; hostility hung in the air of the hot, overcrowded chamber. Roosevelt had a special reason to want to wind up the hearing; the November election was barely more than two months away. Rather than sitting in Albany or Hyde Park, he was determined to present himself to voters on a whistle-stop campaign all over the country.

Meanwhile, Roosevelt sounded out one of the most respected legal minds in the country. Professor Felix Frankfurter of Harvard Law School, a future justice of the U.S. Supreme Court, remembered their private conversation in Hyde Park: "I worked out with Roosevelt the legal theory on which Jimmy Walker had to go, the theory being that when a public official has acquired money during the time that he was in public office, the presumption of wrongdoing lies there unless he can explain why he suddenly came into money that he couldn't have got merely through his salary." It was the same test that Roosevelt and Rosenman had applied in removing Sheriff Tom "Tin Box" Farley.

Some of the old Tammany pros conferred with the mayor to see what could be done to save him. Afterward, they asked Jim Farley to plead Walker's case with the governor—for political if not personal reasons.

"I had known and liked Walker for a great many years," Farley recalled, "and his friends assumed that the only thing necessary was for me to call up Albany, tell Governor Roosevelt to give Jimmy a clean bill of health, and the whole thing would be over." Farley did speak to Roosevelt, but discovered that the Walker case was too hot and too far out in the open for any delay or tampering. The public—that is, voters in New York and around the country—would get the wrong message if Roosevelt seemed to cave in to Tammany pressure.

Walker could see the handwriting on the wall.

"I think Roosevelt is going to remove me," Walker confided to a friend. "Papa made me eat my spinach."

He asked Al Smith, who still carried weight with the power brokers in New York and Catholic voters around the country, for advice.

"Jim, you're through," Smith told him. "You must resign for the good of the party."

It was an ancient script, and Walker could see its merits as well as anyone: resign before you're fired (or, in Walker's case, be suspended temporarily). Never put yourself above your party. The Democrats had great power in New York—the only place where power mattered to Walker—and it would only be lessened if he were mortally wounded but still in office.

On Sunday, August 28, 1932, Jimmy Walker's brother George, who had been confined to a clinic, died of a tubercular condition at Saranac Lake, in upstate New York. This further depressed the mayor. Dr. Schroeder, Jimmy's personal physician, said that he was suffering from "nervous exhaustion." On Thursday morning, September 1, the mayor atttended a solemn requiem mass for his brother at St. Patrick's Cathedral; afterward, the funeral cortege drove to Calvary Cemetery. Among the mourners was Jim Farley, F.D.R.'s national campaign manager. Looking at the mayor's drawn face at graveside, Farley turned to Dan McKetrick, an old friend of Walker's, and whispered, "Jim looks terrible. In fact, he looks worse than George."

At the cemetery, Walker asked his sister, Nan Burke, to take a short stroll with him. They walked toward the nearby plot where Charles F. Murphy, the Tammany Sachem who had advanced Walker's early career, was buried. Walker confided to her, "Nan, I'm going to resign." She asked him when. He replied that he planned to do so that very day.

Governor Roosevelt scheduled the next and perhaps final hearing for Friday, September 2, 1932, at 1:30 P.M. Nearly all the evidence was in; Judge Seabury, satisfied, declined an invitation to add to his conclusions.

The night before the hearing, Roosevelt met with his closest political and judicial advisers in the Executive Mansion in Albany. He turned to Raymond Moley and, half to himself, said, "How would it be if I let the little Mayor off with a hell of a reprimand?" And Moley recalled that Roosevelt answered himself: "No, that would be weak." Sitting around a table in Roosevelt's study were several of the strategists who had helped him gain the Presidential nomination: Jim Farley, Basil O'Connor, Sam Rosenman, Frank Walker, and Arthur Mullen, a Democratic national committeeman from Nebraska. The professional politicians felt that Roosevelt should not remove Walker but, instead, end the case with a severe reprimand.

As the discussion grew hot, O'Connor lit a cigarette, flicked the match at Roosevelt, and angrily said, "So you'd rather be right than President!"

Roosevelt softly replied, "Well, there may be something in what you say."

At that moment, the professional politicians were wrong and Roosevelt's instincts were right. The country was waiting for the governor to be firm, even tough. The national press had reported Jimmy Walker's obviously slippery answers and had praised Roosevelt for his judicious conduct. The Republicans had blown Walker's trial into an issue of Roosevelt and Tammanyism. In his political biography, *Roosevelt: The Lion and the Fox,* James MacGregor Burns observed, "The Governor had walked the political tightrope expertly. He stripped the Republicans of a national issue without losing Tammany."

Roosevelt realized that to cave in with only a censure would have been an obvious retreat—and a losing move in the presidential campaign.

Late in the evening of September 1, 1932, the phone suddenly rang in Roosevelt's study. At 10:40 P.M., the mayor had sent an official message not to Roosevelt but to the Honorable Michael J. Cruise, City Clerk of the City of New York, Municipal Building, New York: It read:

"I hereby resign as Mayor of New York, the said resignation to take effect immediately."

Roosevelt offered no immediate comment to the startling news. The reporters on the late shift in Room 9 at City Hall were thunderstruck. They rushed to the phones to make their late editions.

Judge Seabury was in his townhouse on East Sixty-third Street, preparing material for the resumption of hearings in Albany the following day. After midnight, the phone rang with the news. Seabury then called George Trosk to come over. They sat up all night discussing what moves they should make next. Trosk later said, "We were about to delve further into Walker's finances and the details would have completely destroyed him." From his kitchen early that morning, Seabury told reporters:

"The charges were fully proved and corroborated by documentary evidence. The Mayor's resignation in the face of this record is equivalent to a confession of guilt."

⌒

Roosevelt's triumph was clear, though he now had to worry about Tammany's support in the November election.Tammany, for its part, had to pick up the pieces. Which course should it take? Threaten to refight the battle? Appeal to the courts? Let Walker twist in the wind? Or compromise to survive?

On Friday, September 2, 1932, at 1:30 P.M., Governor Roosevelt entered the hearing chamber for the last time. After thirteen sessions and two thousand pages of testimony, he issued a final statement:

> I desire to read into this record the following telegram received by me this morning:
> HON. FRANKLIN D. ROOSEVELT. IN VIEW OF THE RESIGNATION OF THE HON. JAMES J. WALKER, MAYOR, WE WILL NOT BE PRESENT IN THE EXECUTIVE CHAMBERS AT 1:30 P.M. FOR THE SCHEDULED HEARING.
>
> > CURTIN & GLYNN, ATTORNEYS.

No other comment was needed.

TWELVE

The Knave of Hearts

WALKER RESIGNS, DENOUNCING THE GOVERNOR;
SAYS HE WILL RUN FOR THE MAYORALTY AGAIN,
APPEALING TO 'FAIR JUDGMENT' OF THE PEOPLE

The page one banner headline that stretched across five columns of *The New York Times* on September 2, 1932, informed Americans that a surprising new battlefront was being opened in the city as well as in the presidential election.

Jimmy Walker was out, but he was fighting mad, and it showed. In an unplanned maneuver, he now threatened to make a sham of his resignation. His "weapon" would be the electorate—the people who had chosen him twice before in overwhelming numbers.

An hour after resigning, Walker cabled Betty Compton in Paris. She was delighted to hear from him; he promised to join her soon. They had not seen each other for eighteen months. Out in the cold once again was Allie Walker.

Walker next issued a tough statement calling his trial a "travesty" and declaring that he planned to seek vindication by running for reelection. The tone was quite unlike the diplomatic and measured

"Your Excellency" language that he had directed at the Democratic presidential candidate in Albany:

"Instead of an impartial hearing, the proceeding before Governor Roosevelt developed into a mock trial, a proceeding in comparison to which even the practice of a drumhead court-martial seems liberal. The Governor denied me the right, to which I am entitled under the Constitution and the law, to confront accusing witnesses and cross-examine them, and by his treating accusations as self-proved, without supporting evidence."

Walker again argued that the accusations against him covered not only matters relating to his official conduct but also his "private affairs" and the private affairs of others having "no official relation" with the City of New York.

"Even in England," Walker said, "the King yielded to the courts in order that no one would suffer from an unjust or illegal act of the Executive or the Crown. I must submit to being outraged by the unlawful acts of the Governor. I did not believe that in this day and age any man in this country would assert the right to act above the law, to exercise arbitrary and unlawful power."

In charges that foreshadowed those leveled at special prosecutors in the latter part of the twentieth century, Walker complained, "The Governor has announced that he will persist in his illegal course. He has so announced at a time when I am informed that if the rights which he denies to me were granted, the alleged charges would have to be dismissed. But I am told that I am without remedy in the courts because the Governor asserts and stands on an immunity from the process of the courts. This has not been claimed even in England since the time of George III, whose assertions of arbitrary power provoked the American Revolutionary War."

It was the kind of extravagant claim that might have impressed Walker's pals at Toots Shor's saloon or the showbiz crowd at the Friars Club, but the comparison would not have held up in a court of law or even in the wised-up court of public opinion. With the counsel of Sam Rosenman and other legal experts, Roosevelt had sealed Walker's fate. As for the public, the hearings were over, Walker had resigned, and now attention turned to the presidential election.

Roosevelt was accused by Walker of being "studiously unfair" and of acting like "a prosecutor" instead of as "an impartial judge." In an insulting crack about Roosevelt's legal knowledge, Walker said that the governor required questions to be answered that "even a first-year law student would recognize were not permissible and without binding force upon me." If he expected any redress, that was the wrong thing to say at the wrong time. Walker had already experienced F.D.R.'s hot temper.

The angry ex-mayor wound up his furious protest with a rhetorical question: "Shall I permit myself to be lynched to satisfy prejudice or political ambition?" And he answered himself: "Why, then, continue before him [Governor Roosevelt] when there is another forum open to me? To that forum, the people of the City of New York, I leave my case in the spirit of true democracy, conscious of the rectitude of my official acts and with faith in the fair judgment of my fellow-citizens."

John Curtin followed up with a letter that attacked Roosevelt as well as Seabury. He stated that the governor lacked "cold neutrality." As for Seabury, Curtin called his charges "a mountain of snow which quickly melts in the sunlight of analysis." In *his* closing, Curtin described himself as only "a humble lawyer" protecting his client's liberty under the Constitution. This fawning self-description brought winks and chuckles to his fellow members of the New York bar; one characteristic he definitely hadn't shown at the hearing was humility.

What was Roosevelt's response to these personal attacks?

The dignity and the strength of silence.

"Why should he answer Mr. Walker's virulent and hysterical attack upon him for the manner in which he has conducted the hearing in Albany? The thing speaks for itself," *The New York Times* editorialized. "If Governor Roosevelt occasionally pressed a searching cross-examination, it was because he knew the case better than did the lawyer for the defense."

The editorial reaction elsewhere around the country to Walker's resignation was almost unanimously hostile to the ex-mayor. The nation's press deplored Walker's attacks against Governor Roosevelt's judicial mien. To be sure, some of this criticism represented old-fashioned heartland attitudes about wicked New York City.

Walker's letter was a big story at home and abroad:

"Neither the belligerent tone of the statement accompanying Mayor Walker's resignation nor his implied threat that he may seek vindication at the hands of the people can conceal the fact that his action was nothing more nor less than abject surrender."—*The Philadelphia Inquirer*

"The Mayor's dilatory tactics and feeble defense were a fitting prelude to his resignation. His statement seems the most ridiculous feature of all. The resignation did not astonish persons who had been reading his testimony."—*The Boston Herald*

"The resignation of Mayor Walker forestalls what was generally conceded to be certain removal from office. There will be universal approval of the stand of Governor Roosevelt, and his standing, not only in New York but the country over, will be strengthened."—*The Atlanta Constitution*

"All the clatter of Walker's talk about unfairness and perversion of executive power, all the pettifogging resort to legal quibbles by his lawyer, cannot hide the fact that Walker has had full and free opportunity to explain the facts which discredit him. Governor Roosevelt has never shown to better advantage than in his clear-headed service to the cause of good government."—*The Chicago Tribune*

"The American people have never been able to understand the admiration of the people of New York City for Mayor Walker. He has seemed to be a contemptible rather than an admirable figure, and his whining complaints of mistreatment by the Governor can cause no sympathy for him outside the metropolis."—*The St. Louis Globe-Democrat*

"Out of it all comes the one clear fact that Walker was the visible front, the symbol, of a corrupt and vicious machine government. Even if all his personal and official actions were shown to be blameless, that stigma would still lie upon his name."—*The New Orleans Times-Picayune*

"The resignation of Mayor Walker does not lend itself to wisecracking on the part of the spruce little Tammany favorite. Walker virtually confesses that a nimble and gamin-like turn of mind could not beat the rap. Flippancy has failed its most distinguished practitioner."—*The Portland Oregonian*

There was one reaction that pleased the business community. The day after Walker's resignation, Wall Street traders reported that the prices of New York City bonds advanced sharply. Brokers believed that Acting Mayor Joseph V. McKee would introduce economies in government and bring a greater measure of stability to the marketplace.

From Germany, which had welcomed Jimmy Walker twice during his mayoral junkets abroad, came a sympathetic response. The *Vossische Zeitung* of Berlin said that "Jimmy" had charm, elegance, ready humor, and optimism. Quite accurately, the newspaper said, "New York without him does not seem the same New York that so readily wins the hearts of all foreign visitors going there without any prejudices or blinkers."

But another view of the Walker-Roosevelt encounter came from England. Commenting on the ex-mayor's charge that the hearing was an inquisition, an editorialist in *The Manchester Guardian* wrote: "A close reading of the transcript shows nothing that could be considered unfair in Governor Roosevelt's questioning. Now the Mayor threatens to seek a verdict from the people by standing for election. He might embarrass Roosevelt considerably if he did, but he would embarrass his own allies in Tammany still more. Had he come through the hearing with flying colors, Tammany would have made a hero of him. Now he likely will be made a scapegoat."

Presciently, *The Guardian* added: "Tammany doesn't like backing losers."

Fielding President Hoover again, the Republicans sounded gleeful. Their New York leaders felt that Walker's resignation deprived Roosevelt of the chance to remove the mayor and emerge as a courageous personality. They believed that Roosevelt thus lost some of his glamour with voters in the western and midwestern states, where Tammany was a byword for corruption. The Republicans also believed that the mayor's claim of not getting a fair hearing would harm Roosevelt with voters who still cherished Jimmy Walker's image.

It was clearly Walker's intention to run again in the special election to be held in November because of his resignation. (The regular mayoral election would have been in 1933, an off year.) Under the rules of succession, aldermanic president McKee would be acting mayor until a new mayor was sworn in, in 1933.

This did not necessarily please Tammany leaders John Curry of Manhattan and John McCooey of Brooklyn, because McKee was the choice of another boss, Ed Flynn of the Bronx, who, in turn, was a Roosevelt confidant and booster. What's more, McKee had fought for Roosevelt at the Chicago convention while the Tammany regulars, and Walker, were making a futile attempt to nominate Al Smith. McKee was from the Bronx, and his selection as president of the Board of Aldermen was due largely to Flynn's influence. Flynn was no fan of the resigned mayor: "Under Walker we had perhaps the worst example of the spoils system that could be imagined," he later observed.

Walker's immediate aim was to create a large enough groundswell of public support that the Tammany leaders could not ignore him even if he had embarrassed them. Despite the exposure of his financial shenanigans, Walker wanted to test his popularity with the electorate once again.

"My case is in the hands of the people of New York," he confided to a small group of trusted reporters. "I am not going to urge my case. All the effort I have made to help New York City is reciprocated in thousands of messages I've received from as far west as the States of Washington and California. They express support for my contention that I have not had a fair trial. My record as Mayor is all I have to offer. The Democratic party and the people have my case. I am not going to urge them one way or the other. I want their frank and definite judgment. I want the fellow in the street—the man and woman in the street—to decide it. My record, which is without any distinction in race, color or creed, must be judged by the people themselves."

For Governor Roosevelt, the mayor's decision to run again was more than bizarre; it could be an impediment on the road to the White House. If Roosevelt and Walker were on the same Democratic line in November, it would confuse New York voters, especially if there was an attractive independent alternative candidate on the ballot who might cause voters to split the ticket.

"The prospect that James J. Walker's candidacy for Mayor this fall will cause a Democratic feud even greater than those which existed when Samuel J. Tilden and Grover Cleveland were running for President has made it doubtful that Governor Roosevelt, the Democratic nominee for President, can carry New York State," wrote James A. Hagerty, the canny *New York Times* political correspondent. "The result could be that he may lose the Presidency entirely on the Walker issue unless something can be done to bring Tammany his support." (Both Tilden and Cleveland served as New York governors and fought against the excesses of Tammany Hall.)

Walker and his allies mobilized some of his steady supporters to show that he still had some of "the people" on his side. Among them was Joseph P. Ryan, president of the Central Trades and Labor Council, who was able to bring out crowds for Walker at political rallies. "The labor movement in the City of New York regrets that political expediency has deprived them of a Mayor whose every official act has been in conformity with the Americanistic policies of organized labor," Ryan said. "We realize that you have taken the only step possible to protect yourself. We will welcome the opportunity to assist you in every possible way to see that you are restored to your former post."

Much would depend on which way the old Tammany wheelhorses moved. Despite all the evidence of Walker's "beneficences," did they still stand behind him? Certainly Tammany leaders had reason to seek revenge against Governor Roosevelt. And earlier Seabury investigations had put a damper on Tammany's business climate. In addition to giving Walker a third crack at the mayoralty, another way to wreak vengeance was by refusing to nominate Lieutenant Governor Lehman, Roosevelt's choice to succeed him.

Ethnicity always remained a factor in any New York election. The Sachems knew that if Lehman was chosen to head the state ticket, his appeal to the city's Jewish voters would go far toward overriding any action Tammany took to punish Roosevelt for Jimmy Walker's resignation.

Tammany had a lot at stake. The mayoralty was its key point of entry into the patronage chain. The mayor could name magistrates and fill courtroom posts; commissionerships and hundreds of jobs in all the city departments were up for grabs. Many were appointive rather than civil service positions. The mayor didn't rule the city when he took orders from Tammany's boss—but the boss couldn't run the city without a compliant mayor. Tammany had to decide whether it needed F.D.R. more than he needed it.

There was talk of harming Governor Roosevelt by deposing Jim Farley, national chairman of the Democratic party, from his post as chairman of the New York State party committee. Farley, as everyone on the scene knew, had been instrumental in gaining Roosevelt the presidential nomination and had strong connections to Democratic leaders all over the country.

The decision whether to support Walker, depose Farley, and un-hinge Roosevelt's campaign would be made by three men: Curry, the Tammany boss in Manhattan; McCooey, the Brooklyn boss; and their ally Edward J. O'Connell, the Albany boss.

The Roosevelt forces now showed genuine fear about gaining their own state's forty-seven electoral votes. The pros cherished an old but fairly accurate political maxim, one dating from before the pollsters and bean counters of later years told candidates how to think and talk about the issues. It went: To win New York State, a Democratic candidate must have at least 750,000 votes "leaving the Bronx" (meaning all of New York City and Long Island), or he could not overcome the up-state voters who invariably favored the Republicans.

For the rest of September and early October, Roosevelt planned to make a train trip covering twenty-three states. Despite his physical in-firmity, he decided against sitting at home as a back-porch candidate. F.D.R. had already begun his "fireside chats" over the radio while gov-ernor, but he wanted to speak to the people by personal appearances.

An influential voice of support soon came from William Randolph Hearst, in a signed editorial in his *New York American:*

WALKER'S UNJUSTIFIABLE ATTACK ON ROOSEVELT

"Jimmy Walker is not an evil person. He is merely an irresponsible one. He is irresponsible in his personal behavior, which is deplorable, but apparently not unforgivable in the eyes of his fellow-citizens," Hearst wrote. The editorial ended by saying that the Hearst papers were "sincere and devoted supporters" of Governor Roosevelt and, furthermore, that any possible support for Walker depended on a "change in his attitude" toward the governor. Once again, "the Chief" was trying to unify the Democrats and add to his own strength as a national force in publishing.

That viewpoint put Jimmy Walker on the spot; in effect, it asked him to retract what he had written in anger after resigning. It also threw down the gauntlet to the Tammany Sachems, warning them that support of Walker for mayor and hostility to the Roosevelt candidacy would lose them the support of the Hearst press and its readership. That was a message the Manhattan and Brooklyn bosses had to ponder.

In the world of Democratic politics, it was interpreted as another good sign for F.D.R. when Mayor James Curley of Boston went on a national speaking tour in behalf of the Roosevelt candidacy. Curley, a close ally of the Kennedys of Massachusetts, had been an original Roosevelt backer at the presidential convention. He was indebted to Joseph P. Kennedy, one of F.D.R.'s financial supporters. Curley was as strong a boss among Irish voters in Boston as his Tammany counterparts in New York City.

Even in 1932, long before the federal government became a powerhouse in city as well as national affairs, mayors and other local officials wanted a friend in the White House. Curley's motives were simple. The Boston boss saw Roosevelt as a political comer whom he could use to advance his own ambitions to win the governorship of Massachusetts. Roosevelt's oldest son, James, had gone into the insurance business in Boston and was eager to dabble in politics. Curley established a solid alliance with him, which pleased F.D.R. Curley had nothing at stake in Manhattan, except the enmity of Walker and Al Smith.

For once, Walker lapsed into momentary silence with the press, describing himself as "Private Citizen Jimmy." He left his Mayfair Hotel apartment and went to the Larchmont home of his friend A. C. Blumenthal, for the Labor Day weekend. Dr. Schroeder said that the ex-mayor was exhausted; as usual, he could be counted upon to recommend that his patient go away for a nice rest. Walker had given his personal doctor the lucrative post as administrator of the Sanitation Department.

Asked if his $100,000-a-year offer to Walker to help him in the management of the Florenz Ziegfeld theatrical enterprises still held good, Blumenthal said he would be glad to have his assistance at any time. "But don't forget that he's going to run again and be vindicated," the showman said. "He got a dirty deal and I told him all along he should have resigned instead of tolerating it from the Governor."

In a lighthearted sidewalk interview after a weekend at the Blumenthal estate, Walker told reporters: "I am trying to give an imitation of being a private citizen, but you fellows won't let me. You boys have had enough quotes from me in the last few days. In Paris, when I was there, they called me God's gift to the newspapermen. I feel like it now, but I have nothing to say at the moment. I didn't want to go away before, but I want to take a vacation as soon as I can."

With no fresh news about Walker's plans, the reporters were reduced to describing his wardrobe. They wrote that he was dressed in one of his seventy-five suits—a gray checked number with a white silk shirt and a black necktie. In other less than stop-press news, six suits that Mayor Walker had kept in his auxiliary wardrobe at City Hall "for emergencies" were shipped back to his suite at the Mayfair. While in his suite, reported the august *Times* on page one, he wore blue-flowered silk pajamas.

Only hours after Governor Roosevelt declared the hearings over, Judge Seabury and his wife took their first vacation in more than two years. He and Maud hastily packed their steamer trunks and embarked on the French liner *Paris* for a month on the Continent and in England where, as in the past, he would search for English common-law first editions in old bookstores.

"No intelligent person will be misled by the Mayor's attempt to substitute for a defense an assault upon the good faith and motives of the legally constituted authorities to review his acts while in office," Seabury said at dockside. "The elimination of Mr. Walker as Mayor of this city is a distinct victory for higher standards of public life, and in the elevation of this standard Governor Roosevelt did much to contribute by the manner in which he conducted the hearings."

Roosevelt, who had a long memory, did not return the compliment.

On September 10, 1932, eight days after resigning, Jimmy Walker sailed for Europe on the Italian liner *Conte Grande,* saying he planned to visit Paris. Accompanying Walker were his secretary, George Collins; a valet; and a dog. Waiting for him was Betty. Walker promised to be back in New York for the convention of the city's Democratic delegates at Madison Square Garden on October 6, 1932. At that time, Walker said, he would offer himself as a candidate for renomination in the special mayoral election on November 8, 1932.

It was not to be.

On October 4, Walker embarked on the German liner *Bremen* for the trip home—obviously too late to attend the nominating convention. He was at sea in more ways than one when it opened. Walker cabled a message to the chairman, who read it to the convention delegates:

> I CANNOT SEE HOW I COULD CAMPAIGN WITHOUT DAILY REMINDING THE PUBLIC OF THE UNFAIR NATURE OF THE HEARINGS CONDUCTED BY THE GOVERNOR. THIS IN MY OPINION WOULD DO THE DEMOCRATIC PARTY NO GOOD. MUCH AS I FEEL AGGRIEVED BY THE TREATMENT I HAVE RECEIVED, I AM NOT ONE OF THOSE WHO THINK HE IS BIGGER THAN THE PARTY. I REQUEST THAT MY NAME BE WITHHELD FROM THE CONVENTION.

Walker's name had already been put in nomination, but it was quickly withdrawn. This was not his decision alone to make; behind the scenes, others were deciding his fate.

While he was in Europe, the Tammany leaders had lapsed into ominous silence. There was a realistic reason for their hesitation. Word had reached Curry and McCooey that Al Smith, still the most powerful influence among Catholic voters in New York City, would not go out of his way to support Walker for mayor. Furthermore, the bosses were aware that if they renominated Walker, Governor Roosevelt would not appear on the same podium with him. Finally, unsubtle criticism was beginning to come from "the powerhouse"—the bishopric at St. Patrick's Cathedral on Fifth Avenue—deploring the former mayor's extramarital wandering and lifestyle.

In short, a Walker candidacy would be opposed in powerful quarters and, though he might still win, Tammany would thereby alienate key supporters and officials in New York, Albany, and Washington.

In a sudden switch before the state convention, Boss Curry ordered the state Democratic Committee to pledge its "active and loyal support" to Governor Roosevelt and his running mate, House Speaker Garner. A resolution urged "the united Democracy of New York State" to help in bringing about their "triumphant election." No attempt was made to oust Jim Farley, Roosevelt's chief political operative, from his post as state Democratic chairman, nor to deny the succession to the governor's chair of Lieutenant Governor Herbert Lehman.

Immediately afterward, Governor Roosevelt invited Curry and McCooey to meet him for a friendly little chat at the Executive Mansion in Albany. The cards were now face up on the table; everybody in the game read them clearly. Jimmy Walker—the knave of hearts—held a losing hand and he was about to be trumped. In order to live and thrive another day, the Tammany bosses had retreated.

THIRTEEN

"Jimmy, You Brightened Up the Joint!"

The 1932 presidential election was now set for a sweeping Democratic victory, but there were still some surprises in store.

Walker had already made some decisions about his personal life. After the *Conte Grande* docked in Naples, he telephoned Betty in Paris and asked her to meet him in Italy. The two lovers held a warm reunion in the ancient town of Pompeii.

They discussed his chances of obtaining a divorce from Allie; it would be easier, and quieter, to do so in Europe than in New York. Afterward, they would be free to get married; it was only a question of timing. Despite his bold public statements, Walker had not yet made up his mind about attending the special nominating convention. At this point, he was still sure he could be elected again. He promised Betty that after serving out the year to complete his second term, he would retire from office gracefully, and they could wed.

But Betty argued against his running again. She noticed that his health was frail; another year in City Hall, she insisted, would kill him. Walker felt that he owed it to his friends and supporters to offer himself to the electorate one last time. She reminded him that he also owed something to *her*—time to enjoy a normal life together.

Before he departed for Europe, a friendly reporter had told him,

"Everyone is for you, Jim. All the world loves a lover." Walker corrected him. "You're mistaken. What the world loves is a winner."

Walker's contacts in New York informed him that Tammany's Sachems had had a change of heart and that he no longer figured in their plans for the mayoralty. Suddenly, the decision had been made for him. He may have been bitter but, like a good party man, he tried not to show it.

In his place, the Tammany bosses had picked Surrogate Court Judge John P. O'Brien, a loyal hack. He was a prominent Catholic layman who was reported to wear his holy medals even while exercising in a gym suit. Among his honors, he was a Knight of the Equestrian Order of the Holy Sepulchre and president of the Friendly Sons of St. Patrick. His detractors called him "the wild bull in the china shop" because they could never be quite sure what might issue from his mouth. He could be forgetful on the platform. Once, before a Jewish audience, he praised "that scientist of scientists, Albert *Weinstein*." Another time, he told an audience in Harlem, "I may be white but my heart is as black as yours."

Playing the game, Walker had sent a cordial message from the *Bremen* to O'Brien. It read: "Perfect nomination. Very happy."

At dockside in New York, Walker was asked whom he would support in the November election. He replied that he was for the full ticket: O'Brien for mayor, Lehman for governor, Roosevelt for president. Then he borrowed a phrase from Al Smith: "I'm still a Democrat, though very still."

With the full-court press of Tammany, Surrogate O'Brien won the special election. Despite Tammany's efforts to weaken Acting Mayor McKee by stripping him of his financial powers and killing his plans to put more buses on the streets, he received 260,000 write-in votes against O'Brien. It became clear that something was shaky in Tammany Hall's grip on the electorate. But you couldn't prove it by the new mayor. When O'Brien was asked who his police commissioner would be, he replied, "I don't know—they haven't told me yet."

In the contests for president and governor, Roosevelt had everything going for him: The Depression demanded a change in leadership; he had the Roosevelt family's name recognition and popularity; and he had shown himself to be above the corruption of the city. Despite this last, Tammany worked hard for his ticket. Across the country, in the crucial two months before election day, F.D.R. was perceived as a strong but fair advocate against dishonesty in government. With his own brilliant political instincts, and a superb staff of strategists, he had managed to take on a symbol of Tammany misbehavior and, at the same time, succeeded in enlisting Tammany Hall on his side. Roosevelt and Lehman won by wide margins.

To be sure, the times were ripe for the right man. Roosevelt's running mate, Cactus Jack Garner, had confidently told him, "All you've got to do to be elected is stay alive." Hoover had done little to fight the Depression and, fairly or not, he was singularly blamed for it.

In a coast-to-coast campaign, F.D.R. promised unemployment relief, repeal of Prohibition, lower tariffs and (in a contradiction that foreshadowed Ronald Reagan's budget promises) a cut in Hoover's excessive deficit spending. What Roosevelt confronted were more depressing numbers than faced any twentieth-century president: fourteen million jobless and tens of millions more living marginally. He preached a politics of public relief to make up for the shortcomings of private corporations, which he attacked as much as he did his Republican opponent for failure to do something about unemployment. "I do not believe that in the name of that sacred word, individualism," Roosevelt said, "a few powerful interests should be permitted to make industrial cannon fodder of the lives of half the population of the United States."

Today, Roosevelt's words sound not simply liberal but positively radical. He lamented the fact that about six hundred corporations controlled two-thirds of American industry. He called for "distributing wealth and products more equitably." Inevitably, Hoover and the conservative Republican press attacked him as an "agent of revolution." Indeed, they were right: the New Deal wrought a revolution in American economic and social life for the remainder of the twentieth century (only President Reagan attempted to reverse some of the New Deal benefits—unsuccessfully).

F.D.R. carried all but six states and won by a popular vote of 22,809,638 to Hoover's 15,758,901. Norman Thomas, the Socialist party candidate, attained 881,951 votes. William Z. Foster, the Communist party candidate, received 102,785.

"No cosmic dramatist," wrote Robert E. Sherwood, the playwright and future F.D.R. speechwriter, "could possibly devise a better entrance for a new President—or a new Dictator, or a new Messiah—than that accorded to Franklin Delano Roosevelt."

After the election, on December 27, 1932, Judge Seabury filed his final report: "In the Matter of the Investigation of the Departments of the Government of the City of New York." His salutation simply read, "Sirs." Privately, he told his friends he would not address the legislators as "Gentlemen" because that would be inaccurate. As a courtesy, he sent a copy to President-elect Roosevelt "with kind personal regards and best wishes for a Happy New Year."

The report summarized his findings of corruption by city officials but was mainly devoted to a review of the case against the former mayor. Seabury said that Walker was a person of questionable credibility whose career had been "an affront to New York's citizens" and who had resigned "to avoid being removed."

The notorious Paul Block brokerage account from which Walker drew $250,000 in profits although he had invested nothing and been absolved by his benefactor from all risk was again emphasized, as it had been during the Albany hearings. It was in this connection that the name of Betty Compton found its way into the record. Referring to a $7,500 check drawn out of the account "to a person who, before the State legislative committee, was called the 'unnamed person,'" the report noted:

"While the hearings before the Governor were in progress, Mayor Walker disclosed that the person who had received this check was Betty Compton. This fact was widely published, and no further reason exists for referring to her as the 'unnamed person.' The principal significance lies in the fact that the payee is the same person with whom several financial transactions were cleared through the bank and brokerage accounts carried in Sherwood's name."

Russell T. Sherwood—still a fugitive from justice, somewhere in Mexico—handled Walker's personal business transactions and shared a safe-deposit box with him. Betty Compton was one of the beneficiaries of this secret account, which at one time or another held nearly a million dollars. In addition to the $7,500 check, a $16,500 letter of credit was purchased for her, and Sherwood gave her about $42,000 in bonds and securities.

"The City of New York has been relieved of the presence of a Mayor whose career was an affront to its citizens, but it is with a sense of shame that we must admit those who were responsible for him still control the government of the greatest city in the world," Seabury concluded. "How long this will continue rests primarily with the legislature of the State, in whose power it lies to grant or withhold from the people of the city a measure of freedom at least sufficient to accord them the opportunity, by revision of the city's charter, to secure a better government."

President-elect Roosevelt delivered his last word about Tammany corruption and the mayor on December 29, 1932. He didn't twist the knife in Jimmy Walker's mortal wound but instead established a record for future governors.

The official statement for his successors in Albany contained neither self-justification nor vindictiveness toward the ex-mayor. Walker was far from City Hall—in fact, he was back in Europe with Betty Compton—when Roosevelt issued what amounted to a memorandum for the files.

"The purpose of this memorandum is to record for convenient reference the proceedings incidental to the hearing," he wrote, "including the controversies that arose during its progress relative to the Governor's power of removal and to his conduct of the inquiry."

After summarizing the events that led to the Executive Chamber in Albany, Roosevelt said that, ordinarily, the mayor's resignation would render any report unnecessary. But in this case, the governor's right to remove the mayor of the City of New York had been challenged. That made it necessary to cite the precedents in constitutional history behind Governor Roosevelt's jurisdiction.

"It is to maintain the principle of accountability to the State, against wrongdoing by Government officials, that the Governor is invested with the power of removal," the memorandum declared, adding that the governor exercised that power not as a judge or arbitrator but "in the interest of the people of the State of New York."

The memorandum referred to the discovery of the Tweed Ring frauds in 1871, a scandal that spurred legislation and judicial decisions upholding the governor's right of removal. Roosevelt concluded that "the justification for the position taken by the present Governor was actuated by the same consideration which served as guides for his illustrious predecessors, Governors Tilden, Cleveland and Hughes."

True to his word, the ex-mayor remained a Democrat but very still during the unexciting special election that brought in John P. O'Brien. As a reward for his devotion to Tammany Hall, Mayor O'Brien was elected a sachem to succeed Walker. The new mayor had once said, "Join Tammany and work for it. Stay loyal. Stay put. Reward will come." Once again, the Tammany bosses were counting on business as usual.

Jimmy Walker stayed mainly in seclusion at A. C. Blumenthal's estate during October. In early November, Betty Compton and her mother arrived in New York, ostensibly to wind up some business affairs. When Miss Compton was asked why she had returned to the city, she coyly said, "To eat oysters."

Rumors circulated that Walker and his mistress were preparing to go back to Europe for an indefinite stay. In the background hovered his and Allie Walker's creditors. "They woo you on the way in and sue you on the way out," Walker said. All during the investigations, neither Jimmy nor Allie had given up their stylish living habits. A strong possibility existed that the government would be looking more closely at Walker's tax returns, scrutinizing the admitted "beneficences" as well as any unreported ones.

On November 10, 1932, Walker, Betty, and her mother, Mrs. Florence Compton, boarded the *Conte Grande* for Italy and the French Riviera. They occupied first-class cabins. Who paid for their costly passage, whether Walker had borrowed or received new money from old friends, remained a matter of speculation. Some critics guessed that Walker's missing accountant had banked money for him abroad, but this allegation was never proved. What is known is that for the next three years, while he and Betty traveled around Europe, they managed to live well.

Walker told his friend Gene Fowler sentimentally, if not exactly accurately, "I had little more in the way of money than my father possessed when he arrived from Ireland so long ago. I thought of the thrill he must have felt at seeing a much lower skyline than I now looked upon. I saw the skyscrapers, their many windows glowing, then the tip of Manhattan receding. From my side of the ship I could not see the Torch of Liberty. A sad feeling came over me, but New York still seemed an enchantress, even to the eyes of one who was going away."

A few months after settling in Nice, Walker telephoned his wife in Florida to say he wanted her to file for divorce. With regret, Allie complied, charging that Jimmy had deserted her in 1928. They never saw or spoke to each other again. Allie ended her days running a religious bookstore at St. Patrick's Roman Catholic Church in Miami Beach.

James J. Walker, age fifty-one, and Betty Compton, age twenty-eight, were married on April 19, 1933, in a civil ceremony performed at City Hall by the mayor of Cannes.

Only days before, Walker had read a New York newspaper clipping that said he might be considered to be living in sin, and unable to receive the sacraments, if he remarried outside the church. The possibility worried him—"I don't want to be outside looking in," he wrote to the rector of the American College in Rome. But he didn't mail the letter.

His fears were unfounded; no action was taken against him. He was never excommunicated.

In 1933, a federal grand jury in New York examined Walker's income tax returns. The mysterious Russell T. Sherwood turned up after he was given immunity from the contempt-of-court citation issued by the state legislative committee. Loyal to the end, the accountant denied that he had colluded with Walker during the Seabury investigation to avoid providing information about the mayor's personal finances.

The case against Walker for tax evasion was dropped in August, several months after his marriage. However, the government continued to check his financial records for another two years, and he was pursued by lawsuits arising from his own and his former wife's debts. Walker claimed that he lived abroad for health reasons rather than to avoid being hounded by the courts or creditors.

Most of the time, Walker and Betty stayed in England. Once they visited her birthplace on the Isle of Wight, and Jimmy told reporters that he would like to own a little farm there. However, in his wanderings the Greenwich Village boy proved to be more of a city dweller. While in London, they stayed at the luxurious Park Lane Hotel, facing Hyde Park. Their main base was a modest house in Surrey, near the village of Dorking. From there Walker would take an hour-long train ride into London to meet friends. Sometimes with Betty and sometimes alone, he traveled to Paris, Cannes, Rome, and Venice. Old theatrical acquaintances he encountered at fashionable resorts found him weary and dispirited.

Finally, in the summer of 1935, Walker received notice that the government was ending its tax case against him. It was the signal the homesick couple had been waiting for. A *New York Times* editorial on August 31, 1935, set a tone of forgiveness: "If and when he comes, he will have a triumphant reception in this city. It would be a kind of opening of hearts and hands for one who always was a popular favorite here."

When the Walkers arrived in New York aboard the liner *Manhattan* on October 31, 1935, boat whistles greeted them in the harbor. Tugboats were hired by the Friars and Grand Street Boys to salute his arrival. Thousands of people cheered the ex-mayor, Betty, and Mrs. Compton as they stepped down the gangplank. Jimmy Walker waved his derby as a loudspeaker played a recording of "Will You Love Me in December as You Do in May."

The mayor of New York City was now the feisty Fiorello H. La Guardia. His three terms in office, from 1934 to 1945, coincided with President Roosevelt's New Deal, covering the era of social reform that ruled the city and the country through the Depression and the end of the Second World War.

La Guardia ran as both the Republican and City Fusion party candidate for mayor (many New York Democrats couldn't bear to pull a Republican lever, hence the independent Fusion line on the ballot). His coalition administration linked disillusioned Tammany Democrats, Roosevelt New Dealers, and reformers of various stripes. To those who worried about the fact that he also ran on the Republican line, the enigmatic Fiorello liked to describe himself as a Lincoln Republican. No one could say with certainty where Lincoln would have stood on the complex issues facing Roosevelt, but the sixteenth president's name was magical on the hustings.

After Walker's downfall, the 1933 election of the flamboyant half-Italian, half-Jewish ex-congressman from East Harlem puzzled many New Yorkers. Judge Seabury had practically had veto power over the mayoralty ever since his investigation. Indeed, the nomination had first been offered to him, but he declined to run.

Why did Seabury handpick La Guardia?

"Because he's absolutely honest, he's a man of great courage, and he can win," Judge Seabury said. He might have added that both had nurtured a longtime enmity toward Tammany Hall. At political rallies, Republican and Fusion party balladeers parodied the Tammany theme song:

> Tammany, Tammany,
> Better stay in your tepee,
> Watch a Fusion victory,
> Tammany, Tammany,

Crack 'em, smack 'em, rock 'em, sock 'em,
Tammany!

In his first successful run for mayor, La Guardia handily defeated his two opponents: Mayor John O'Brien, who was Boss Curry's regular Democratic candidate, and Joseph McKee, the former acting mayor, who ran on the Recovery party ticket. After his election, La Guardia chose to be sworn in as mayor in Judge Seabury's home on the Upper East Side of Manhattan, and he did so both times he was reelected.

During his three terms in office, La Guardia did more than read the Sunday comics during a newspaper strike, chase fire engines in his borrowed fireman's hat, and conduct orchestras whenever he was handed a baton. He restored the city's credit during the Depression; unified the transit system; built small parks, cleared slums, and began low-cost housing; and reorganized the police and sanitation departments. Although La Guardia cut a few corners and infuriated some of his subordinates, he filled important jobs with qualified individuals who were attracted to his clean administration.

Like F.D.R. in Washington, the Little Flower lifted the spirits of the citizens and gave New York City soul.

After returning to New York, Jimmy and Betty rented an apartment in a nondescript building at 132 East Seventy-second Street, off Lexington Avenue, and settled down to a relatively quiet life. They adopted two children. He spent time with friends at the Friars and the Grand Street Boys, spoke at charitable functions, and devoted more time to his family. His financial condition was still something of a mystery.

When some of his friends in the state Senate urged him to run for office again, Walker replied, "I did my very best and the record must tell the story. I have no vindictiveness and no ill feelings." Although he made it clear that he was through with politics, he openly supported President Roosevelt's policies and reelection campaigns.

In what was interpreted as a crack against his old mentor, Al Smith, and the right-wing Liberty League, with which Smith had affiliated himself, Walker said, "President Roosevelt has become the symbol of liberalism as opposed to reaction. Reaction goes hand-in-hand with racial and religious bigotry and with anti-Semitism. I shall always be on the side of the masses against their oppressors."

James A. Farley—now President Roosevelt's postmaster general—arranged for Walker to pay a social call at the White House in May 1938. The visit amounted to an imprimatur for the tarnished ex-mayor. Even during the investigations that had brought him down, he and Farley had remained good friends. While Walker lived abroad in self-imposed exile, Roosevelt had often asked Farley how he was faring. Despite the hearings and the harsh words that followed, Farley said, the president had always liked Walker as a person. They had known each other since before the First World War, when both were New York State senators.

Shortly after Walker's White House visit, Mayor La Guardia invited him in for a talk at City Hall. As he emerged afterward, Walker wisecracked to reporters, "We were trying to find out if Diogenes was on the level." Walker graciously called the Little Flower the greatest mayor in the city's history.

In a gesture that was almost universally admired, Mayor La Guardia appointed Jimmy Walker as impartial chairman of the garment industry at a salary of $20,000 a year, plus $5,000 for expenses. Judge Seabury interpreted the mayor's appointment as an attempt to gain voters for Roosevelt's third term among New Yorkers who still admired Walker. La Guardia replied, "The Walker selection by the dress industry is not an issue in this campaign. Coming from Judge Seabury, a man I admire so much and am so fond of, it hurts me personally." They soon reconciled.

People on both sides of the negotiating table agreed that Walker did a creditable job settling labor disputes.

His skills at urging compromises helped him in his new role as a mediator; so did his humor: "If a man makes good suits, he'll go broke. If he makes bad ones, he'll go to jail." He joked about the disputed parties he dealt with: "They are always *buttonholing* me."

In 1940, Betty showed signs of restlessness and unhappiness. She complained that her individuality was being lost and began to see a psychoanalyst. In 1941, she obtained a Florida divorce on vague but legally required grounds of "extreme cruelty." They shared in the custody of their adopted children and remained close friends, even attending the theater together. A marriage, her fourth, followed in 1942 to Theodore Knappen, a consulting engineer, whom she met on a cruise ship to South America. She had always wanted a biological child, and she gave birth to a son in 1944. Six months later, mourned by her husband and Jimmy Walker, the beautiful former Betty Compton died of cancer at the age of forty.

For the next two years, Jimmy Walker continued to play the role of the good New Yorker, salving his loneliness by speaking at rallies to help the war effort and participating in hundreds of charitable and social events all over the city. After resigning as impartial chairman of the garment industry in 1945, he became president of Majestic Records, a subsidiary of a radio and television company. He explained that his job was to plug the company's music. "I used to press suits," he said. "Now I'm pressing records."

In one of the last talks he gave, at a communion breakfast, he said, "The glamour of other days I have found to be worthless tinsel, and all the allure of the world just so much seduction and deception. I now have found in religion and repentance the happiness and joy that I sought elsewhere in vain."

Toward the end of 1946, Walker often complained of dizziness, headaches, and breathing difficulties. Doctors were called in. It was found that he had a blood clot on the brain. In a coma, he was taken to Doctors Hospital—the same hospital where Betty had died. Now it was his time. The nurses drew the blinds in his darkened room.

On November 18, 1946, at the age of sixty-five, James J. Walker died, unaware that the last rites of the Roman Catholic Church had been administered to him. Thousands of people visited Campbell's Funeral Home and attended the high requiem mass at St. Patrick's Cathedral. He would have been thrilled by the big turnout and tipped his gray derby and waved his malacca cane to his beloved crowds.

In the words of the popular song that he had written early in his career as an aspiring lyricist, they still loved him in December as they did in May.

After drinking through the night, Arthur "Bugs" Baer, the humorist, and Toots Shor, the saloonkeeper, went to Campbell's at four o'clock in the morning to get a last look at him. The sentimental Shor stood at the casket and, through his tears, cried out, "Jimmy! Jimmy! When you walked into the room you brightened up the joint!"

So recalled Gene Fowler, the romanticizing Hearst newspaperman and Walker companion. Palship overflowed the funeral parlor; politics was forgotten.

Two of his old friends spoke through mist-filled eyes: "I think there's a special place for Jim in Heaven." "If there isn't, then I don't want to go there."

William O'Dwyer, then mayor of New York, said, "He was more of a philosopher than the public could ever believe or know."

Among the city's rabid sports fans, he was remembered as the father of the law that legalized boxing in New York State and sponsored legislation allowing Sunday baseball. He was also a favorite of the tabloid newspapers; no mayor had ever provided reporters with livelier copy. If nothing else, they could always write about his bespoke duds.

That Machiavellian master builder, Robert Moses, contrasted Beau James and the Little Flower: "La Guardia could speak real Yiddish where Jimmy Walker's vocabulary was limited to *gefilte fish* and *bagels and lox*. Fiorello reveled in Italian of the street variety where Jimmy knew only *arrivederci* and *pasta*. Walker had to make a quick exit to get a big hand. La Guardia had persistence and knowledge and could afford to stick around and make a real impression. One was an entertaining, enormously likable mountebank, the other an accomplished showman."

Louis Nizer, a prominent attorney who also liked to occupy center stage, said, "James J. Walker met success like a gentleman and failure like a man."

About his own life and career, Jimmy Walker wistfully yet candidly observed:

"I have lived and I have loved. The only difference is that I was a little more public about it than most people. After all, maybe it isn't a mistake to be one's self and take chances. With all my misgivings, my countless mistakes, with all my multiplicity of shortcomings, I have a single regret. I have reached the peak of the hill and must start the journey downward. I have carried youth right up to the fifty-yard mark." And then he added:

"I had mine and made the most of it."

Epilogue

A New Political Era

The subway and bus and trolley riders from the ethnic neighborhoods of New York City remembered Beau James as a bon vivant who was as much at home in the cafés of Montmartre as in the speakeasies of Manhattan, a Broadway boulevardier in spats who symbolized the good times and street smarts of a boozy era. Baghdad-on-the-F.D.R.-Drive was no City Upon a Hill, but it was a helluva lot of fun while it lasted—except, of course, for the unemployed, the victims of racial and religious discrimination, and the idle poor who pressed their noses against the closed windows of opportunity.

Death was not the time to talk about Jimmy Walker's trial by fire before Governor Roosevelt, or to describe the steadfastness of the Seabury investigation, or to mention that he resigned the mayoralty and fled to Europe rather than face legal problems because of his conduct, or to recall the parade of Follies girls who floated through his life, or to reminisce about Betty Compton, his gorgeous mistress.

In the general public's memory, Jimmy Walker is enshrined not for his larceny but for his lighthearted personality—for being a fun mayor who reflected a gay era in the life of the city and country. He did that, true, but it would conceal his record not to add that he was also a corrupt mayor who was for sale and who kept and used illegally obtained funds—laughingly known as beneficences—in hidden bank and brokerage accounts. In this respect, he failed the trusting people of his beloved New York.

None of that—not even the fact that he was a loyal Tammany man who honored the Tweed-like system of boodle—detracted for a moment from Walker's undeniable charm and appeal to the electorate during the Roaring Twenties and the early years of the Depression. Eventually, both Roosevelt and La Guardia extended the hand of friendship to Walker the man, not Walker the Mayor.

Jimmy Walker's early mentor, Al Smith, rose from the sidewalks of New York and became a strong advocate of social legislation. But he wound up an unhappy warrior, the victim of religious prejudice in the 1920s. The Ku Klux Klan burned crosses against his candidacy—and against the supposed "evils" of New York. Hate literature prophesied that "bootleggers and harlots would dance on the White House lawn" if he was elected.

In the more open-minded American society of the 1960s, after the biggest war in history, the lessons learned from Smith's presidential race helped to elect John F. Kennedy as the first Catholic president. Smith did not live to see it happen. Toward the end of his life, Smith's liberal reputation was harmed by his volte-face in favor of big business and his denunciation of the New Deal. As a champion of the conservative Liberty League, he attacked the "socialistic heresies" of the Roosevelt administration.

In the second half of the twentieth century, Tammany Hall no longer owned City Hall. The bosses lost their absolute power to name and elect mayors, judges, and commissioners. The resignation of Mayor Walker, Tammany Sachem and symbol of rule by bossdom, was a body blow from which the organization never fully recovered. F.D.R. kept getting reelected, with or without Tammany's support. Mayor La Guardia consistently denounced the Hall, and also kept getting reelected. The popular Little Flower was able to break the Democrats' long-held habit of voting only for every star on the ballot.

Something new was happening in Gotham. You could no longer buy a family's loyalty and votes with a free turkey at Christmastime. During the 1930s, the federal government was providing what the state and city could not: employment opportunities, through such make-work agencies as the Federal Writers' Project of the Works Progress Administration, and unemployment insurance and disability payments funded directly with federal money or with federal money funneled through the states. Although these payments were often low, a dollar went a long way during the Depression. A full dinner at a good restaurant cost $1.50; for the well-fixed, a room at the elegant Plaza Hotel was $8 a night.

In the wonderful lyrics of Betty Comden and Adolph Green in *On the Town,* the Bronx was still up and the Battery down, but the neighborhoods and ethnic backgrounds of their residents were changing. People in Manhattan and the other boroughs were better educated and more independent; votes were no longer dominated by malleable immigrants. You didn't have to be named O'Brien, Sullivan, Murphy, McCooey, McQuade, Hylan, Foley, or Flynn to become a district leader or a mayor, a commissioner or a sheriff. In addition to officials of Irish ancestry, there were now borough presidents who were Italians, Hispanics, Jews, and blacks. (Soon enough, they dispensed their own patronage.)

A sign of its diminution of power was that Tammany Hall's impressive stone and brick building on Seventeenth Street and Union Square, which served as headquarters from 1929 to 1943, had to be abandoned for lack of funds. After several moves, the organization wound up in rented rooms in an office building at 62 East Forty-second Street. Leaving the Wigwam was a psychological blow to the New York County Democratic Committee, the formal name for what was once informally called Tammany. The Hall's last boss was Carmine DeSapio, who successfully supported Robert F. Wagner, Jr., for mayor in 1953. When Wagner decided to run for a third term in 1961, he ran on an anti-Tammany platform. That ended DeSapio's leadership.

The rise of the Democratic reform clubs in the 1950s and 1960s introduced a strong new force in New York that marked finis for Tammany. Simultaneously, Governor Adlai E. Stevenson of Illinois, an eloquent voice for progressive government in the New Deal tradition, was nominated twice to run for president. Among the reformers who supported Stevenson and played leading party roles, nationally and locally, were two highly respected old New Yorkers who represented the best in Democratic politics: former Governor Herbert Lehman and Eleanor Roosevelt.

During the La Guardia years in City Hall, the Republican-Fusion mayor was a powerful ally of Roosevelt's New Deal. He often went directly to the White House to plead for his city and its people. It helped, of course, that the President and the mayor were on the same wavelength.

Neither F.D.R. nor the Little Flower won their elections by the current means of electoral politics—market surveyors and pollsters who solicit the opinions of a supposed cross-section of voters and then tell the candidates what's in the air and how to shift with the wind. In the White House and City Hall, Roosevelt and La Guardia were surrounded by intelligent advisers from academe, but they thought for themselves and followed their own gut instincts. To be sure, they courted the press, but they didn't depend on the punditocracy to approve their programs.

La Guardia's accomplishments have been overshadowed by his flamboyant personality, so well satirized in the musical *Fiorello!* He's best remembered for reading Dick Tracy and the other comic strips over WNYC, the city's radio station, during a newspaper shutdown, for showing up at fires, for smashing slot machines, and for declaring war on gamblers, burlesque houses, and kiosks that carried "smutty" magazines. Though civil libertarians complained about his high-handedness and censorship, the public at large cheered him on.

But La Guardia's more important achievements are still visible in New York. As president of the U.S. Conference of Mayors for nearly ten years, he fought for more federal assistance to the cities. Under the La Guardia administration, there was an upsurge of public housing for the poor, including blacks in Harlem. He and his commissioners built more parks, sewer systems, hospitals, health centers, bridges, and airports than any of his Tammany predecessors. There is no Tweed Courthouse to tarnish La Guardia's record.

F.D.R. changed the direction of the government and the country between 1933 and 1945. No matter what it's called, he created the underpinnings of a welfare state that didn't destroy but—with all its flaws and opportunities—actually preserved the American free enterprise system. In his third inaugural address, on January 20, 1941, Roosevelt declared: "The hopes of the Republic cannot forever tolerate either undeserved poverty or self-serving wealth." In similar forms, that contest still continues today.

To read Roosevelt's words now is to become newly aware that his successors, both Democratic and Republican, have lacked his vision and failed to equal his achievements in the White House. It's a largely forgotten event, but his courage was first displayed in full flower when, against the legal odds, he served as judge and jury in the Albany hearings that brought down Jimmy Walker and Tammany Hall. Thereafter, F.D.R. went on to become the commanding president of the twentieth century.

A Note on Sources

In the course of reporting and writing about American history, politics, and the judiciary over the years, I interviewed or corresponded with a number of individuals who provided background material for some of the facts and conclusions in this and related books. These materials can be found in the Herbert Mitgang Papers in the Manuscripts and Archives Section, New York Public Library, Fifth Avenue and Forty-second Street, New York City. There are no restrictions on these papers; they are open to scholars and authors who apply for permission to the Special Collections Office at the Library.

New material will be added to the papers within a year after publication of this book.

The bulk of the material about the Seabury investigations, Governor Franklin D. Roosevelt's role, and the trials of Mayor James J. Walker and members of his administration, including the district attorney and other officials, can be found in scattered official city and state reports and judicial documents. No one institution contains all the reports mentioned below.

Major sources include the Franklin D. Roosevelt Library at Hyde Park, New York; the mayoral papers of the different administrations in the Municipal Archives and Records Center, New York City; the library of the Association of the Bar of the City of New York; the Columbia University School of Law library; the Collection of Tammaniana and the Oral History transcripts of various personalities at the Columbia University library.

An invaluable source of information is the Newspaper Division of the New York Public Library, which contains editions of *The New York Times, New York Herald Tribune, New York Sun, New York World-Telegram, New York Journal-American, Daily News,* and other publications about events covered by this book. *The New York Times* especially proved itself the newspaper of record by printing transcripts from the hearings before the state legislative committee in Manhattan and Governor Roosevelt in Albany.

These are the official records used for the book:

Magistrates' Courts public hearings, transcript of testimony, 299 witnesses, 1930–1931.

In the Matter of the Investigation, under commission issued by Governor Franklin D. Roosevelt of the State of New York, of charges made against Honorable Thomas C. T. Crain, District Attorney of New York County, 1931.

In the Matter of the Investigation of the Magistrates' Courts, First Judicial Department, Supreme Court, Appellate Division, final report, 1932.

Joint Legislative Committee to Investigate the Departments of the City of New York, transcript of testimony, 320 witnesses, 16 volumes, 1931–1932.

In the Matter of the Investigation of the Departments of the Government of the City of New York, pursuant to joint resolutions adopted by the New York State Legislature, intermediate report, 1932.

In the Matter of the Investigation of the Departments of the City of New York, pursuant to joint resolutions adopted by the New York State Legislature, second intermediate report, 1932.

In the Matter of the Investigations of the Departments of the City of New York, pursuant to joint resolutions adopted by the New York State Legislature, final report, 1932.

Hearings before Governor Franklin D. Roosevelt, Albany, in the Matter of the Charges against Mayor James J. Walker, brought by

Samuel Seabury, William J. Schieffelin, as chairman, on behalf of the
Committee of One Thousand, James E. Finegan, and others. Transcript
of testimony, 34 witnesses, led by Mayor Walker, 5 volumes, 1932.

Individuals I interviewed or corresponded with in the past, both while
writing about the Seabury investigation and in researching *New York
Times* articles and editorials on the judiciary and municipal affairs, include:

Adolf A. Berle, Jr., Chamberlain of New York City, counsel to the
Board of Estimate on transit, occasional Roosevelt Brain Truster;
William M. Chadbourne, Fusion party leader and Bull Mooser; Edward Corsi, La Guardia associate, U.S. commissioner of immigration;
Thomas E. Dewey, district attorney, governor of New York, Republi-
can presidential candidate; Edward R. Finch, presiding justice, Appel-
late Division, Supreme Court, First Department; Felix Frankfurter,
associate justice, U.S. Supreme Court; Judge Learned Hand, U.S.
Court of Appeals, Second Circuit; Roy W. Howard, publisher, Scripps-
Howard newspapers; Mrs. Fiorello H. La Guardia; Reuben A. Lazarus,
consultant on municipal affairs, New York State Assembly, member of
Mayor Walker's legal staff.

Also, Walter Lippmann, New York *Herald Tribune* columnist; David
C. Mearns, chief, manuscript division, Library of Congress; Raymond
Moley, professor of public law, Columbia University, and Roosevelt
Brain Truster; Robert Moses, New York City parks commissioner, con-
struction coordinator, member of the City Planning Commission; Allan
Nevins, Columbia University history professor, founder, Society of
American Historians; Joseph M. Proskauer, lawyer, state Supreme
Court justice; Eleanor Roosevelt, for her views of Governor Roosevelt's
stand on the Walker hearings; Samuel I. Rosenman, counsel to Gover-
nor Roosevelt, speechwriter, state Supreme Court justice.

In addition, I spoke with these members of Judge Samuel
Seabury's staff: George Trosk, chief of staff; W. Bernard Richland,
aide and former New York City corporation counsel; Seabury's three

nephews, Andrew Oliver, William B. Northrop, and John B. Northrop; and twenty Seabury "boys," among them Irving Ben Cooper, Philip W. Haberman, Jr., and William G. Mulligan, all of whom played major roles in discovering Jimmy Walker's secret accounts.

This is a selected list of relevant publications:

Allen, Oliver E. *The Tiger: The Rise and Fall of Tammany Hall.* Addison-Wesley Publishing, 1993.

Atkinson, Brooks. *Broadway.* Limelight Editions, 1985.

Bernard Bellush. *Franklin D. Roosevelt as Governor of New York.* Columbia University Press, 1955.

Bendiner, Robert. *Just Around the Corner: A Highly Selective History of the Thirties.* Harper & Row, 1967.

Berger, Meyer. *The Story of The New York Times.* Simon and Schuster, 1951.

Berlin, Isaiah. *The Proper Study of Mankind: An Anthology of Essays.* Farrar, Straus & Giroux, 1998.

Burns, James MacGregor. *Roosevelt: The Lion and the Fox.* Harcourt, Brace, 1956.

Caro, Robert. *The Power Broker: Robert Moses and the Fall of New York.* Knopf, 1974.

Chambers, Walter. *Samuel Seabury: A Challenge.* The Century Company, 1932.

Connable, Alfred, and Edward Silberfarb. *Tigers of Tammany.* Holt, Rinehart & Winston, 1967.

Evans, Harold. *The American Century.* Alfred A. Knopf, 1998.

Faragher, John Mack. *The American Heritage Encyclopedia of American History.* Henry Holt, 1998.

Foner, Eric, and John A. Garraty. *The Reader's Companion to American History.* Houghton Mifflin, 1991.

Flynn, Edward J. *You're the Boss.* The Viking Press, 1947.

Fowler, Gene. *Beau James: The Life and Times of Jimmy Walker.* The Viking Press, 1949.

Hamburger, Philip. *Mayor Watching and Other Pleasures.* Rinehart, 1958.

Fuller, Hector. *Abroad with Mayor Walker.* Shields Publishing, 1928.

Gribetz, Louis, and Joseph Kaye. *Jimmy Walker: The Story of a Personality.* Dial Press, 1932.

Gunther, John. *Roosevelt in Retrospect: A Profile in History.* Harper & Brothers, 1950.

Heckscher, August, with Phyllis Robinson. *When La Guardia Was Mayor: New York's Legendary Years.* W. W. Norton, 1978.

Jackson, Kenneth T., Editor. *The Encyclopedia of New York City.* Yale University Press, 1995.

Josephson, Matthew, and Hannah Josephson. *Al Smith: Hero of the Cities.* Houghton Mifflin, 1969.

Kennedy, William. *Legs.* Penguin Books, 1983.

Kluger, Richard. *The Paper: The Life and Death of the New York Herald Tribune.* Alfred A. Knopf, 1986.

Lankevich, George J. *American Metropolis: A History of New York City.* New York University Press, 1998.

Leuchtenburg, Willaim E. *The FDR Years: On Roosevelt and His Legacy.* Columbia University Press, 1995.

Manners, William. *Patience and Fortitude: Fiorello La Guardia.* Harcourt Brace Jovanovich, 1976.

Miner, Margaret, and Hugh Rawson. *American Heritage Dictionary of American Quotations.* Penguin, 1997.

Mitgang, Herbert. *The Man Who Rode the Tiger: The Life and Times of Judge Samuel Seabury.* Fordham University Press, 1996.

Northrop, William B., and John B. Northrop. *The Insolence of Office: The Story of the Seabury Investigations.* G. P. Putnam's Sons, 1932.

Phillips, Cabell. *From the Crash to the Blitz, 1929–1939.* Fordham University Press, 1999.

Roosevelt, Eleanor. *This I Remember.* Harper & Brothers, 1949.

Roosevelt, Franklin D. *The Public Papers and Addresses of Franklin D. Roosevelt.* With a Special Introduction and Explanatory Notes by President Roosevelt. Five volumes, 1928–1936. Random House, 1938.

Sann, Paul. *The Lawless Decade.* Crown, 1957.

Schlesinger, Arthur M. Jr. *The Age of Roosevelt.* Vol. 2: *The Coming of the New Deal.* Houghton Mifflin, 1960.

Siegfried, André. *America Comes of Age.* Harcourt, Brace, 1927.

Tugwell, Rexford G. *The Democratic Roosevelt.* Doubleday, 1957.

Walsh, George. *Gentleman Jimmy Walker: Mayor of the Jazz Age.* Praeger, 1974.

Ward, Geoffrey C. *A First-Class Temperament: The Emergence of Franklin Roosevelt.* Harper & Row, 1989.

Whalen, Grover A. *Mr. New York: The Autobiography of Grover A. Whalen.* G. P. Putnam's Sons, 1955.

Wilson, Edmund. *A Literary Chronicle: 1920–1950.* Anchor Books, 1956.

Acknowledgments

A warm salute to the editors, librarians, and friends who helped to inspire this book and guide it into print:

Bruce K. Nichols, senior editor, The Free Press, who saw the historical need for a fresh interpretation of the trials of Mayor Jimmy Walker against the background of the Jazz Age, Prohibition, and a political era that led to the demise of Tammany Hall and the ascendancy of Mayor Fiorello H. La Guardia and Governor Franklin D. Roosevelt to the presidency. Other Free Press members who also deserve credit for creative assistance include Dan Freedberg and Jolanta Benal.

Marilyn Annan and John Moytka, dedicated and knowledgeable librarians at *The New York Times;* Whitney Bagmall, librarian, Columbia University law library; Miriam Bowling, curator of manuscripts, New York Public Library; W. Bernard Richland, aide to Judge Samuel Seabury, and former New York City corporation counsel; twenty members of the Seabury legal staff; Sheldon M. Harnick, lyricist, *"Fiorello!;* Brooks Atkinson, former *New York Times* drama critic and essayist; John B. Oakes, former editor of the editorial and op-ed pages, *New York Times,* and A. H. Raskin, deputy editor; Bethuel M. Webster, attorney, diplomat, president of the Association of the Bar of the City of New York.

And once again, to Shirley Mitgang, for devotion and wise counsel, and to Esther, Lee, Laura, Gina, and Caroline Mitgang and David Goodman, for rations, quarters, and inspiration.

Index

Acuna, Chile Mapocha, 113–15
Adams, Hattie, 48, 49
Adler, Polly, 111, 112, 120
Adonis, Frank, 129–30
Advertising Club, 96
Age of Innocence, The (Wharton), 91
Ager, Milton, 79–80
Alice Adams (Tarkington), 91
Allen, Janet. *See* Walker, Janet Allen
Ambassador Hotel, 195
America Comes of Age (Siegfried), 46
American Newspaper Guild, 119
American Tragedy, An, 88
Anti-Saloon League, 3
Arrowsmith (Lewis), 91
Asbury, Herbert, 30
Atkinson, Brooks, 87, 88
Atlanta Constitution, 208
Attell, Abe, 11
Auden, W. H., 173
Autobiography of Lincoln Steffens, The, 106

Babbitt (Lewis), 91
Baer, Arthur ("Bugs"), 21, 229

Ball, Ernest R., 65
Baltimore Sun, 172
Bankers Club, 103
Banton, Joab H., 88
Barrymore, Ethel, 88
Barrymore, Lionel, 88
Belasco Theatre, 23
Belmont Park, 8
Bender, Albert, 10
Berle, Adolf A., Jr., 51, 163
Berlin, Irving, 72, 93, 94
Berlin, Isaiah, 173, 175
Berry, Charles W., 110
Beyer, Robert S., 197
Beyer Tile Company, 197–98
Biltmore Hotel, 62
Black, William H., 135
Blackstone, Sir William, 24
Block, Billy, 151
Block, Max, 151
Block, Paul, 93, 150–52, 170–72, 196–98, 220
Blue, Wednesday, 34
Blumenthal, A. C. ("Blumey"), 55, 195–96, 214, 222
Bogart, Humphrey, 88
Bolton, Guy, 81
Bonagure, Guy, 128

Bontemps, Arna, 92
Bonus Army of World War I veterans, 176–78
Boston Herald, 208
Bourdet, Edouard, 88–89
Brenner, Dorothy, 160
Bridge of San Luis Rey, The (Wilder), 91
Brodsky, Louis B., 117–18
Brooklyn Bar Association, 137
Brooklyn College, 27
Brooklyn Dodgers, 64
Broun, Heywood, 119, 126, 144–45, 165
Bruckner, Henry, 28
Buffalo Evening News, 172
Bunk of 1926, 88
Burke, Nan Walker (sister of Jimmy), 202
Burns, James MacGregor, 166, 203

Calvary Cemetery, 201–2
Campbell's Funeral home, 228
Cantor, Maurice F., 12
Cappel, Peter, 195
Captive, The, 88–89
Cardozo, Benjamin N., 136
Cather, Willa, 91
Cayuga Democratic Club, 23
Central Trades and Labor Council, 211
Chevalier, Maurice, 128
Chicago Tribune, 208
Chicago White Sox, 6–7, 11, 84
Church of the Annunciation, 100
Cincinnati Reds, 6–7
Citizens Union, 99, 106
City Affairs Committee, 133
City Club of New York, 125–27, 131

City College of New York, 27, 174
Clean Books Bill, 69–70
Cleveland, Grover, 39, 166, 168, 211, 222
Clinton, DeWitt, 63
Cloth Shrinkers Union, 131
Coen, Irene Luzzatto, 50
Collier's, 90
Collins, George, 215
Columbia University, 163
   Law School, 102, 175
Columbus, Christopher, 96
Combs, Earle, 84
Comden, Betty, 233
Commodore Hotel, 85
Communist Party, 27–28, 220
Community Church, 133
Compton, Arthur H., 174
Compton, Betty ("Monk")
   charges against, 220–21
   death of, 228
   described, 80
   divorce from Walker, 227–28
   in *Oh, Kay!,* 80–81, 83
   married life with Walker, 224, 226
   marries Walker, 223–24
   as mistress of Walker, 1–2, 34, 80–83, 110, 180, 205, 215, 217, 220–24, 231
Compton, Florence, 222–24
Conboy, Martin, 183–84, 192
Connolly, Maurice E., 70
Coolidge, Calvin, 38, 66, 87
Cooper, Irving Ben, 104, 112, 119–20
Copeland, Royal S., 93
Cordes, John, 17–18
Cosden Oil, 189
Costello, Frank, 129–30
Cotton Club, 92

Coughlin, Father Charles E., 199
Coward, Noël, 88
Cradle Snatchers, The, 88
Crain, Thomas C. T., 125–32
Crater, Joseph Force, 23–25
Croker, Richard, 72, 75, 136
Cross, Guernsey T., 159–60, 167
Cruise, Michael J., 203
Cullen, Countee, 92
Curley, James, 213
Curry, John Francis, 126, 210, 226
   testimony of, 135–36
   Walker's post-trial attempt to
     run in special mayoral elec-
     tion and, 212, 216
Curtin, John J., 179, 184–88,
   191–92, 199, 204
   post-trial personal attack on
     Roosevelt and Seabury, 207
Cuvillier, Louis, 110

Davis, Matthew L., 41
Dawn, Elaine, 24
Debs, Eugene V., 72
Delmonico's Restaurant, 44
Dempsey, Jack, 22
Depression of the 1930s
   described, 85–86, 219, 233
   Hoover and, 85, 105, 162,
     176–78, 219
   Roosevelt and, 86, 218, 219, 225
DeSapio, Carmine, 233
De Witt Clinton Hotel, 181
Diamond, Jack ("Legs"), 11, 90
Dilagi, Michael, 98
Doctors Hospital, 228
Dodsworth (Lewis), 91
Dos Passos, John, 91
Doyle, Dr. William F. ("Horse
   Doctor"), 134–36
Dreiser, Theodore, 88

Dugan, Joe, 84
Dugan, William, 89
Duke of Duluth, The, 66

East Hampton Star, 34, 99
Ederle, Gertrude, 77
Einstein, Albert, 32, 218
Einstein, Isadore ("Izzy"), 32–33
Eisenhower, Dwight D., 178
Elmer Gantry (Lewis), 91
Empire State building, 13
Empire Theatre, 89
Equestrian Order of the Holy
   Sepulchre, 218
Equitable Coach Company, 73,
   146, 148, 150, 154–55, 170,
   190
Equitable Trust Company of New
   York, 194
Evening Graphic, 24

Fageol, Frank R., 146
Fairfield Hotel, 5–6
Fallon, William J., 8
Farewell to Arms, A (Heming-
   way), 92
Farley, James A. 140, 163, 164,
   201, 202, 212, 216
   Walker invited to Roosevelt
     White House, 227
Farley, Thomas ("Tin Box"),
   107–9, 123, 160, 172, 201
Thomas M. Farley Association,
   107
Faulkner, William, 91–92
Fay, Larry, 90
Fay, Lorraine, 24
Fears, Peggy, 195
Federation Bank and Trust Com-
   pany, 131
Ferber, Edna, 91

Fertig, Maldwin, 183, 192
Fiorello!, 107, 123, 234
Fitzgerald, F. Scott, 6–8, 79, 92
Fitzgerald, Zelda, 79
Flood, Patrick, 12
Flynn, Edward J., 54, 70, 210, 233
Foley, James A., 70, 75, 233
Ford, Henry, 51
Foster, William Z., 220
Fowler, Gene, 21, 83, 223, 229
Franco, Francisco, 174, 175
Frankfurter, Felix, 104, 200–201
Free Milk Fund for Babies, 82
Free Synagogue, 133
Friars Club, 206, 226
Friedman, Jeann, 61
Friendly Sons of St. Patrick, 218
Front Page, The, 88
Fuller, Hector, 94, 95
Fulton Fish Market, 68, 128–30
Fusion Party, 225–26, 234

Gaiety, the, 91
Gardner, Charles W., 48
Garibaldi, Giuseppe, 63
Garner, John Nance, 158, 164, 165, 179, 216, 219
Gehrig, Lou, 84
General Theological Seminary, 100
General Tire and Rubber Company, 146
George III, king of England, 206
George V, prince of Wales, 95–96
Gershwin, George, 81, 86
Gershwin, Ira, 81, 86–87
Girones, Jose, 128
Glynn, John J., 179, 204
Godkin, Edwin L., 47
God's Trombones (Johnson), 92
Goering, Hermann, 85

Golden Rule Pleasure Club, 48–49
"Good-by Eyes of Blue" (Walker), 65
Good Government advocates ("Goo-Goos"), 2, 15, 58, 79, 159
Goodier, James H., 103
Gopher Gang, 11
Gordon, Vivian, 119–21, 125
Grabowski, John, 84
Grand Central Terminal, 179, 194–95
Grand Street Boys Association, 33, 93, 226
Great Gatsby, The (Fitzgerald), 6–8, 92
Green, Adolph, 233
Green, John, 12
Greenpoint People's Regular Organization of the Fifteenth Assembly District, 139–40
Groton, 175
Guinan, Texas (Mary Louise Cecilia), 89–90
Gunther, John, 175–76
Gustavus Adolphus, crown prince of Sweden, 77
Guys and Dolls, 6

Billy Haas's Restaurant, 23
Haberman, Philip, 103–4, 181
Hagerty, James A., 211
"Hail, Hail, the Gang's All Here," 194–95
Hammond, Fred, 68
Hampden, Walter, 88
"Happy Days Are Here Again," 166
Harding, Warren G., 38
Harlem Renaissance, 92

Harnick, Sheldon M., 123
Harper's Weekly, 43
Harrison, William H., 97
Harvard University, 175
  Law School, 104, 200–201
Hastings, John A., 146, 170, 197
Hayes, Patrick Cardinal, 93
Hearst, Mrs. William Randolph, 82
Hearst, William Randolph, 49
  Roosevelt supported by, 164–65, 179, 213
  on Walker, 178–79, 199, 212–13
Hecht, Ben, 2, 88
Hemingway, Ernest, 92
Herwitz, Oren, 103, 181
Hill, David B., 166
Hines, Jimmy, 11
Hitler, Adolf, 173–75
Hofstadter, Samuel, 181
  described, 133
  Seabury investigation and, 133, 135, 136, 144, 148, 149, 159, 171, 189
Holmes, John Haynes, 133
Home to Harlem (McKay), 92
Hoover, Herbert, 38, 87, 136
  Bonus Army of World War I veterans and, 176–78
  Depression of the 1930s and, 85, 105, 162, 176–78, 219
  1928 presidential campaign, 8–9, 13, 35, 56, 72
  1932 presidential campaign, 35, 105, 141, 162, 209, 219
  Prohibition and, 35
Hoover, J. Edgar, 27
Hornblow, Arthur, Jr., 88–89
Hotel Astor, 96
Hotel Owners Association, 82
Hotel Ten Eyck, 180, 189

Hotsy Totsy Club, 11, 90
House, Edward, 160–61
Howe, Louis, 140, 160
Hoyt, Waite, 84
Hudson Dusters, 45
Hughes, Charles Evans, 222
Hughes, Langston, 92
Hurston, Zora Neale, 92
Hylan, John F. ("Red Mike"), 20, 71–73, 76, 233
  New York Times on, 70

"I Like Your Way" (Walker), 65
Imperial Theatre, 80
International Workers of the World, 27
Interstate Trust Company, 190
Irving, Washington, 79

Jackson, Andrew, 41
Jacobs, Joe, 180
Jamaica Racetrack, 7
Jazz Age, described, 79–80
Jazz Singer, The, 88
Jefferson, Thomas, 30
Jessel, George, 61–63
Jimmy the Well-dressed Man (Kaufman), 154–56
Johnson, James Weldon, 92
Johnston, Alva, 76
Jolson, Al, 88, 93
Jones Beach, 74

Kaufman, George S., 86–87, 154–56
Kearney, Philip, 88
Kelly, "Honest John," 43, 75, 136
Kennedy, John Fitzgerald, 156, 232
Kennedy, Joseph P., 156, 213
Kern, Jerome, 86

Kerrigan, Charles F., 76, 109–10
Knappen, Theodore, 228
Koenig, Mark, 84
Kosciuszko, Thaddeus, 63
Kresel, Isidor Jacob
  described, 102
  Seabury investigation and, 102,
    104, 111, 114, 116–17, 121
Krock, Arthur, 156–57, 200
Ku Klux Klan, 73, 232
Kurzman, "Tough Jake," 130

La Follette, Robert, 72
La Guardia, Achille, 50
La Guardia, Fiorello H., 30
  Bonus Army of World War I
    veterans and, 177
  City Hall, Walker's visit to, 227
  described, 3, 19, 50, 51, 229
  elected mayor, 225–26
  Fiorello!, 107, 123, 234
  Fusion Party and, 225–26, 234
  garment industry appointment
    for Walker, 227, 228
  legacy, 226, 234–35
  mayoral campaign, unsuccess-
    ful, 3, 51–53, 144
  Prohibition and, 51
  Roosevelt compared to, 234
  Seabury, supported by, 225
  Tammany Hall reform efforts,
    3, 50, 51, 53, 225–26, 232–33,
    235
  U.S. Conference of Mayors, as
    president of, 234–35
  Walker compared to, by Robert
    Moses, 229
Lanza, Joseph ("Socks"), 129–30
Lardner, Ring, 7–8
LaSalle School, 64
Lawrence, D. H., 69

Lawrence, Gertrude, 81
Lazzeri, Tony, 84
Lee, Robert E., 55
Legal Aid Society, 122
Lehman, Herbert H., 178, 211,
  216, 218, 219, 234
Levy, George B., 103
Lewis, Sinclair, 91
Liberty League, 226–27, 232
Lincoln, Abraham, 30, 42, 51, 225
Lindbergh, Charles A., 77, 84–85
Lindbergh, Charles II, 180
Lindemann, Leo "Lindy," 5, 6
Lindemann, Mrs. Leo, 6
Lindy's, 5–6, 16–18, 180
Lippmann, Walter, 4, 106, 156,
  162–63, 183
"Little Augie," 130
"Little Tin Box" (Harnick), 123
Livingston, Nick, 181
Long, Huey, 178
Lopez, Vincent, 1–2
Louise, princess of Sweden, 77
Low, Seth, 67
Luciano, Lucky, 129–30
Lulu Belle, 88

MacArthur, Charles, 88
MacArthur, Douglas A., 177–78
MacDonald, Ramsay, 77
Macy, W. Kingsland, 25–26
Madden, Owney, 90
Madison, James, 30
Madison Square Garden, 153–54,
  215
Madison Square Presbyterian
  Church, 47, 49
"Maggie Murphy's Home," 95
Main Street (Lewis), 91
Majestic Records, 228
Malone, Dudley Field, 62

Manchester Guardian, 209
Manhattan Transfer (Dos Passos), 91
Marie, queen of Rumania, 77
Mast, Jane, 89
Mastbaum, Jules, 55
Maya, 89
Mayfair Hotel, 180, 213–14
McAdoo, Eleanor Wilson, 165
McAdoo, William Gibbs, 164–65
McClure's, 105
McCooey, John H. ("Uncle John"), 70, 76, 139, 216
    explains patronage job for his son, 137
McCooey, John H., Jr., 137
McGoldrick, Joseph P., 163
McGuinness, Peter J., 137, 139–40
McKay, Claude, 92
McKee, Joseph V., 209, 210, 218, 226
McKeon, John J., 146
McKettrick, Dan, 202
McKinley, William, 39
McLaughlin, Andrew G., 120–21
McManus, George, 16–21
McManus, Thomas ("Hump"), 18–19
McNaboe, John J., 150
McQuade, Francis X., 117, 137, 233
McQuade, James A. ("Jesse James"), 137–39, 233
McQuade Brothers, 138
Meade, Edmund, 12
Medalie, George, 172–73
Mellon, Andrew, 66
Melniker, Harold, 103, 181
Mencken, H. L., 3, 15
Merchant of Venice, The, 88

Merritt, Ed, 68
Methodist Board of Temperance, 31
Meusel, Bob, 84
Mezzacapo, Joseph, 131
Middle Atlantic Fisheries Association, 130
Miller, Gilbert, 89
Miller, Marie, 24
Miller, Marilyn, 88
Mr. New York (Whalen), 29
Moley, Raymond, 102–3, 140, 163, 202
Molloy, Louis, 150, 181
Montauk Island Club, 34
Mooney, William, 40
Moore, Wiley, 84
Moore, Victor, 81
Morning Telegraph, 83
Morris, Robert E., 116
Moses, Robert, 63, 74
    Walker compared to La Guardia by, 229
Mozart Hall faction, 42
Mullen, Arthur, 202
Mulligan, William, 104, 181
Mulrooney, Edward P., 114, 115, 120, 121, 154
Murphy, Charles Francis, 15, 45, 69, 70, 75, 117, 136, 202, 233
    described, 43–44, 76
Murray, James, 21
Mussolini, Benito, 94–96, 174, 175

Nast, Thomas, 43
Nation, The, 47
    on Walker, 154–56
New Orleans Times-Picayune, 208
New York American, 178–79, 199, 212–13

New York City Police Depart-
    ment, 36, 95, 98, 195, 218
    Crater disappearance and,
        23–25
    Police College, 153–54
    Prohibition and, 31, 33
    prostitution and, 111–16,
        119–21
    "Red scare" and, 26–30
    Rothstein murder and, 9–11,
        15–22, 25, 26, 53, 97
    Seabury investigation and, 104,
        111–16, 119–23, 125, 140, 147
    Tammany Hall and, 20–21, 45,
        47, 49, 64, 100, 104, 111–16,
        119–23, 140
    Whalen appointed commis-
        sioner, 20–21, 29–30
New York Daily News, 111,
    147–48
New York Giants, 64, 117
New York Herald Tribune, 90,
    156
    on Roosevelt, 183
    on Seabury investigation, 106
    on Walker, 55, 183
New York Jewelers Exchange,
    195
New York Law School, 65
New York Sun
    on Rothstein, 19
    on Tweed, 42
New York Times, 87, 98–99, 132,
    173–74
    on Hylan, 70
    on La Guardia, 52–53
    on Roosevelt, 13–15, 159,
        190–91, 200, 205, 207, 211
    on Rothstein, 9
    on Seabury investigation, 111,
        145–46, 153, 156–59

on Tweed, 42–43
on Walker, 51–52, 55–56, 67,
    72–73, 99, 128, 145–46, 153,
    156–59, 171–73, 190–91, 196,
    200, 205, 207, 211, 214, 224
New York World, 7
    on Tweed, 42
    on Walker, 96
New York World-Telegram
    on Seabury investigation, 111
    on Walker, 119
New York Yankees, 64, 84
Night Hawk, 89
Nizer, Louis, 229
Norris, Jean H., 117

O'Brien, John P., 218, 222, 226,
    233
Ochs, Adolph S., 9
O'Connell, Edward J., 212
O'Connor, Basil, 140, 202
O'Connor, Thomas, 195
O'Dwyer, William, 229
Of Thee I Sing, 87
Oh, Kay!, 80–81, 83
Oliver, Roland, 89
Olvany, George W., 45–46, 70
Omley, Claire, 22
Once in a Lifetime (Kaufman),
    154
O'Neil, William, 146
O'Neill, "Honest John," 43
One of Ours (Cather), 91
On the Town, 233
Ottinger, Albert, 56

Padlocks of 1927, 89
Palmer, A. Mitchell, 27
Pani, Joe, 1
Park Central Hotel, 8, 10, 16–19
Parkhurst, Rev. Charles H., 47–50

Pegler, Westbrook, 79
Pennock, Herb, 84
Pfeiffer, Peter J., 116
Philadelphia Inquirer, 208
Phillips, Jesse, 68
Piker, The, 88
Pilatsky, Charles C., 130
Pius XI, Pope, 82
Plaza Hotel, 79
Plunkitt, George Washington, 40
Polo Grounds Athletic Club, 117
Polyclinic Hospital, 10, 17
Portland Oregonian, 208
"Pretty Girl Is Like a Melody, A,"
    91
Progressive Party, 72, 99
Prohibition, 1, 3, 103, 181, 232
    clubs (speakeasies), 11, 23,
        31–34, 48, 90, 231
    effects of, 30–34, 36
    Eighteenth Amendment (enact-
        ment) described, 30
    Roosevelt and, 35–36, 219
    Rothstein's bootlegging, 5, 9
    Tammany Hall and, 90
    Twenty-first amendment (re-
        peal) described, 30, 34–35
    Walker and, 31–36, 73, 90, 147,
        231

Quinlivan, James, 116
Quintano, Joe, 194–95

Raymond, Nathan ("Nigger
    Nate"), 16–17, 21–22
Reagan, Ronald, 219
Recovery Party, 226
Rector's, 66
Reiman, Eugene, 17
Reuben's, 114
Richmond Times-Dispatch, 172

Ritz, Sally Lou, 23
Ritz-Carlton Hotel, 84
Roberts (Jimmy's valet), 84
Roberts, Kiki (Marion
    Strasmick), 11
Rogers, Lindsay, 163
Rogers, Will, 4
Roman Gardens, 97–98
Roosevelt, Eleanor, 38, 79, 166,
    176, 234
Roosevelt, Franklin Delano, 19,
    34, 43–44, 46, 51, 54, 79, 80,
    92, 103, 106
    Albany trial of Jimmy Walker,
        167–73, 175–76, 178–209,
        215, 220, 231, 235
    Bonus Army of World War I
        veterans and, 178
    Depression of the 1930s and,
        86, 218, 219, 225
    described, 4, 14–15, 38–39, 167,
        175–76, 219
    elected president, 219–20
    Hearst, supported by, 164–65,
        179, 213
    La Guardia compared to, 234
    legacy, 235
    New York Herald Tribune on,
        183
    New York Times on, 13–15, 159,
        190–91, 200, 205, 207, 211
    1928 gubernatorial campaign,
        3, 8–9, 13–14, 56
    1932 Democratic National Con-
        vention in Chicago, 163–66,
        185
    1932 presidential campaign, 26,
        35, 105, 133, 140–41, 145,
        153, 156–66, 168, 173–75,
        179, 182, 185, 200, 202–4,
        209–13, 217–20

Roosevelt, Franklin Delano *(cont.)*
  post-trial official statement on
    Walker and Tammany Hall,
    221–22
  post-trial personal attack by
    Walker on, 205–9, 212–13
  presidential ambitions, 3, 14,
    26, 35, 39, 98, 105, 120, 133,
    140–41, 145, 150, 153,
    156–66, 168, 173–75, 179,
    182, 185, 200, 202–4, 209–13,
    217–20
  Prohibition and, 35–36, 219
  Seabury investigation and, 99,
    102, 109, 120, 121, 125–27,
    131–34, 136, 143, 145, 150,
    152, 153, 156–64, 166,
    169–71, 220
  state programs and policies,
    56–57, 175–76
  Tammany Hall and, 3, 4, 14, 15,
    23, 25–26, 36, 37, 39, 56, 58,
    98, 99, 102, 109, 120, 121,
    125–27, 131–34, 136, 143, 145,
    150, 152, 153, 156–64, 166,
    169–73, 175–76, 178–216,
    219–22, 231, 232, 235
  Walker and, 4, 15, 15, 25–26, 36,
    58, 67, 99, 133–34, 141, 143,
    145, 150, 152, 153, 156–73,
    175–76, 178–216, 218, 220–22,
    226–27, 231, 232, 235
  White House, Walker's visit to,
    227
Roosevelt, James, 39, 213
Roosevelt, John, 166
Roosevelt, Theodore, 14, 72, 168,
    175, 181, 200
  described, 38
Roosevelt: The Lion and the Fox
  (Burns), 203

Rosenman, Samuel I., 109, 140,
    163, 166, 183, 202, 206
Rothstein, Arnold, 90, 117
  bootlegging and, 5, 9
  described, 5–6, 8
  drugs and, 5, 16, 19, 25
  gambling and, 5–10, 12, 16–19,
    25, 45, 111, 125
  murder of, 2–4, 8–11, 15–22, 25,
    26, 53, 56, 97, 119, 121, 125
  real estate and, 9, 16
  Tammany Hall and, 3, 4, 9, 12,
    19, 45
  Walker and, 2, 6, 19
Rothstein, Caroline, 12
Runyon, Damon, 8
Ruth, Babe, 84
Ryan, Joseph P., 211
Ryskind, Morrie, 87

St. Francis Xavier School, 64, 65
St. Joseph's Church, 66
St. Louis Cardinals, 84
St. Louis Globe-Democrat, 208
St. Louis Kid, 18
St. Patrick's Cathedral, 44, 83,
    201, 216
  Walker's funeral, 228
Sartoris (Faulkner), 91
Schmeling, Max, 180
Schroeder, Dr. William, Jr., 73,
    201, 214
Schultz, Dutch (Arthur Flegen-
    heimer), 11–12
Schurman, Jacob Gould, Jr., 104
Scotch Ann, 48–49
Seabury, Maud, 103, 181, 215
Seabury, Samuel, 214, 227
  Albany trial of Jimmy Walker
    and, 168, 181–82, 184–88,
    195, 199, 202–4, 215

described, 99–101
final report of, 221–22
investigation, 2–3, 58, 99–123,
    125–41, 143–64, 166, 169–72,
    180, 185, 189, 191, 194, 196,
    198, 207, 211, 220–21, 224,
    225, 231
La Guardia supported by, 225–26
post-trial comment on Walker,
    215
presidential ambitions, 160
reforms proposed, 121–22
Walker testimony, 2–4, 129,
    143–63, 171
Service Bus, 148
Sex, 89
Shakespeare, William, 80
Shame of the Cities, The (Steffens),
    40, 105
Shardinsky, Max, 148
Sheldon, Edward, 88
Shelton, Yvonne ("Little Fellow"),
    67
Sherman, Henry L., 135
Sherwood, Russell T.
    charges against, 146, 152, 161,
        169, 171, 192–93, 221, 224
    as fugitive, 146, 152, 192–93,
        221
    testimony of, 224
Shocker, Urban, 84
Shor, Toots, 229
Toots Shor's saloon, 206
Show Boat, 86
Shubert, Jacob J., 89
Shubert, Lee, 89
Shubert, Sam S., 89
"Sidewalks of New York," 95
Siegfried, André, 46
Silverman, Sime, 85–86
Sisto, J. A., 146, 189–90

Smith, Alfred E., 54, 74, 179, 213
    described, 3, 46–47, 68
    legacy, 232
    Liberty League and, 226–27, 232
    1924 presidential campaign, 15,
        44
    1928 presidential campaign, 3,
        8–9, 13–15, 35, 56, 72, 164
    1932 Democratic National Con-
        vention in Chicago, 163–66,
        185
    1932 presidential campaign,
        105, 141, 158, 161–66, 185
    Prohibition and, 3, 35, 232
    as state legislator, 67–69
    Tammany Hall and, 15, 39, 44,
        46, 47, 67, 70, 76, 141, 163
    Walker and, 15, 47, 67, 69, 70,
        73, 83, 93, 161–65, 175, 201,
        216, 218, 226–27, 232
Smith, J. Allen, 146–47, 150
Smith, Moe W., 32–33
So Big (Ferber), 91
Socialist Party, 53, 72, 144, 220
Society for the Prevention of
    Crime, 47
"Someone to Watch Over Me," 81
Sound and the Fury, The
    (Faulkner), 92
Spirit of St. Louis, 84–85
Stalin, Joseph, 175
Steffens, Lincoln, 40, 105–6
Stein, Harry, 120
Steingut, Irwin, 110, 144, 150
Stevenson, Adlai E., 234
Strike Up the Band, 86–87
Sullivan, Big Tim, 44–45, 233
Sulzer, William, 102
Sumner, John S., 69–70
Sun Also Rises, The (Hemingway),
    92

Sunny, 88
Swope, Herbert Bayard, 7–8

Tammany Hall, 5, 11
  Albany trial of Jimmy Walker,
    167–73, 175–76, 178–209,
    215, 220, 231, 235
  Crater and, 23, 24
  decline and fall of, 232–35
  Good Government advocates
    ("Goo-Goos") reform efforts,
    2, 15, 58, 79, 159
  Greenpoint People's Regular
    Organization of the Fifteenth
    Assembly District, 139–40
  inner workings described,
    37–38, 40–51, 74–75
  La Guardia's reform efforts, 3,
    50, 51, 53, 225–26, 232–33, 235
  Mozart Hall faction, 42
  New York City Police Depart-
    ment and, 20–21, 45, 47, 49, 64,
    100, 104, 111–16, 119–23, 140
  origins of, 40–41
  Parkhurst's reform efforts, 47–50
  Prohibition and, 90
  Roosevelt and, 3, 4, 14, 15, 23,
    25–26, 36, 37, 39, 56, 58, 98,
    99, 102, 109, 120, 121, 125–27,
    131–34, 136, 141, 143, 145,
    150, 152, 153, 156–64, 166,
    169–73, 175–76, 178–216,
    219–22, 231, 232, 235
  Roosevelt's post-trial official
    statement on, 221–22
  Rothstein and, 3, 4, 9, 12, 19, 45
  Seabury investigation, 2–3, 58,
    99–123, 125–41, 143–64, 166,
    169–72, 180, 185, 189, 191,
    194, 196, 198, 207, 211,
    220–21, 224, 225, 231

  Smith and, 15, 39, 44, 46, 47,
    67, 70, 76, 141, 163
  Tepecano Democratic Club,
    97–98
  Tweed Courthouse, 235
  Tweed Ring, 2, 42–43, 133, 222,
    232
  Walker and, 2–4, 15, 19, 20,
    25–26, 29, 36, 37, 40, 44, 46,
    47, 51, 53–55, 58, 59, 64, 66,
    67, 69–71, 74–76, 78, 79, 83,
    99–123, 125–41, 143–64,
    166–73, 175–76, 178–216, 218,
    220–22, 224, 225, 231, 232, 235
Tarkington, Booth, 91
Tepecano Democratic Club,
  97–98
Terminal Taxicab Company, 146
Terranova, Ciro, 98
Theofel, John, 137
Thomas, Norman, 53, 72, 132, 220
Thurman, Wallace, 92
Tibbetts, Harland B., 104
Tilden, Samuel J., 211, 222
Tin Pan Alley, 64, 65, 71–72
"Today and Tomorrow" (Lipp-
  mann), 162–63
Toomer, Jean, 92
Trosk, George, 132, 181, 187, 203
Truman, Harry S., 177–78
Tugwell, Rexford G., 25, 140, 163
Tuttle, Charles H., 25
Twain, Mark, 30–31
Tweed, William Marcy, 42–43, 50,
  75, 154, 181
Tweed Courthouse, 235
Tweed Ring, 2, 42–43, 133, 222, 232
Twin Coach Company, 146

United Sea Food Workers, 130
Untermyer, Irwin, 127

Untermyer, Samuel, 118, 126–29,
    143
U.S. Conference of Mayors, 234–35

Van Wyck, Robert A., 181
Variety, 85–86
Viggiano, Prosper, 130
Virgin Man, The, 89
Vitale, Albert H., 97–98, 117
Voorhis, John R. 64
Vortex, The, 88
Vossische Zeitung, 209

Wagner, Robert F., 39, 93
Wagner, Robert F., Jr., 233
Wales Padlock Law, 89
Walker, Frank (no relation), 202
Walker, George (brother of
    Jimmy), 201–2
Walker, James J. (Jimmy), 45, 50,
    91
  Albany trial, 167–73, 175–76,
    178–209, 215, 220, 231, 235
  baseball and, 84
  boyhood years, 60, 64–65, 100
  Broadway and, 80–83, 86–90,
    180, 206, 231
  bus system under, 73, 148, 150,
    154–55, 169–70, 190
  City Hall, invited to La
    Guardia's, 227
  Clean Books Bill and, 69–70
  Compton, Betty, as mistress of,
    1–2, 34, 80–83, 110, 180, 205,
    215, 217, 220–23, 231
  death of, 228–29, 231
  divorce from Allie, 223, 224
  divorce from Betty, 227–28
  education of, 64, 65, 69
  election campaign, 60, 70–73,
    184

  estrangement from Allie,
    83–84, 180, 205, 217, 222–24
  funeral of, 228
  garment industry appointment
    from La Guardia, 227, 228
  hospital system under, 73
  La Guardia compared to, by
    Robert Moses, 229
  lateness, famous for, 66, 168
  law career, 20, 66, 69, 100, 196
  legacy, 231–32
  Majestic Records, as president
    of, 228
  married life with Allie, 67, 82,
    83, 93, 94, 151, 152, 179, 190
  married life with Betty, 224, 226
  marries Allie, 66
  marries Betty, 223–24
  The Nation on, 154–56
  New York American on,
    178–79, 199, 212–13
  New York Herald Tribune on, 55
  New York Times on, 51–52,
    55–56, 67, 72–73, 99, 128,
    145–46, 153, 156–59, 171–73,
    190–91, 196, 200, 205, 207,
    211, 214, 224
  New York World on, 96
  New York World-Telegram on, 119
  as Night Mayor of New York,
    76, 96, 159, 184
  1932 Democratic National Con-
    vention in Chicago, 163–65
  one-liners, memorable, 2, 3, 59,
    70, 105, 118–19, 144, 148,
    153, 168, 180, 188, 189, 214,
    218, 227, 229–30
  parks and playgrounds under,
    73–74
  post-trial comment from
    Seabury on, 215

Walker, James J. (Jimmy) *(cont.)*
  post-trial official statement by
      Roosevelt on, 221–22
  post-trial personal attack on
      Roosevelt by, 205–9, 212–13
  Prohibition and, 31–36, 73, 90,
      147, 231
  "Red scare" and, 26–28
  reelection campaign, 3, 51–54,
      62, 144, 171, 184
  religion and, 83, 216, 223–24, 228
  resignation of, 201–6, 208–9,
      213–15, 222, 231, 232
  Roosevelt and, 4, 15, 25–26, 36,
      58, 67, 99, 133–34, 141, 143,
      145, 150, 152, 153, 156–73,
      175–76, 178–216, 218,
      220–22, 226–27, 231, 232, 235
  Rothstein and, 2, 6, 19, 53
  salary and perks as mayor, 74
  sanitation services under, 73
  Seabury investigation, 2–3, 58,
      99–123, 125–41, 143–64, 166,
      169–72, 180, 185, 189, 191,
      194, 196, 198, 207, 211,
      220–21, 224, 225, 231
  Shelton, Yvonne (mistress), re-
      lationship with, 67
  Smith and, 15, 47, 67, 69, 70,
      73, 83, 93, 161–65, 175, 201,
      216, 218, 226–27, 232
  songwriting career, 64–66,
      71–72, 229
  special mayoral election, post-
      trial attempt to run in, 205–18
  speeches, parades, ceremonies,
      61–64, 77–78, 85, 93–96,
      153–54, 180, 194–95, 224–25,
      228
  as state legislator, 20, 43, 61,
      66–73, 100, 184, 227, 229

  subway system under, 71, 73
  Tammany Hall and, 2–4, 15, 19,
      20, 25–26, 29, 36, 37, 40, 44,
      46, 47, 51, 53–55, 58, 59, 64,
      66, 67, 69–71, 74–76, 78, 79,
      83, 99–123, 125–41, 143–64,
      166–73, 175–76, 178–216,
      218, 220–22, 224, 225, 231,
      232, 235
  testimony in Albany trial, 170–72,
      178, 188–90, 193–99, 209
  testimony in Seabury investiga-
      tion, 2–4, 129, 143–60, 171
  tributes to, on his death, 229
  wardrobe of, 61, 66, 77, 80, 84,
      92, 94–96, 129, 143–44, 147,
      168, 179, 195, 214
  water supply under, 74
  Whalen appointed police com-
      missioner by, 20–21, 29–30
  White House, invited to Roo-
      sevelt's, 227
  womanizing, 1–2, 34, 47, 67,
      80–83, 110, 180, 205, 215–17,
      220–23, 231
  Workmen's Compensation Act
      and, 69
Walker, Janet Allen ("Allie," wife
      of Jimmy)
  at Albany trial, 180, 189
  courtship and wedding, 66
  divorce, 223, 224
  in *The Duke of Duluth*, 66
  estrangement, 83–84, 180, 205,
      217, 222–24
  married life, 67, 82, 83, 93, 94,
      151, 152, 179, 190
Walker, Mrs. William (mother of
      Jimmy), 64, 66
Walker, William (father of
      Jimmy), 55, 67, 94, 223

described, 64, 100
Tammany Hall and, 64, 66, 75,
     100
Walker, Dr. William H. (brother
     of Jimmy), 198
Walsh, George, 61
Warner Theater, 88
Warren, Joseph A., 20
Washington and Jefferson Col-
     lege, 159
Waterman, Frank D., 71, 73
Weary Blues, The (Hughes), 92
Wende, Assemblyman, 68
West, Mae, 89
Whalen, Grover Aloysius, 77
   appointed police commissioner,
        20–21, 29–30
   autobiography *(Mr. New York)*,
        29
   described, 21
   Prohibition and, 33
   "Red scare" and, 26–30
   Rothstein murder and, 21, 26
Wharton, Edith, 91
White, E. B., 78
White, George, 158

Wilder, Thornton, 91
Willebrandt, Mabel W., 31–32
Williams, Alexander S., 49
"Will You Love Me in December
     as You Do in May" (Walker),
     65–66, 225, 229
Wilson, Dudley, 137
Wilson, Woodrow, 14
Wilson Bros., Inc., 137
Winchell, Walter, 11, 83
"Wintergreen for President," 87
Wise, Rabbi Stephen S., 133
Wodehouse, P. G., 81
Women in Love (Lawrence), 69
Wood, Fernando, 41–42
Woodmansten Inn, 1–2
Workmen's Compensation Act,
     69
World's Work, 45–46

Yankee Stadium, 84
Yellen, Jack, 79–80

Ziegfeld, Florenz, 24, 214
Ziegfeld Follies, 11, 23, 24, 59,
     195, 214, 231